166-77

The Humanities
and
Humanistic Education

James L. Jarrett
University of California, Berkeley

Addison-Wesley Publishing Company
Reading, Massachusetts
Menlo Park, California • London • Don Mills, Ontario

To Carroll Grabo

Preface

Stupor of knowledge lacking inwardness—
What book, O learned man, will set me right?

Theodore Roethke

Much pro-Humanities rhetoric has been a combination of nostalgia and hypersensitiveness to recent criticism or—more especially—neglect. The scientists are getting all the money and all the acclaim, the aggrieved ones cry. Or: Think of what it costs to launch a moon rocket! They cry down technology, sometimes making it the supervillain of our villainous times. And they cry up their own fields as the only remaining hopes for spiritual salvation. So far from winning sympathy, such laments seem mainly evocative of counterthrusts: Shall we then double the number of teachers whose principal feat it is to make Shakespeare both dull and trivial? To require more students to take the sort of music course wherein they mainly confirm their impressions that "serious music" is a sorry joke? Or bring out yet another volume of academic philosophy to prove the slightness of its connection with life as lived?

It is time to raise the dispute to a higher level. It seems altogether possible that we humanists, as a group, pretty much deserve our present estate, and that nobody will take seriously our demands for more attention, time, and money until we have changed our ways.

For one thing, we have to induce our own identity crisis. We are not any longer confined to classical scholarship. We are not aesthetes and not just aestheticians. If not all practicing historians, philosophers, and religious scholars belong in our ranks, a considerable number *do,* and we would be impoverished by their absence. It is less important to decide whether literature is at the very center of the humanities, or just *primus inter pares,* than to recognize how much the nonverbal arts contribute to our field. We are teachers and scholars and critics; but we are also poets, composers, choreographers, and film-makers. And much else. But not everything. He who for fear of invidious exclusion nervously includes all teaching, all scholarship, all creativity, succeeds only in making the humanities meaningless.

We humanists need also to question the chic dichotomy between teaching and being. The teacher of the humanities has an especial obligation to be, as best he can, like unto the quality of his own subject matter. Though the terms must for the present remain vague, we would assert that the one essential quality for teaching humanistically is *being* humanistic. Like all councils of perfection, this one can be a wet blanket or an empty pontification; but it is intended to be a plea not to settle for too little, and a reminder of the peculiar integralness of the field. Most of us have known at least a few persons we would call humanistic, not merely by profession, but in their human being. It is they who make us discontent with a radical separation between vocation and calling.

This book has been helped along by a number of students who have, sometimes gently, sometimes indignantly, disputed with its author. Some found it unhappily divisive, especially in suggesting some differences between the sciences and the humanities. Some argued that "humanistic" has almost nothing at all to do with "humanities," and that only when we accomplish wholesale social and economic reform will there again be time for aesthetic values. Still others suggested—I remember Holly Wilson, particularly—that in its heavy dependence upon discursive argument and intellectual analysis, the book is not stylistically consonant with its burden and its plea.

One chapter has appeared separately in *The Educational Forum;* part of another chapter, in *The Journal of General Education.*

Some of the persons who helped most were innocent of its being written. I mean not only Plato, Santayana, Dewey, Jung, Stephen Pepper and DeWitt Parker, but also Brewster Ghiselin, Edwin Clapp, and Philip Wheelwright. Ralph Smith, Karon Conrad, Harry Broudy, Jane Cauvel, and Hans Krimm read and commented on one or more of the chapters. James Stone of the Humanities Department of San Francisco State College accomplished such a painstaking, thorough, and perceptive working through of the entire manuscript that he deserves hearty thanks; obviously, the remaining deficiencies of the book are in spite of his assistance. My sons Dennis and Devin helped too; the first by extensive criticism, the second by collating. She to whom the book is dedicated discussed with me every topic, read and reread every page, and made important improvements, both stylistic and substantive—if such antihumanistic distinction may be allowed, even in a preface.

J. L. J.

Berkeley, 1972

Contents

	Introduction	xiii
1	Ancient Greece and Rome	1
2	The Rise of Humanism in the Renaissance	13
3	From the Renaissance to the Twentieth Century	27
4	Some Recent Definitions of the Humanities	47
5	The Sciences and the Humanities	63
6	Toward a New Characterization of the Humanistic	81
7	Humanists and Their Vices	95
8	The Humane, the Humanitarian and the Humanistic	105
9	Value and the Humanities	121
10	Humanistic Teaching	141
11	Humanities Curricula	165
12	Humanistic Learning	187
13	The Humanities and the Whole Man	211
	Notes	221
	Index	247

61449

Introduction

Rousseau said near the beginning of *Emile:* "All that we lack at birth and need when grown up is given us by education."[1] Now, two hundred years later, the power we attribute to education is no less—at least if we can judge by the number of words and dollars spent on the schools, by the fine hopes that accompany the latest proposals for reform, or by the faults that are laid at the classroom door.

Somehow—it is commonly proclaimed—if only formal education could become what it ought to be, then both society and individual human beings would become efficient, productive, gentle, sensitive, intelligent, kind, and free, with an end to fear, crassness, and brutality.

But there is no agreement as to how these brave ends are to be achieved. Some resonate to the promise contained in the words "accountability," "performance criteria," "behavioral objectives," and "computer-assisted instruction." Some predict wonders from a thoroughgoing scientific overhaul of instruction, with top-to-bottom "systems" orientation and close budgetary monitoring. But we also hear praise of "alternative schools" and "open classrooms"—even of "de-schooling"—and warnings about inhumanity, impersonalism, facelessness, mechanization, rigidity, and alienation in today's schools.

Some who employ these polemical terms are ardently political in bent, seeing the inadequacies of the schools as a function of a corrupt society, and despairing of any reform short of total revolution. Others think that, however great the need for political and economic overhaul, and however essential the teaching of scientific, critical thinking, our greatest needs today are for teachers characterized by trust, compassion, sensitivity, caring, and for greater emphasis upon the achievement of beauty, love, joy: in short, upon the positive qualities of humanity. All of which brings to mind, or some minds: the humanities.

Crisis in the Humanities[2]—this title of a recent book sounds a note familiar in our time. We are much given to crises, real or imagined, and often we seem to doubt that anything less urgent than a crisis has any motivating force for action. But, crisis or no, the humanities do appear to be attracting more attention just now than for many decades. If some of the attention is unfavorable, with mutterings about intellectual and cultural snobbism, exploitative capitalism, emotive subjectivism, and pedantic traditionalism, in most circles any rhetoric which rings the changes on the word "human"—humane, humanitarian, humanism, humanistic, humanities—invites applause. Thus we hear of schools built to the human dimension, of humane teachers, of reforms to humanize the curriculum, of the resurgence of the humanities after many years of subservience to the sciences, and so on.

That opinions differ on what these words signify will be quickly shown by an arbitrary gathering of some recent definitions of just one of them:

> Howard Mumford Jones: "The humanities are those branches of knowledge (and activity) that have a special capacity, if rightly interpreted by humane learning, to mature the intellectual and moral powers and to quicken the sensibilities of the individual."[3]

> New York State Education Department: The humanities: " . . . those areas which have to do with the expression of man's ideals."[4]

> Jerry L. Walker: "The proper studies of the humanities are those uniquely human activities, the creation and use of symbols."[5]

> Charles Keller: " . . . The humanities acquaint man with the thoughts, creations, and actions of his predecessors, through the ages and mankind around him. . . . They have to do with making man more human."[6]

> J. H. Billington: "Both the subject and object of humanistic study are the whole man—where mind and passion meet, where creativity and criticism interact. Humanistic studies—history and philosophy, arts and letters—directly involve man in the anguish, achievements, and aspirations of other people, and in enduring human questions of artistic form, moral value, and personal belief."[7]

> Jon Roush: "The humanities . . . share at least the task of connecting the past and present as they are manifested in the works and acts

of men. . . . The objective of a humanistic education is competence in the judgment of human creations, with that judgment informed by an awareness of pertinent historical contexts.[8]

All of these—and dozens more could be cited—are by persons who love, honor, and cherish what it is they call the humanities. But there are others who will regard a book on the humanities—particularly when it is discovered that in certain respects the humanities and the sciences are distinguished and even contrasted—as a piece of divisive mischief: knowledge is unified, life is single, the world is one, the child is whole; so let there be an end to distinctions, which are bound, anyway, to be invidious. For instance, Harold Taylor has said,

> . . . I question the whole idea of the "humanities" as a special area of the curriculum designed to take care of human values which, presumably, the rest of the curriculum can then safely ignore while it goes on ladling out its generous supply of facts.[9]

True it is that all fields of study and other endeavor are related. That is, they can *be* related, for as Jacques Barzun somewhere said, "All subjects are interrelated through the single mind of man."

Of course mathematics is intimately related to physics and astronomy, and one cannot proceed very far in the study of chemistry without doing some physics too, and it is hard to think how a political scientist could remain oblivious of economics, or a dancer of music; and today we hear too about such subjects as biophysics, about the use of chemistry in the history of art, and about poets who are expert botanists and medical doctors who are passionate violists. Is graphology a science? —Opinions differ. How in the Middle Ages could scholars come up with such a grouping as arithmetic, geometry, astronomy, and music, the famous quadrivium? One gets along fine with Thomas Aquinas' theories about art until, without warning or embarrassment, he shifts his examples from music and sculpture to juggling and cobbling. Then there was Thomas Jefferson, who extended the list of fine arts to include landscape gardening, as there are today people who want to include arrangements of lights or of jets of water.[10]

Confronted with such surprising classifications, the suspicion gradually dawns that all definitions, all groupings, are arbitrary: kings can be yoked with cabbages as easily as with queens. Einstein taught us that even such a fundamental distinction as that between matter and energy is not only unsound but obfuscating. Nobody can reliably draw a sharp line between plants and animals, organic and inorganic, man and non-man, man and woman, cause and effect, love and hate, introvert and extravert, arts and sciences, right and wrong, beautiful and ugly, night and day. And the lesson of this may seem to be that of Gorgias, the ancient Sophist, who said that nothing exists, but even if it did, it couldn't be known; and furthermore even if it could be known, it couldn't be communicated to another.[11]

And yet we cannot quite stop celebrating the difference between men and women, or finding useful the distinction between hot and cold, and odd and even. Indeed, with the weakening of the belief in absolute categories, characterizations, and distinctions, we are prompted to proliferate, not abandon, them.

Anyone who sets out to show that a great gulf naturally and necessarily separates the natural from the social sciences, or the humanities from the sciences, faces a task as hopeless as that of showing exactly where elementary education must stop and secondary education begin, or the exact distinction between "solid" and "frill" subjects. But concepts and classification are also challenges. If one senses or feels or intuits a connection between things, the task of discovering and expressing the nature of that connection may be not only interesting but fruitful in future thinking and learning and teaching. John Dewey spent most of his life trying to get clear about what it is that characterizes the scientific, and (equally) the democratic; his discoveries, or anyway his proposals, profoundly altered the texture and structure of education throughout the world, even though probably only a tithe of educators ever completely subscribed to his theories.

Such a job has yet to be done for the concept "humanistic," although a number of thinkers have made commendable progress in this messy and intricate task. Yet, much remains to be done, and if it is done well, big dividends—William James used to speak of the "cash value" of an abstract idea—can be expected to accrue in the way of changed curricula, changed teaching procedures, new, imaginative texts and "packages" of school material—all, of course, in the interest of better learning, better lives.

A fully adequate definition will be found complex and hard to formulate—perhaps even impossible—but provisionally we can manage with what the article on "humanities" says in the 1962 edition of the *Encyclopaedia Britannica:*

> Humanities, a group of educational disciplines distinguished in content and method from the physical and biological sciences and, if less decisively, from the social sciences.

Then the article goes on to mention language and literature, along with the other fine arts, and philosophy, "at least in its more traditional divisions, and, to a less clearly defined extent, history, where the boundary between the social sciences and the humanities is most debatable." This makes a fair beginning in a time when the European tendency to identify the humanities with classical studies is no longer acceptable, and the once prevalent American tendency to make a sharp distinction between scholarly studies of literature, philosophy, history, music (musicology), and the visual arts (art history and criticism) on the one hand, and the creative activities of poets, painters, architects, and composers on the other, is less and less common. If now we take the word "humanist" to mean one who engages in these sorts of studies and related creative activities, identifies with, and prizes them, and the word "humanistic" to stand for the most important values humanists try to enhance through the humanities, we will have at least made a start.

But even in the context of a supportive rhetoric, we humanists are likely to be somewhat uneasy. What *is* our task? What *do* we share? Everyone knows that scientists all employ the "scientific method," but what in the world is the "humanistic method"? Are graduates of humanities programs more likely to be possessed of the qualities of humanness or humaneness (whatever *they* might mean) than others?[12] What value is there, after all, in such studies, that corresponds with that of the sciences and technologies? Why are humanists so often—recently, anyway—given to talking about syntheses and integrations of the humanities? Does this entail opposition to analysis and specialization?

Perhaps, after all, there *is* a crisis in the humanities.

This book, which is openly normative and not merely descriptive, is predicated upon the belief that the humanities warrant a bigger place in our schools than they presently occupy, but only if they earn a better place by changing what they are in practice. It is not so much that students need to know a great deal more *about* literature and the fine arts, history, philosophy, and religion, but that they need to develop and increase their capacity to enjoy and to appreciate the process and the products of these fields; still more, they need to become more humanistic and humane selves, whatever be the specific content of their studies. The time has come to break out of those self-righteous and hardened categories that are the English and Music and Art departments, and to look at fruitful combinations, relations, groupings, and integrations.

True to our own humanistic bent, we begin this work historically: back to the Greeks yet once again. Still, this is backdrop: the action is up front, in the present. So, after criticizing some recent attempts at definition of our key words, we undertake our own. The themes announced in this characterization provide the topics for the rest of the book.

Our next concern is with the values associated with the humanities, but begins by admitting to some vices, especially that of assuming that the humanists monopolize virtue. Then we come to practicalities, applications: the improvement (humanizing) of teaching and the construction of (humanistic) curricula in the interest of the more-nearly-whole child and adult. And finally we arrive, where some would have had us begin: the principal goals of education in the humanities. It is of course hoped and intended that that arrival will also be a terminus *a quo*.

1

Ancient Greece and Rome

It is no wonder that we humanists go back and back and back to the Greeks. No amount of reminding that theirs was a violent civilization based on slavery (and the virtual enslavement of women), a culture with no faith in lasting peace, no conception of a merciful and loving god, no exalted image of the love of man and woman—none of this tarnishes Greece's glory or its fatal fascination. For the Greeks were the most sheerly creative people that ever lived: they invented not only very great works of philosophy and drama and history, but invented philosophy and drama and history. Also pure mathematics, geography, the epic, zoology, and education, or at least educational *theory* in the sense of a detailed consideration of the content and methods of education for the purpose of individual and cultural success.[1]

They taught themselves—for there had been no previous people from whom to learn such a lesson—and they taught us, what it is like to think hard and systematically about man as an individual and men in society, about the nature of law and medicine, about duty, fate, comedy and tragedy, friendship, and justice. They produced not just great creators but great men who have served as models to succeeding generations.

We know them to have been a people who loved games and parties, loved to laugh and have parades and festivals, loved to talk and argue, travel and play the lyre, participate in religious rites and go to the theater —and to do all these human things with a flair and a style that made them somehow worthy of recording and remembering.

During the whole long period of their supremacy, the Greeks were a life-loving people who admired human kind and were exceptionally proud of themselves—indeed, so proud that they early along became intensely conscious of the dread sin of *hubris,* the overweening cockiness over the human ability to control destiny. Always aware of the unpredictability of death and of the dreadfulness of the fate that sometimes

1

overtakes men and even family lines beyond the limits of what they deserve, the Greeks were, if anything, even more impressed with the extent of man's potentiality for greatness. Their faith in man's mind and spirit was almost limitless, but they knew too that mind and spirit need cultivation lest they languish and fester. Aristotle fully enunciated for the Greeks the belief that happiness is inconceivable apart from achievement. Man becomes happy not by an inexplicable access of blissful feeling, but by accomplishing what is in him to accomplish, actualizing that which is his potentiality. Man has it in him to be courageous, spirited, magnanimous, beautiful, just, and wise: he is happy if and only if he lives up to these ideals. And the first condition for this realization is knowledge of himself, the constant theme of the tragic dramatists, the philosophers, and of course of the oracle at Delphi, the navel of the universe.

But even that sublime oracle did not relieve man of the responsibility for pondering and thinking: it spoke in riddles that required unraveling. It was the begining, not the end, of the quest for wisdom, as Plato spoke of philosophy starting always in wonder. But, again, philosophy, the love of wisdom, lies within man's potentiality by virtue of his very being, his human *areté.* As Sophocles had his chorus say, in *Antigone:*

There are many strange wonders, but nothing
More wonderful than man.[2]

If the humanities have to do with man at his full stretch, then the Greek culture, though not perfect, was marvelously humanistic.

When in the early books of *The Republic* Plato has Socrates begin to outline the education of his future "Guardians," the leaders of the ideal state that will at last epitomize justice, his earliest provisions are for the physical development of young children and for the beginning of their musical and literary education, beginning with the tales and poems that they will be told. No contemporary of Plato would have been in the least surprised at these emphases: they were precisely those of the Athenian schools of the time—and had been for decades. But many would have been, and presumably were, shocked at the strictures Plato put upon literary education, for he was extremely critical of most of the poets whom educated Athenians were accustomed to cite continually in their conversations in support of whatever point they were making. It was always, "As Homer said . . . ," and "According to Simonides . . . ," and "Hesiod's words on this subject were . . ."—much as a thirteenth century Scholastic, a seventeenth century Puritan, or a nineteenth century Methodist sought support in scripture for opinions advanced on almost any subject. For anyone, then, to do what Plato did, to say that too often the poets were misleading and even corrupting, must have been almost as shocking as for anyone to suggest to devout Christians that the books of *Job* and *The Gospel According to Matthew* were immoral and standing in need of correction and excision.

Not content with slicing big sections out of the *Iliad* and the *Odyssey,* Plato went ahead to express serious doubts about whether there would be any legitimate place in the brave new world he was projecting for the "imitative" poets and other artists. The trouble with these types was not only that they told untruths about the gods and heroes, but that whereas justice is exemplified by the principle that "every man does one thing," namely, the thing that he really knows *how* to do, poets and dramatists continually wrote as if they were authorities on all sorts of subjects, and encouraged those who acted in their plays and listened to their words, to assume all manner of roles, pretending to be now a king, now a messenger, now a soldier, and again a slave, or a seer.

> It is probable then, that if a man should arrive in our city, so clever as to be able to assume any character and imitate any object, and should propose to make a public display of his talents and his productions, we shall pay him reverence as a sacred, admirable, and charming personage, but we shall tell him that in our state there is no one like him, and that our law excludes such characters . . . ; but for ourselves, we shall employ, for the sake of our real good, that more austere and less fascinating poet and legend-writer, who will imitate for us the style of the virtuous man, and will cast his narratives in those moulds which we prescribed at the outset, when we were engaged with the training of our soldiers.[3]

Modern readers of *The Republic* typically find this projected state less than ideal, for a variety of reasons (in spite of its attractiveness in such respects as basing political power strictly on merit, according equality of opportunity to the female, etc.), and nothing comes in for more criticism than the outrageous proposal that children should be offered a highly expurgated version of the poets, along with tales concocted especially for the healthiness of their morals. Why, readers have asked down through the centuries, should Plato of all thinkers—he who among all philosophers was the nearest thing to a *literary* genius commit this act of supreme ingratitude to writers and artists? Many ingenious answers have been offered by way of explanation, but part at least of the right answer seems clear. Plato is severe on the poets because he takes them seriously. It is easy to be tolerant of what we take to be falsity if it is just all in fun. What does it matter to us that Homer has his gods carouse and have temper tantrums and fits of jealousy? It makes them all the more colorful, more "human." They are not real, in any case; it's all just a good tale. In such circumstances, censorship is absurd. But Plato believed that children are strongly influenced by the stories they hear; he thought that when a poet speaks of the gods (though Plato did not *believe* in their literal, anthropomorphic existence) he speaks of ideal beings, so there must be an implicit endorsement of their character traits. Is there not some serious conflict set up in the child's self, then, if on the one hand you tell him that honesty and sincerity and consistency are great virtues, and on the other hand that the gods were double-dealing, sly, and fickle?

But more generally, Plato believed that all of us are made healthier and more nearly beautiful in our souls by dwelling among beautiful things; conversely, that we are corrupted by "symbols of evil" and ugliness. Hence it is necessary in a just state to supervise all artists and craftsmen, not poets alone, lest their products have mischievous effects on impressionable youth. Music Plato found particularly powerful; thus, especial care is indicated about the kind of music the budding young guardian is allowed to hear. And there is a transfer effect from music too, he says, because

> . . . rhythm and harmony sink most deeply into the recesses of the soul, and take most powerful hold of it, bringing gracefulness in their train, and making a man graceful if he be rightly nurtured, but if not, the reverse? And also because he that has been duly nurtured therein will have the keenest eye for defects, whether in the failures of art, or the misgrowths of nature; and feeling a most just disdain for them, will commend beautiful objects, and gladly receive them into his soul, and feed upon them, and grow to be noble and good; whereas he will rightly censure and hate all repulsive objects, even in his childhood, before he is able to be reasoned with. . . .[4]

Although nobody has gone as far as Plato in supposing that musical innovations—not the words sung to music, but the very modes and instrumentation of pure music—may actually corrupt or overturn a state, there are those today who see an insidious connection between various forms of delinquency and rock music, as well as some who see a beneficent connection between this music and the virtues they applaud in today's youth: a certain liberation of spirit, a freedom, a release from the cramping effects of the Puritan Ethic. And there are not a few enlightened parents of our time who have come to deplore the more grisly parts of the long-loved stories of Hans Christian Andersen and the brothers Grimm. They have also come so to deplore such popular children's fare as "Eenie meenie miney moe" and "Little Black Sambo" that they make strong efforts to substitute "tiger" for "nigger" in the former and to remove the latter from the children's shelves in recognition of the power of such early subtle influences to plant the seeds of racial prejudice.

Yes, Plato did take the arts very seriously, whether or not we can condone his suspicion of the poets and painters or his high-handed censorship of the arts of which he did not approve. And for the ancient Greeks generally, as we know, the arts were not mere amusements or frivolous distractions or ornaments, but powerful and important aspects of life, for people of all ages, so that it was assumed that to be able to look at the Parthenon was somehow refreshing to the soul and an inspiration, to live in the company of the poets was to choose one's companions well, to play the lyre or the flute and to draw were intrinsically worthwhile and likely to have beneficial effects on the rest of one's life. Consequently, these skills of performance and appreciation were an essential part of education.

Yet, it must be remembered that when these Greeks spoke of poetry, they thought, as we generally do not, of something heard, rather than read. One popular occupation among the ancients was that of the Rhapsode who could recite, at astonishing length, book after book of the great epics, and go ahead to interpret the poets' meaning in this or that passage. Everybody, it seemed, had his head full of poetry, there to consult at appropriate moments. Although by the fourth century, literacy was common, writings were rare. Whoever had a handful of papyrus was thought to have a library. When a fine speech was heard, many students would set out to get it by heart, perhaps asking the speaker or one of his close disciples to correct them as they repeated the words; and when men got together, one of their favorite occupations was to give a close account of some interesting conversation they had recently been a party to, or to retell in detail an argument they had heard from somebody who had heard it made by someone such as Parmenides many years ago.

Learning to memorize, getting a great deal of poetry by heart (which was in turn the main source of one's knowledge of the legendary beginnings of Hellas, of the gods, of the heroes, of the virtues attributed to them by the great poets—and thus an important source of moral ideas), listening to speeches and dialogues, *memorizing them*—these apparently constituted a very large part of the education of young men. But not just listening and memorizing: talking, speaking, declaiming, debating, orating, too. The intense desire to become proficient at various kinds of speaking was precisely the root of the Sophists' rise to fame and fortune, even before Plato's time.

Beginning with Protagoras of Abdera in the middle of the fifth century B.C., and continuing with Gorgias, Hippias, Prodicus, and many another self-proclaimed Sophist, this tradition of the itinerant, professional teacher was to last for many centuries, and to constitute a major part of the education (beyond the elementary levels) of young men in the Graeco-Roman world.

Now, some of the Sophists professed the ability to teach anything at all, but Protagoras, at least, promised to make his students into good citizens; and the chief means to this end, he thought, was devotion to literature and public speaking. He said flatly—according to Plato, anyway—that "the most important part of a man's education is to become an authority on poetry. This means being able to criticize the good and bad points of a poem with understanding, to know how to distinguish them, and give one's reasons when asked." Protagoras makes it clear that he is not thinking of poems as purely aesthetic artifacts—indeed the ancient Greeks did not even have a word for "purely aesthetic—or of criticism as literary exegesis: no, the poets provide us texts on all the particular virtues and on virtue in general.[5]

Furthermore, literature was taken by all the Greeks and Romans to embrace history and theology: to them it was so obvious as to require no emphasis that every young man should know his own country's past, know the great lawmakers and statesmen, and military strategists, and to be acquainted with the great accounts of the origins and nature of men and gods. If some of this knowledge came to them through the writings of professional historians, such as Herodotus and Thucydides, a great deal also came by means of the epic and tragic poets.

Although accounts of human virtue and vice, of right action and the good life, and of vivid ways of going wrong were, then and now, the substance of story and drama, Socrates made a strong effort to preempt ethics for philosophy, as distinct from theological or literary or mythic or commonsensical assertion. But, Plato taught, in order to know what man should do, we must inquire into what man is, for surely duty and ideal must be based upon capacity and potentiality. Everything has its *aretê*, its peculiar excellence or power or virtue, and until we discover the *aretê* of man, which we must assume to be different from that of a horse or a god or a knife, we are stumbling blindly in our pursuit of the good life. And if, as Socrates came to think, man's distinctiveness lies in his capacity for reason, for rational inquiry, for reflective discourse, for looking into himself, then his overarching duty must be to cultivate these capacities and to order his life in accordance with his discoveries.

Plato went all the way with his revered master, except in what Socrates left out of account; for if man is indeed a rational animal, one must look to the highest forms of rationality, those exhibited in mathematical reasoning and in the dialectical approach to the cosmos itself, for the best exemplification of human achievement.

As Plato had Socrates argue in *The Symposium,* whereas the lower education properly concerns itself with the perception and love of individual embodiments of beauty, the higher education helps the gifted few to understand that Beauty itself, absolute and pure, is an even nobler object of contemplation and reverence. In short, man's common erotic nature can be sublimated and transfigured into the sublimest love of Truth, Beauty, and the Good; furthermore, since one tends to become like that which one dwells with and upon, it is in concern for these ideal forms that man's yearning for immortality is, if anywhere, to be realized.

Not surprisingly, Plato's love for these higher mysteries had no very wide appeal in his own time. His contemporary and rival, Isocrates, attracted far more students. Isocrates was no philosopher, and his voice was too weak for him to be an orator, but he was apparently a very skillful teacher and writer of speeches. He had contempt for those Sophists who exaggerated their versatility and their effectiveness such as Hippias, who used to boast that he could teach anything from sandal making to statesmanship. Isocrates thought that those who made excessive claims for education only did the profession harm by paving the way for certain disillusionment. "I consider that the kind of art which can implant honesty and justice in depraved natures has never existed and does not now exist, and that people who profess that power will grow weary and cease from their vain pretensions before such an education is ever found."[6] No, a teacher needs good material; his pupils must have a certain aptitude for learning and a reasonably sound character to start with: *then* the right kind of education can get results. And the right kind of education is education for political oratory: "I do hold that people can become better and worthier if they conceive an ambition to speak well, if they become possessed of the desire to be able to persuade their hearers . . ."[7]

As Cicero and Quintilian were to reiterate, centuries later, Isocrates thought that training in oratory was inseparable from character education. A man should learn to embrace just and important causes and to hold before his audience "those examples which are most illustrious and the most edifying." In short, "the power to speak well and think right will reward the man who approaches the art of discourse with love of wisdom and love of honour."[8]

Unlike some of the disreputable Sophists of his own day and later, Isocrates had only scorn for disputatiousness, for logic-chopping and word-splitting, and for winning arguments by fair means or foul. However, he had an abiding belief that there is no higher or nobler calling than true statesmanship, the exercise of which demanded not mastery of the abstruse practices of the philosophers (like Plato), but of the study of politics, and of the ways of putting speeches together, and of delivering them effectively.

Opposed as Plato was, with his lifelong defense of the centrality of philosophic study, to Isocrates' emphasis on rhetoric and oratory, (which Plato saw as putting persuasion above the search for truth), their respective approaches to education were alike in stressing the verbal: logos, the word, was at the center of the curriculum, and that word was far more often oral than written. By the time of Aristophanes, scorn was already being heaped upon those who from following the newer fads in education have, through neglect of physical training, a pale complexion, "narrow shoulders, a narrow chest, a long tongue, small hips and a big thing . . ." and who know only how "to spin forth long-winded arguments on law."[9] But even in the fifth century, Aristophanes was fighting a losing, rearguard battle: education was to become more and more verbal as time went on.

Gradually, the oral tradition would begin to give way before the popularization of writing and the building of libraries[10]—though this movement was to culminate only after the invention of movable type in the fifteenth century and the consequent proliferation of printed books.

But, even in ancient times, texts did accumulate, and increasingly the efforts of the grammarians, rhetors, etymologists, philologists, and other students of language became centered on these texts, with monumental efforts being made to collate them, correct them, provide glosses to fill in lacunae, analyze their constructions, etc.

Although Greek education of the Hellenic and Hellenistic ages was indeed predominantly verbal and rhetorical, it was by no means entirely so. Music, for instance, had a strong and rich tradition in Greece; apparently all or most youth, at one time, learned to play the lyre, both by itself and as an accompaniment to song or dance, and many learned to play the aulos, a kind of oboe. Singing, both solo and choral, was a skill widespread among the populace, and dancing too, though gradually they became more and more professionalized (as the arts became increasingly complex), and in the later ages, gentlemen were wholly content to be spectators and auditors, and even made an invidious distinction between themselves and the professional performers.

Still, Aristotle reserves in his fourth-century curriculum an important place for music and for drawing too. He did observe, though, that playing an instrument, while a desirable skill for a young gentleman, must not be allowed to occupy an undue amount of time. Playing the aulos *well,* takes, for a person of the "leisure class," more time than it is worth; therefore, one should learn to play as an amateur only. Apparently the place of drawing and painting was not so well established, for Aristotle seems to have extended himself a little to defend them as school subjects. Still, he says, drawing is not merely of practical importance (apparently some had argued that one who draws might have a keener sense of lengths and weights that would be useful commercially) but has also a "liberal" worth, in that it is an activity that refines our perceptions of the environment: from drawing we learn to *see* better.

Aristotle indeed was, more than any other thinker of his time, concerned with understanding the nature of liberal education; that is, the education proper to and for the benefit of the free man, the man who can enjoy leisure.

> There is a distinction between liberal and illiberal subjects, and it is clear that only such knowledge as does not make the learner mechanical should enter into education. By mechanical subjects we must understand all arts and studies that make the body, soul, or intellect of freemen unserviceable for the use and exercise of goodness. That is why we call such pursuits as produce an inferior condition of body mechanical, and all wage-earning occupations. They allow the mind no leisure, and they drag it down to a lower level.[11]

Reading and writing, he said, were obviously useful subjects, and gymnastics was important for the promotion of health and courage, but the justification for music and drawing and poetry is of a different order: "the right employment of our time in leisure." And he cites Odysseus' words approvingly: "that the best way of spending time is when men are merry and 'the banqueters throughout the hall give ear to the minstrel, all seated in a row.' "[12]

He concludes that "there is such a thing as a subject in which we must educate our sons, not because it is necessary, but because it is fine and worthy of free men. ... To seek utility everywhere is by no means the way of free men with a sense of their own dignity."[13]

Since probably in Aristotle's own time, as well as ever since, there have been persons disposed to see this kind of appeal as elitist and snobbish, it is to be noted that though Aristotle and Plato did accept and assume the necessity of a slave-based society, and in other ways too a hierarchy of human beings according to their realization of value, they did believe it was something inherent to the human condition that education best serves. Whatever the actual condition of most men, the highest and best life is that in which there is a degree of freedom from drudgery, and an opportunity to enjoy nonutilitarian beauty.

Still, Aristotle, more than Plato—ironically, since we think of Plato as ever so much more poetic than his pupil—saw a high psychological function served by poetry, especially the tragic drama: namely, to purge the self of such clogging emotions as fear and pity by arousing them in a special (we might say, *nonthreatening*) context.

We cannot but agree with Aristotle in thinking that in his culture the theater was a great and powerful educative force, a molder of men's minds and souls, a synthesizer of religious, political, philosophic, moral, and aesthetic qualities; no Greek could have regarded tragic drama as mere entertainment; and comedy, however amusing, was not to be reduced to amusement. Indeed, neither Greek nor Roman was in the least likely to share the modern confusion that identifies education with schooling. We are shaped and formed by the totality of our environment: it follows that we cannot afford to be careless about any aspect of that environment, architectural, legal, ceremonial, erotic, or whatever.

Yet the Romans went even beyond the Greeks in the importance they attached to verbal discourse. With Cicero and Quintilian, rhetoric and oratory were, as with Isocrates, broad in their range, and ethical in their intent—to be a good orator one must be a good man, Quintilian insisted—but a great deal of language study became even more picayune than in Hellenistic Greece, to the point of deplorable pedantry and artificiality. Rules for written composition became ever more dogmatic and the specification of proper intonation and gesture ever more detailed. Catalogs of the allowable figures of speech, rhythms, and other rhetorical niceties became ever longer. And perhaps most damaging of all to the humanistic tradition, rhetoric became more of an occupation for the specialist than a reasonable way of educating the citizen, the leader, the man. Yet even this vice was observable earlier. As Marrou put it: "Hellenistic man was already beginning to be torn between that aspiration toward totality which we with our bad Greek call the 'encyclopaedic' tendency, and the need, no less essential to humanism, to preserve culture as something human, within the limits of some sort of personalism."[14] By the time Roman education was virtually destroyed by the incursions of the Christians from within and the "barbarians" from without, there was little in it genuinely worth preserving in the interest of the great Roman ideal of *humanitas* (the translation of the Greek *paideia*), a concept which somehow synthesized both humanism and humanitarianism.

Still, at least two innovations may be attributed to the Romans. For one thing, unlike the early Greeks, the educated Roman had to know a foreign language: namely, Greek. And second, in the literary portion of his studies, he paid more attention to contemporary and recent writers. The first point became, of course, utterly essential to ideals of humanistic education in and beyond the Renaissance; but, in the other respect, the Greek rather than the Roman ideal has predominated in our own era, at least until very recently.

But the wisest of the Romans went a little way beyond their Greek masters, too, in grappling directly with the problem of what arts are "proper to humanity" that is, the liberal arts, the arts of the free man. It was Cicero to whom the Renaissance humanists returned with particular reverence and awe, over the abyss of a millenium and a half, for his penetration into what it was that poets, philosophers, and politicians had in common: namely, the arts of policy and civility, and the ability to discourse, displaying a proper sense of one's own cultural heritage, upon individual man and collective man in the unending search for a better life.

Although discourses upon man in early Greek thought typically exhibited human shortcomings, and most notably powerlessness in the face of death, in contrast to the blessed and everlasting gods, gradually the contrast came to be oftener in the other direction: man's advantages over the beasts, the civilized Greek's and Roman's over the barbarians.[15] Studies became increasingly secular, and with an ever greater emphasis upon arts and letters, mythology, oratory, history, and philosophy. These were the principal ingredients of *paideia,* that large educational process through which man's latent humanity develops; these were the principal modes of achievement, the most eloquent evidences of *humanitas.*

2

The Rise of Humanism in the Renaissance

With the appearance of Protagoras and Socrates in the fifth century B.C., philosophy became for the first time man-centered. At his trial, Socrates complained of the fact that he was under indictment for an old and unspecified charge, that of inquiring "into things below the earth and in the sky"[1] along with pure sophistry. Aristophanes, for instance, in *The Clouds,* had him walking on air and spouting metaphysical nonsense "about things of which I know nothing whatsoever. I mean no disrespect for such knowledge," he continues; "if anyone really is versed in it . . . but the fact is, gentlemen, that I take no interest in it."[2]

What he *was* interested in, he went on to say, was easily determined by simply noticing the things he talked about day in and day out. Above all else he was interested in discovering who, if anybody, was wise—and this search led him to expose many who pretended to wisdom but who had only fooled themselves as well as others. He was interested in the difference between right and wrong, good and evil, and in the hard question of whether virtue can be taught. "I have never set up as any man's teacher," he said, but he did feel he had a mission from god to persuade "young and old, to make your first and chief concern not for your bodies nor for your possessions, but for the highest welfare of your souls . . ."[3]

Even to the extent that he was interested in divinity, it was mainly divinity as made manifest in one's inner *daemon,* that sets one his life tasks, as it were, and tells him when he is straying from the proper path.

There is a sense in which the humanists that began to appear in Italy in the early fourteenth century, and elsewhere in Europe and in England shortly thereafter, were reacting to the Middle Ages, as Socrates was to the "pre-Socratic" ontologists and cosmologists, the speculators about the ultimate principles and constituents of the universe. Man was their model and their measure, their despair and their hope, and all study, all

13

art, all human accomplishment was for man and the amelioration and brightening of his lot.

If philosophy as a discipline fell off after the great medieval scholars, Anselm, Abelard, Aquinas, Occam, Roger Bacon, and the others,[4] it was because elaborate proofs of the existence of God, technical elaborations of Aristotelian logic, debates about whether if angels were immaterial one angel could be told from another, and speculations about form, matter, and substance began to seem too far removed from the life of man. The philosophic interests of the humanists were in large measure ethical —though some were enraptured by a Platonic and neo-Platonic mysticism—and their ethical interests, again, were not in the abstract elaborations of the medievalists, but in the search for better models for living, living well, living beautifully, fully, even exuberantly. And this search for models was not rewarded by the writings of the immediately preceding centuries; with the gradual and then the accelerated rediscovery of ancient texts, it became ever clearer that the best models were provided by Cicero, Quintilian, Virgil, and Horace; by Homer, Hesiod, the great tragic dramatists, and the Platonic Socrates. The ancient poets were particularly popular, but Cicero was everybody's favorite as the master prose stylist of all time. As Jacob Burckhardt has written:

> From the fourteenth century Cicero was uncontested as the purest model of prose. This was by no means due solely to a dispassionate opinion in favor of his choice of language, the structure of his sentences, and his style of composition, but to the fact that the Italian spirit responded fully and instinctively to the amiability of the letter writer, to the brilliancy of the orator, and to the lucid exposition of the philosophical thinker.[5]

Amiable, lucid, brilliant—yes, these were qualities much esteemed in the Renaissance, more esteemed it must be said than profundity or ratiocinative rigor. The Renaissance is a time of arts and letters, not of philosophy. Indeed what philosophers of the first rank can be named between Thomas Aquinas and René Descartes, a gap of three centuries? Duns Scotus? Occam?—fine minds, without question, but still solidly within the medieval tradition. Bruno? Campanella?—interesting, adventurous spirits, doubtless important in preparing the way for the efflorescence of the seventeenth century, but scarcely major. Or the name may be proposed of the dashing, impetuous, daring, incredibly learned young man Pico della Mirandola—he died at thirty, having mastered at least five ancient and who knows how many modern languages, drunk at the major intellectual fountains of Europe, offered to debate with anyone on some nine hundred questions of gravity. And true it is that his *Oration on the Dignity of Man* delivered when he was twenty-four, came quickly to seem almost a creed to the humanists. Yet there is little in it that can be called "philosophy" if that term stands for reasoned argument. No, it is what it pretends to be, an oration, an enthusiastic burst of rhetoric praising man as only a little lower than the angels; indeed at times Pico contrasts the angels rather invidiously with his favorite among all created beings, for brutes *and* angels are both predetermined in their nature.

> But upon man, at the moment of his creation, God bestowed seeds pregnant with all possibilities, the germs of every form of life. Whichever of these a man shall cultivate, the same will mature and bear fruit in him. If vegetative, he will become a plant; if sensual, he will become brutish; if rational, he will reveal himself a heavenly being; if intellectual, he will be an angel and the son of God.[6]

All this needs saying, Pico wrote, in order that man *appreciate* his full potentiality, and realize it. "Let a certain saving ambition invade our souls so that, impatient of mediocrity, we pant after the highest things and (since, if we will, we can) bend all our efforts to their attainment."[7]

This most Romantic of Renaissance men was true to his age in his near worship of Plato and the Platonists—especially that about them which was impassioned in its search for truth. Characteristically he lauds "Those Socratic frenzies which lift us to such ecstasy that our intellects and our very selves are united to God. And we shall be moved by them in this way if previously we have done all that it lies in us to do."[8]

Stung by those who spoke scornfully of his youth, Pico concludes his oration by abandoning any pretense to modesty: "I have wanted to make clear in this disputation, not only that I know a great many things, but also that I know a great many things which others do not know."[9]

And there too is the Renaissance man speaking, the man who wanted to excel, to leave his particular mark on the world.

There was no shortage of philosophers in the age, just a shortage of those who attained to great heights. Pico for all his passion and industry did not. Ficino too did not, though he managed an interesting definition of man in terms of love. He too derived from Plato—indeed

he invented the phrase "Platonic love"—but like so many of the humanists concerned himself particularly with the Latin word *humanitas,*
which, as Kristeller says, . . . "is ambiguous since it stands both for the
human race and for humane feeling as a personal virtue. This ambiguity
reflects the ancient Roman stoic ideal of *humanitas* that combined with
the standards of cultural refinement a high respect for other persons as
fellow human beings."[10] Ficino elaborated the notion by saying that
"Man proves himself a member of the human race by loving other men
as his equals, by being humane. When he is inhumane and cruel, he
removes himself from the community of mankind and forfeits his human
dignity."[11]

    In a search for philosophic thought in this period one is even more
likely to go to persons not easily classified—which is part of what it was
to *be* a "Renaissance man" no doubt—Rabelais, Montaigne, Erasmus.
If one adopts Crane Brinton's distinction between the exuberant and the
spare humanists,[12] Rabelais, bawdy, roaring, gleeful, obscene, with a
Gargantuan appetite for wine, women and books—it is Rabelais with his
absolute devotion to excess, who exceeded all others in exuberance. But
where Rabelais shouted with laughter, Erasmus displayed a quiet, sly,
somewhat wry smile over the folly of man; his book in praise thereof was
the most popular book of an age that invented books as we know them,
and made them popular. (It has been said that Gutenberg himself had
no real conception of the power of the press, but entertained the more
modest desire to make books cheaply available to students and the
clergy.) Montaigne, too, must be counted on the spare side of the ledger,
for all of his insistence that the right way to educate a young man is to
let him experience the rougher pleasures and pains of living, along with
the smooth: "Let the young man laugh, carouse, and debauch with his
prince; I would have him, even in his excesses, surpass his companions
in ability and vigour, so that he may not refrain from such pleasures
through lack of power and knowledge but for lack of will."[13]

    Over and over again from Renaissance writers on education we hear
caning and other violence deplored. Compulsion or violence, Montaigne
said, "dulls and degenerates a well-born nature. If you would have a
child fear shame and punishment, do not harden him to them."[14] Although Montaigne would be at great pains that a young man not turn
into a pedant, or become bookish to the exclusion of other more direct
sources of wisdom, he obviously believed that his own education had

appropriately equipped him to draw upon the insights of the great classical authors, so that almost every page of his *Essays* is dotted with quotations from Seneca, Cicero, Juvenal, Horace, Propertius, Horace, Plutarch, or Plato, yet he "would have the tutor make the child examine and thoroughly sift all things, and harbour nothing in his head by mere authority or upon trust."[15] Like so much of Montaigne's writing, and so much of that of a hundred of his contemporaries, this was a deep thrust at medievalism, as it is when he says, "Away with your crabbed, logical subtleties; they are abuses, things by which our lives can never be made better."[16] And that is the criterion, always: making our lives better. But the successful employment of this criterion depends upon recognizing that man is naturally and properly an integrated being: "I would have his manners, behaviour, and bearing cultivated at the same time with his mind. It is not the mind, it is not the body we are training: it is the man, and we must not divide him into two parts."[17]

Probably no one directly applied Montaigne's theories to the education of children; certainly *he* was no schoolmaster, and was probably too busy with his civic duties (twice he served, reluctantly but efficiently, as mayor of Bordeaux) and with his own reading and writing to pay more than cursory attention to the education of his own children. For the most famous of Renaissance schools, we have to go back in time to the early fifteenth century, and Vittorino's *La Giocosa,* established under the sponsorship of the wealthy Marquis of Mantua for the education of his own children (including one daughter) and those of other members of the nobility. Indeed, over seventy pupils were enrolled at one time. La Giocosa quickly became well known through Italy as a very fountainhead of humanism. Everything about the school bespoke enlightenment, from the airiness of the school building and the beauty of its surroundings, to the emphasis upon sports and outdoor recreation, the freedom from dreariness and the prevalence of an atmosphere of joy in learning. Although mathematics and astronomy and music (carefully supervised as to the permissible harmonies) were not entirely neglected, the curriculum was very heavily slanted toward literary and rhetorical studies. Latin and Greek were effectively and thoroughly taught, and then used in the mastery of almost the whole catalogue of classical writers, from Homer and Hesiod to Caesar, Livy, Virgil, and Ovid. Heavy emphasis was still put on memorization and declamation—whole orations of Demosthenes and Cicero, and entire books from the great epics, were commonly repeated by the children—for at this time books were still few; but throughout the study, it was the ethical lessons which could be drawn from the great writers of the past that received primary attention, for the end of this education was the development of the complete citizen.

It is a safe guess that most of the graduates of La Giocosa, within the limits of their not inconsiderable fortunes, established their own libraries, for the private collecting of books did not wait for Gutenberg. Petrarch had the best private classical library of the fourteenth century, some two hundred volumes, and we know from Chaucer's tale of the Clerk of Oxford that even a poor student would have his own books:

> For hym was levere have at his beddes heed
> Twenty bokes, clad in blak or reed,
> Of Aristotle and his philosophie,
> Than robes riche, or fithele, or gay sautrie.
> But al be that he was a philosophre,
> Yet hadde he but litel gold in cofre;
> But al that he myghte of his freendes hente,
> On bokes and on lernynge he it spente.[18]

This is the very clerk, it will be remembered, of whom Chaucer said, in a line to become famous: "And gladly wolde he lerne and gladly teche." The gladness with which the Renaissance humanists learned and taught was perhaps their most memorable quality. Hard as it is to imagine anyone exceeding Petrarch and Boccaccio and Machiavelli in their love of old books and learning in general, one senses that the invention of movable type did indeed make possible and actual an even more exuberant love of reading.[19] With Rabelais, as already remarked, we get a man who drank in and gobbled down books as avidly as he did flagons of wine and platters of roast duck. The great letter of Gargantua to his son, Pantagruel, is deserving of extensive quotation:

> Now it is, that the minds of men are qualified with all manner of discipline and the old sciences revived, which for many ages were extinct. Now it is, that the learned languages are to their pristine purity restored, viz., Greek, without which a man may be ashamed to account himself a scholar, Hebrew, Arabic, Chaldaean, and Latin. Printing likewise is now in use, so elegant and so correct, that better cannot be imagined, although it was found out but in my time by divine inspiration, as by a diabolical suggestion on the other side,

was the invention of ordnance. All the world is full of knowing men, of most learned schoolmasters, and vast libraries; and it appears to me as a truth, that neither in Plato's time, nor Cicero's, nor Papinian's, there was ever such conveniency for studying, as we see at this day there is. Nor must any adventurer henceforward to come in public or present himself in company, that hath not been pretty well polished in the shop of Minerva. I see robbers, hangmen, freebooters, tapsters, ostlers, and such like, of the very rubbish of the people, more learned now than the doctors and preachers were in my time.

What shall I say? The very women and children have aspired to this praise and celestial manna of good learning. Yet so it is, that at the age I am now of, I have been constrained to learn the Greek tongue —which I contemned not like Cato, but had not the leisure in my younger years to attend the study of it,—and I take much delight in the reading of Plutarch's Morals, the pleasant Dialogues of Plato, the Monuments of Pausanias, and the Antiquities of Athenaeus, in waiting on the hour wherein God my Creator shall call me, and command me to depart from this earth and transitory pilgrimage. Wherefore, my son, I admonish thee to employ thy youth to profit as well as thou canst, both in thy studies and in virtue. Thou art at Paris, where the laudable examples of many brave men may stir up thy mind to gallant actions, and hast likewise, for thy tutor and pedagogue the learned Epistemon, who by his lively and vocal documents may instruct thee in the arts and sciences.

I intend, and will have it so, that thou learn the languages perfectly; first of all, the Greek, as Quintilian will have it; secondly, the Latin; and then the Hebrew, for the Holy Scripture-sake; and then the Chaldee and Arabic likewise, and that thou frame thy style in Greek in imitation of Plato; and for the Latin, after Cicero. Let there be no history which thou shalt not have ready in memory;—unto the prosecuting of which design, books of cosmography will be very conducible, and help thee much.

Of the liberal arts of geometry, arithmetic and music, I gave thee some taste when thou wert yet little, and not above five or six years old. Proceed further in them, and learn the remainder if thou canst. As for astronomy, study all the rules thereof. Let pass, nevertheless, the divining and judicial astrology, and the art of Lullius, as being nothing else but plain abuses and vanities. As for the civil law, of that I would have thee to know the texts by heart, and then to confer them with philosophy.[20]

Similarly, Castiglione required of his courtier that he be

more than passably accomplished in letters, at least in those studies that are called the humanities, and conversant not only with the Latin language but with the Greek, for the sake of the many different things that have been admirably written therein. Let him be well versed in the poets, and not less in the orators and historians, and also proficient in writing verse and prose, especially in this vulgar tongue of ours; for besides the enjoyment he will find in it, he will by this means never lack agreeable entertainment with ladies, who are usually fond of such things.[21]

Some of the same optimism remains in a figure as late as John Amos Comenius (1592-1671). Though the infinitely pious Comenius would have been shocked down to the soles of his tidy boots to be put in the company of such as Castiglione and Rabelais, yet it is not to be forgotten that Comenius believed he had come upon a method of "teaching all things to all men." The advertisement for *The Great Didactic* read as follows:

A certain Inducement to found such Schools in all the Parishes, Towns, and Villages of every Christian Kingdom, that the entire Youth of both Sexes, none being excepted, shall QUICKLY, PLEASANTLY, & THOROUGHLY Become learned in the Sciences, pure in Morals, Trained to Piety, and in this manner instructed in all things necessary for the present and for the future life, in which, with respect to everything that is suggested Its Fundamental Principles are set forth from the essential nature of the matter, its TRUTH is proved by examples from the several mechanical arts, Its ORDER is clearly set forth in years, months, days, and hours, and finally, AN EASY AND SURE METHOD is shown, by which it can be pleasantly brought into existence.[22]

But Comenius had left behind both the literary and the principally secular character of humanism. Principally secular? Here one must be cautious. It is easy to exaggerate the extent to which Renaissance humanism turned away from the Church. Certainly many of its most famous figures were deeply Christian, even when they castigated the Middle Ages for its confining dogmatism. Petrarch was a loyal churchman, one of his strongest defenses of the study of the classics being that the best of the ancient authors were proper handmaids to Christianity, and in no sense inimical to Christian piety. Erasmus, who went so far as to say that a man ignorant of letters was no man at all, was a person of deepest faith. Thomas More and Vives, similarly, were far from secularism. Still there was, especially as the Renaissance progressed, a kind of weakening of interest in Church doctrine, certainly a weakening of interest in theology and the writing of the Church fathers. Luther could not countenance Erasmus' secular interests for all of his faith, saying gravely, "In him the human carries more weight than the divine."[23]

Religious superstition came to be commonly censured, along with the supposition that writers in the Christian tradition had any monopoly on truth. Interest sharply fell away from otherworldliness and supernaturalism. Though ethics if anything gained in prominence as compared with medieval times, the good life now envisioned was far from monastic. "Do What Thou Wilt" was the motto inscribed on Montaigne's Abbey of Theleme, and freedom was strongly and even invidiously contrasted with the locked-in qualities of medievalism.

It is less in deliberate attacks on medieval Christianity, however, than in an important change of emphasis that Renaissance humanism reveals its secularism. In advice on how to live, in lists of what are the important things to teach, in celebration of the best authors, one notes how little is said about Christianity. In the famous observation of Michelet, the revival of learning was marked by two great achievements, the discovery of the world and the discovery of man. And the humanists were not particularly interested in geography: for them, man had been too long denigrated as the essentially unworthy creature of an awesomely powerful God. "The medieval man," Brinton has written, "*felt* as truth ... that this is the best of all possible worlds. Not a happy but a contented world, for in such a world man would usurp the place of God. It was, quite simply, God's world."[24] The humanist could not bring himself specifically to deny that this is God's world; but he could not help proclaiming that it is also man's.

This is not to say that man in general was worshipped. Perhaps no age has been more elitist, more aware of the differences among men, more appreciative of the greatest men, of the "best that has been thought and said in the world." The distinctions they made among authors were as to better or worse, and hardly at all with respect to epoch or specialization. They spoke little of history as a separate discipline, but much of Herodotus and Seneca; they were completely uninterested in deciding whether Plutarch should be classed with the philosophers: he was an interesting and rewarding writer; some of them might prefer Latin to Greek, but they knew Homer and Virgil were alike great epic poets, and it did not matter much that they were separated by many centuries and much water. The great writers were great and worthy of poring over for what they communicate to men about how to be human. As Sandys has said, the discovery of man in the Renaissance may above all

> be illustrated by the re-awakening of the human spirit from the trance or the half-broken slumber, of the Middle Ages; by the acceptance of the old classical literature, and primarily (in point of time) the old Latin literature, as the *litterae humaniores*—the studies that, in comparison with all others, were regarded as distinctively humane, distinctively humanizing; and lastly, by the recognition of the essence of humanism as consisting in a new and vital perception of the dignity of man."[25]

From a careful study of the ancients, one could extract not only specific moral lessons and guides, but the best possible improvement of one's own style. Thus Lionardo Bruni (1369-1444), writing on the proper education of a lady, advocated immersion in Latin literature: "To her knowledge of facts she must add finish of form, and her highest distinction is to be found in breadth of learning combined with grace of style."[26] But style was more than an ornament: it was a quality of life. It was that which made self-expression, (one of man's principal needs) more than an effusion, even possibly attaining to true creativity.

The Renaissance was not all humanistic. Copernicus' life ranges over almost exactly the same time as that of Erasmus and Sir Thomas More and Melancthon. Galileo was born when Montaigne was at the height of his powers. Then too Leonardo da Vinci's is a name to remind us that a consuming interest in the arts need not exclude an interest in science and technology. Yet, though the Renaissance humanists, for all their diatribes against logic, did not specifically set humane letters over against mathematics and the sciences, they were not typically any more

interested in physics and astronomy than they were in technical philosophy. To us, perhaps the most curious lack among the humanists was
much interest in the visual arts. Of course it is not rare today for ap-
preciators of one art to have no competence or even interest in the others,
but somehow "Renaissance" for us stands for versatility, sweep, breadth,
so that we might expect those who were rediscovering the virtues of
classical literature and cultivating their own expressive style to be interested too in the vase paintings and the sculpture and architecture of
Greece and Rome. Yet the combining of these interests was not to
become common for a long further stretch of time. Nor were these
humanists much concerned, apparently, with the marvelous effflores-
cence of all the visual arts of their own time. And the artists thought of
themselves as craftsmen, exalted artisans, linked more closely with engineers than with scholars.

No, humanism was a verbal enterprise. Not literary in a narrow
sense, the interests of these humanists were in almost everything that can
be written or spoken, always excepting the logic and dialectic they hated
as medieval scholasticism. As Symonds has said about higher education
in the Renaissance:

> The medieval curriculum offered no defined place for the new learn-
> ing of the Revival, which had indeed no recognized name. Chairs
> had therefore to be founded under the title of rhetoric, from which
> men like Chrysoloras and Guarino, Filelfo and Politian expounded
> orally to hundreds of eager students from every town in Italy and
> every nation of Europe their accumulated knowledge of antiquity.
> One mass of Greek and Roman erudition, including history and
> metaphysics, law and science, civic institutions and the art of war
> . . ., domestic manners and religious rites, grammar and philology,
> biology and numismatics, formed the miscellaneous subject-matter
> of this so-styled rhetoric. . . . Each large town established its public
> study, academy or university—similar institutions under varying
> designations—for the exposition of the *litterae humaniores.* The
> humanists, or professors of that branch of knowledge, became a
> class of the highest dignity.[27]

Rhetoric, indeed, was an encyclopaedic discipline; and yet at its
center was the explication of classical literary texts. Rhetoric was again
the Queen of the Disciplines, as it had been for Gorgias and Isocrates,
Cicero and Quintilian. It was a rhetoric big enough, in the hands of most

of them, to include history and ethics, as well as grammar and philology, but it was the rhetorical analysis of literary texts that was their great and abiding preoccupation. Richard McKeon has caught the spirit of the humanists, both in what they were for and against in this passage from his essay "Culture and the Humanities":

> The revolt of the Renaissance was a revolt against the medieval arts and encyclopaedia. It was a return from the technicalities of the verbal logics and speculative grammars of the late Middle Ages to a renewed use of rhetoric to effect the shift from verbal structures and consequences to structures of expression and communication. The study of man was reoriented from the ends formalized in theology to the ends expressed in Greek art and in the Scriptures conceived and interpreted as literature and history. The arts became fields rather than disciplines, and *litterae humaniores,* the more human literature, became the distinguishing mark of man, not as superior achievement in the use of language which distinguished him from animals, nor as the exercise of disciplines distinct from those used in the interpretation of divine letters, but a branch of learning distinct from the emerging new sciences.[28]

Finally, a word about the Renaissance as the time in which literary culture became primarily visual. W. J. Ong, Eric Havelock, and Marshall McLuhan among others, have shown how Plato is the climactic figure in the West in the deterioration of the old oral-aural culture. Socrates was of course not a writer but a talker. Plato wrote his philosophy in the form of dialogues, even when as in the *Timaeus* and the *Parmenides,* they have almost no give-and-take discussion left in them. Still, as Ong has written,

> ... Plato's ideas, the "really real," were polarized at the maximum distance from the old oral-aural human life-world. Spoken words are events, engaged in time and indeed in the present. Plato's ideas were the polar opposite, not events at all, but motionless "objective" existence, impersonal, and out of time.[29]

After Plato, there was no going back. Right on through the Hellenistic, Roman, and Medieval times culture was predominantly visual, according to Ong[30]; but only with the invention of movable type in the middle of the fifteenth century was the spoken word put into eclipse. Before that, after all, the lecture still remained the principal means of getting texts before audiences; but after that, lecturers became virtually unnecessary: most, if not all of what they had to say, could be then or soon read.[31] The book came to be the center of culture.

3

From the Renaissance to the Twentieth Century

We have noted that the Renaissance humanists were a group singularly devoted to the rhetorical analysis of classical literature, and that there was among them but little concern for technical philosophy, history, or the fine arts. If some of the minor philosophers of the time, such as Ficino, speculated about the nature of beauty, drawing of course upon Plato,[1] still aesthetics as a particular subject of interest was not yet ready to emerge. However, there was, especially in the sixteenth century, a growing amount of interest in literary criticism, art criticism, and music criticism; and some of the critics made at least half-hearted attempts to link their own favorite art with some of the others, if only by making invidious comparisons. Alberti, for instance, stung by the apparently common assumption that painters and sculptors were little more than menial artisans, insisted in his book *On Painting* as early as the middle of the fifteenth century that the painter deserved respect (and the sculptor too though perhaps less so) because his art was a difficult one, one requiring genius for the production of beautiful works. He argued that the good painter required a liberal education in order that he understand human beings, and that he should be a student of science in order that he be able correctly to see and represent his subjects.[2] Leonardo da Vinci's *Treatise on Painting* written about 1500, similarly defends painting as an art, asserting its superiority to both poetry and music, not alone in beauty but also in truth. His famous pronouncement, "That painting is most praiseworthy which conforms most to the object portrayed" was the ground for the great attention he paid to the laws of linear perspective,[3] a matter which Albrecht Dürer also wrote upon, while confessing that the nature of Beauty, as an abstract property, eluded him.

Musical theorists, in turn, defended the high place of their art, citing the testimonies of Plato, particularly; indeed, like the humanists, they became fascinated with the music and (particularly since they had little

27

success in finding much out about the actual music itself) the music theories of the ancients. But they went on from there to explore the relationships between certain rhythms and harmonies and in the late sixteenth and seventeenth centuries gradually led music into an ever-broadening range of representation of nature and human feelings.

Particularly interesting was the group of poets, philosophers, and musicians who took to frequenting the home of Giovanni Bardi, Count of Vernio. These Florentine Camerata, as they came to be called, believed they had found in the theories of the ancients a justification for condemning the prevailing polyphony, especially as exemplified in the ubiquitous madrigal, and for proposing instead the composition of lyrical/dramatic works in which the music took its cues from the verses. Here were the beginnings of oratorio and opera, and of centuries of speculation about the fruitful modes of combining arts into syntheses more powerful than any productions since the tragedies of the Athenian theater.

In poetics the devotion to the ancients in the sixteenth century took the form, in such critics as Scaliger and Castelvetro, of defense of the "unities," that is, the rule that a drama must not offend our imagination by skipping around in time and place, but confine its setting to a single place, or to nearby places, and its time to a single day. By this time, Aristotle, who had said, "Tragedy endeavors, as far as possible, to confine itself to a single revolution of the sun or but slightly to exceed this limit. . . . ,"[4] though he was no longer The Philosopher (as with Aquinas) still carried a powerful authority. Thus only, it was thought, could the poet persuade us that we were witnessing a true *mimesis* of life. However, in the seventeenth century such strictures were increasingly softened, as the authority of the ancients declined; for instance, Sidney in his famous "Defense of Poesie" (1595) defended his art against the attacks which derived from Plato, arguing that poetry encompasses both history and philosophy, making universal truths concrete, even though in a strict sense—thus protecting the poet against the charge of telling falsehoods—he "nothing affirmeth . . . and therefore never lieth."

When the seventeenth century is called the "age of science," it is obviously not because of any sparsity of superb creations in literature, art, and music (Shakespeare, Donne, Milton, Corneille, Rembrandt, Hals, Purcell, Monteverdi, et al.) but because of the steep escalation of scientific and mathematical and technological achievement, most notably in Newton's *Principia Mathematica,* which finally fulfilled the promise of mathematically unifying the cosmos. This is not of course meant to suggest that Newton believed science to be a sufficient explanation of man and the world. He was a deeply religious man and prized his own theological writings as much as his scientific, though poetry he considered to be no more than a kind of ingenious nonsense.

This did not stop a poet's writing,

God said, Let Newton be, and all was light.

Pope's celebration of the chief hero of this age was echoed in the words of poets, divines, and philosophers.[5] Indeed, the philosophers of the time were so smitten with the actualities and the promises of scientific knowledge that it comes near being true that they could think of nothing else, much less the arts.[6] And increasingly they conceived of the philosophic enterprise as linked to the sciences and mathematics: the attempt over and over—at least on the part of philosophers—was to blur the distinctions.

Descartes, for notable instance, though he did indeed write a youthful work on music (which managed to ignore the sensuous aspect of music in favor of its mathematics), had little to say about beauty or the arts, but of course felt that he himself had been able to extract from mathematical practice the methods which accounted for its successes, and to show their applicability to the long intransigent problems of philosophy. No humanist he, but a man of the present, ranging from his invention of analytical geometry through his engineering services to the Dutch armies (the list of famous men who devoted much of their energy to the art of fortification is impressive), to the freeing of the whole material world, including the body of man, from the constraints of theology and opening it to the experimentation of science. Mathematics, science, technology, and the new philosophy (become rigorously mathematical) were the promise of an almost completely demystified universe.

If anything, Spinoza went even further in his rationalism and in his exclusion of letters and the arts from any meaningful contribution to that adequate knowledge of the universe through which man's salvation—the term befits the wholly religious mind of this "atheistic" Jew—is alone attainable.

Leibniz, the most encyclopaedic mind of the age (and very nearly of any age), grudgingly allowed a small place for the arts, saying however that, in contrast with the ideals for thought of clarity, distinctness, and adequacy, literary expression was distinctly unclear, its charms resulting from a "je ne sais quoi." He ranked Halley four times as important as Dryden, and Newton ten times, and said in a letter something that pretty well summarizes his feeling about artistic achievement: " 'I am sorry about the loss by fire of the Holbein paintings in Whitehall. Yet I feel after all a little like the Czar of Russia who told me that he more admired certain pretty machines than all the beautiful paintings he had been shown in the King's palace.' "[7]

Francis Bacon, though he gives in "Of the Advancement of Learning" a legitimate place to poetry and to the imagination which is its instrument, "accommodating the shows of things to the desires of the mind," claimed that the power that is knowledge was to be achieved through philosophy and science alone. Thomas Hobbes was somewhat more generous in the place he accorded poetry and the fancy, even suggesting that there were ways in which the philosopher and the poet are allies; but John Locke, for all of the fact that his empirical psychology gave rise to a new aesthetics and a new poetics,[8] himself rather sourly spoke, when he spoke at all, of the ornamental language of literature as a departure from the precision and rigor of science and philosophy:

> ... If we would speak of things as they are, we must allow that all the arts of rhetoric, besides order and clearness, all the artificial and figurative applications of words eloquence hath invented, are for nothing else but to insinuate wrong ideas, move the passions, and thereby mislead the judgment, and so indeed are perfect cheats.[9]

The tongue-clucking tone about moving the passions and *thereby* misleading the judgment is a fair sample of the attitude of both the rationalists and the science-infatuated empiricists toward the feelings of men.

There even began to be a few criticisms—foreshadowing the near avalanche of criticisms in the nineteenth century—of the humanistic domination of school and college curricula. Thus, John Webster in his Examination of the Academies (1654) set down advice concerning the reform of the schools by dividing "Humane learning" into three parts: " 'the purely instrumental studies of grammar, logic, and mathematics; the studies which give substantive knowledge, such as natural philosophy, metaphysics, politics, ethics, and economics; and the merely ornamental arts of oratory and poetry.' "[10] The "merely" tells clearly the part of the curriculum he thinks has been overemphasized; yet it is interesting that there is in this line of thinking a very broad conception of "humane learning," however different its parts.

Even those who were professionally dealing with literature and the arts at this time were emphasizing the importance of reason, clarity, method, regularity, order—in short, the whole array of virtues that the new scientific writing strove to embody and that Descartes, Bacon, and Locke were prescribing for philosophy. In "Of Dramatic Poesy" in 1688 Dryden, representing a dialogue on the question of the comparative merits of the ancients and the moderns, which for many decades was one of the most fascinating of the disputes among men of letters, bespeaks the hope of his age that the arts may soon begin to show the same striking progress that the sciences had done, and by the same means essentially: understanding nature better.

> I deny not what you urge of arts and sciences, that they have flourished in some ages more than others; but your instance in philosophy makes for me: for if natural causes be more known now than in the time of Aristotle, because more studied, it follows that poesy and other arts may, with the same pains, arrive still nearer to perfection. . . .

Or again, certain playwrights are criticized, for having

> failed in laying of their plots, and in the management, swerving from the rules of their own art by misrepresenting Nature to us. . . .

Only a few years before, in a didactic poem which Dryden (along with Sir William Soame) translated, Boileau's "The Art of Poetry," it was said:

> Whate'er you write of pleasant or sublime,
> Always let sense accompany your rhyme.
> Falsely they seem each other to oppose:
> Rhyme must be made with reason's laws to close;
> And when to conquer her you bend your force,
> The mind will triumph in the noble course.
> To reason's yoke she quickly will incline,
> Which far from hurting, renders her divine;
> But if neglected, will as easily stray,
> And master reason, which she should obey.
> Love reason then; and let whate'er you write
> Borrow from her its beauty, force, and light.[11]

At about the same time another French critic, René le Lossu was writing:

> The arts have this in common with the sciences, that the former like the latter are founded on reason and that in the arts one should allow himself to be guided by the lights which nature has given us.[12]

And in the early part of the eighteenth century, Pope followed this same line, urging his fellow poets to "follow nature," but not, of course in the sense of anarchic romanticism: god forbid!

> Those RULES of old discovered, not devis'd,
> Are nature still, but Nature methodized.[13]

For after all, this is what scientists presumably did, to methodize nature.

In art criticism, and in art itself, there began to be in the seventeenth century a shift from representation of nature as the ideal (da Vinci) to a kind of "ideal imitation"—that is, where there is a faithfulness not to nature on its seamier side, but as made worthy of emulation by those striving to be of good character. This meant, for one thing, a searching for the form within the thing, a revealing of the "characteristic" more than what happens to be actual, and a directing of the attention to the general and the abstract, just as the scientist moves from particulars to laws and theories. As late as the 1780's, Sir Joshua Reynolds was advocating the elimination of "accidental deficiencies, excrescences, and deformities of things," in order to reveal "the perfect state of nature, which the artist calls the ideal beauty."[14] The "beauty of which we are in quest," he said, "is general and intellectual." Similarly, Dr. Johnson had spoken of the poet's business as being "to examine, not the individual, but the species ...: he does not number the streaks of the tulip. ..."[15]

Yet though this kind of rationalistic neoclassicism was, of course, to extend, (as we have seen in the last two artists quoted) almost through the eighteenth century, there began to develop early in this period a counter-trend that was to culminate, in one sense, in the nature philosophy of Rousseau, but in another to continue developing right through German, French, British, and American nineteenth century romanticism.

Anthony Ashley Cooper, third earl of Shaftesbury, shortly before his death in 1713, published works which, in his own brand of Platonism (though deriving to a degree from the so-called Cambridge Platonists), envisioned the universe not as a great mathematically perfect machine —its microcosm being the much-discussed watch found on the desert island—but as a marvelously beautiful, perfectly harmonized organic whole. It was the Plato of the *Symposium* and *Phaedrus*—not the Plato of the *Timaeus* or (much less) the *Laws*—that here furnished the guide. The good is the beautiful, and it is beauty that best guides us to the good life. But we know beauty, he argues, not by the reason, but by the feelings, by a kind of "aesthetic sense" whose workings are not reducible to method or law. "It is not a head merely, but a *heart* which must complete the real philosopher," Shaftesbury said, half a century before Rousseau did. He was, Randall has argued, "the first, certainly the most influential, moralist to base his ethics squarely on psychological experience."[16] And from Shaftesbury sprang a distinguished line of moralists all of whom found human feelings to be at the center of the moral life: Hutcheson, Hume, Adam Smith—and then in the nineteenth century, Bentham and both Mills.

And the greatest of the lot was Hume, the sceptical empiricist, who went so far toward undermining confidence in science and reason as to throw serious doubt upon the very principle of induction and the supposition that *cause* is anything but a psychological expectation based upon habit.

Hume was not only convinced that morals and criticism, dealing respectively with goodness and beauty "are not so properly objects of the understanding as of taste and sentiment. Beauty whether moral or natural, is felt, more properly than perceived."[17]

In his astonishingly precocious work, the *Treatise on Human Nature,* Hume had set it down in his introduction that the study of man is the proper foundation for all other studies, from mathematics to natural (i.e., nonrevealed) religion, and he made clear that this study comprised the four "moral sciences": logic, morals, criticism, and politics.

The sole end of logic is to explain the principles and operations of our reasoning faculty, and the nature of our ideas; morals and criticism regard our tastes and sentiments: and politics consider men as united in society, and dependent on each other. In these four sciences of *Logic, Morals, Criticism,* and *Politics,* is comprehended almost everything, which it can any way import us to be acquainted with, or which can tend either to the improvement or ornament of the human mind. . . .

There is no question of importance, whose decision is not compriz'd in the science of man; and there is none, which can be decided with any certainty, before we become acquainted with that science. In pretending therefore to explain the principles of human nature, we in effect propose a compleat system of the sciences built on a foundation almost entirely new, and the only one upon which they can stand with any security.[18]

He meant the foundation of "experience and observation," which admittedly yield only probable conclusions in contrast to the certain demonstration available in mathematics.

Hume clearly thought of himself as doing for the inner world what Newton had done for the outer. He had no notion of pretending competence in natural philosophy, but only in the philosophy of mind and the passions—which is to say sentiments, feelings, inclinations, and taste. And one implication of this is that he allied himself, unlike Descartes, Leibniz, Spinoza, Bacon, and Locke, with men of letters and humane investigators, not with the scientists. "My ruling passion is the love of literary fame," he blithely confessed in his autobiography, and his essays on politics, tragedy, polygamy, taxes, miracles, taste, and civil liberty *(inter alia)*, put him, in his own eyes as well as the eyes of some of his contemporaries, in the company of Cicero and Montaigne, no less than of the Scottish and English moralists of his own time. He specifically mentions Locke, Shaftesbury, Mandeville, Hutcheson and Butler as the philosophers "who have begun to put the science of man on a new footing. . . ."[19]

The "criticism" of which Hume often speaks, a pursuit combining philology, history, literary criticism, and aesthetics (which though the term had been introduced by Hume's contemporary Baumgarten, in Germany, was not yet widely recognized as a branch of philosophy), was well described by Gibbon in his *Essai sur L'etude de la Litterature,* written in 1764:

Criticism is, in my opinion, the art of forming a judgment of writings and writers; of what they have said, of what they have said well, and what they have said truly. Under the first head are comprehended grammar, a knowledge of languages and manuscripts; a capacity of distinguishing supposed from genuine performances, and of restoring the true reading of corrupted passages. Under the second, is included the whole theory of elocution and poesy. The third opens an immense field, the enquiry into the circumstances and truth of facts. Thus the whole generation of critics may be distinguished under three, grammarians, rhetoricians, and historians.[20]

Thus Hume's (and Gibbon's) "criticism" or even more generally his "moral science" may, as R. S. Crane has shown, be properly considered to have descended from humanistic rhetoric. Crane notes some five important resemblances:

(1) The subject matter of what Hume calls his metaphysics ... is concerned with problems which had originally emerged in rhetoric —namely the nature of probable arguments and the analysis of the passions. (2) The fundamental divisions of problems throughout Hume's system into theoretical and practical and general and particular are distinctions which had been made important in the tradition of rhetoric. (3) His treatment of morals and of criticism is a rhetorical treatment in the sense that what is inquired into is primarily not the nature of actions or virtues or of works of art but the psychological causes which lead men to judge actions and characters or literary works as they do. (4) The devices of argument which Hume employs involve an easily recognizable selection from among the commonplaces of rhetoric as set forth, for example, by Cicero and Quintilian (two favorite authors of his). (5) Finally, as a writer ... Hume is constantly preoccupied with questions of style. ...[21]

Although eighteenth century humanities, in contrast with that of the Renaissance, was more commonly philosophical, frequently deeper, far more likely to deal with contemporary writers and not confine its attention to the ancients, it was still continuous with the older tradition, representing, as we have seen, a return after an age of adulation of the mathematical and natural sciences. And it was, perhaps, the last age in which the humanities was widely respected as an obviously valuable, indeed indispensable, part of education.[22] After that, much philosophy was again to become technical, abstruse, and lofty; much history was to aspire to a scientific model; and many men of letters were to become defensive in their insistence upon the value of their favorite field. If the humanities retained a central place in the curriculum of the schools and universities as it did (in both Britain and the United States, the sciences were relatively unimportant parts of the curriculum until after the middle of the nineteenth century), the reason was more because of a kind of snob value attributed to their study than through a better-grounded defense of their importance.

Nevertheless, it is only with Romanticism—and whatever the extent to which Hume celebrated the centrality of human passions, he was in temperament, attitude, and belief miles away from Romanticism—that we see the full flowering (or as some would prefer to say, the overblooming and decay) of a movement that started by trying to do justice to the nonrational side of man.[23]

Jean-Jacques Rousseau was at once a child of the Enlightenment and a father of Romanticism. *Nature* was, of course, his rallying cry, whether his immediate subject was the arts and sciences, politics, or education, and he meant by the words, at one time or another in his voluminous writings, very nearly everything that *can* be meant, from the chronologically original state of man, to man's native endowment, to the fullest development of human nature, the fruit of a genuine education and a just society.

His *Emile* was an attempt to show how a child might conceivably be rescued from the corrupting influences of a corrupt society, by taking him away from its manners and morals into an atmosphere in which he may learn, principally without books, to observe nature and trust his own feelings. The education he proposed was in some respects as distant from that typically associated with humanism as any that could be imagined, for Emile, totally unlike Pantagruel, would not be plunged into philosophy, literature, medicine, rhetoric, music—and everything else that man has written about. Quite the contrary. Thus Emile's tutor said, "I hate books. They only teach us to talk about what we do not know."[24]

However, Emile would, Rousseau believed, emerge into young manhood at once innocent and capable of learning, *wanting* to learn; yet he would still be able to test everything presented him for his learning against the genuineness of his own uncorrupted feelings.

It is said that the only occasion on which Immanuel Kant failed to go for his morning walk was the day when the long-awaited copy of *Emile* appeared in his mail. To be sure, Kant went well beyond Rousseau in the moral instruction which he came to advocate when he addressed himself to problems of education. Yet he, too, however forbiddingly intellectualistic and rationalistic he appears to readers of his first two

Critiques, had a profound respect for the feelings of man, as did Rousseau and Hume.

Although Baumgarten before him had written an Aesthetics, it remained for Kant to establish the subject upon firm philosophical foundations. In aesthetic judgment, he taught, unlike the judgments employed in science and morality, we consult our feelings not our concepts. Beauty has to do not with things seen objectively but with things we, their beholders, take first as the source of a disinterested pleasure and then shape, using the free play of our imaginations. In all experience of beauty, whether in art or nature, there is a sense of purposiveness, even though we are unable to assign a definite purpose to its particular reality. "Nature is beautiful because it looks like art; and art can only be called beautiful if we are conscious of it as art while yet it looks like nature."[25]

With the appearance of this aesthetics from Kant, the least poetical of philosophers, poets, novelists, and art lovers all over the civilized world felt they had been given a justification for the full celebration of their humanistic interests, felt that they had been liberated from the rationalism of the eighteenth century. As Randall has said, in describing the effect of Kant's aesthetics upon the burgeoning tide of German (and other nations') *sturm und drang,*

> ... Romanticism burst asunder the tight little world of Newtonian science. It called men back to experiences, facts, and values forgotten in the first enthusiasm for mathematical interpretation of nature and human life. Physics might be a marvelous tool: (but) . . . it failed to understand man and his eternal interests, art, religion, moral striving, and aspiration; and it ended by failing to understand even itself.[26]

In Germany, suddenly philosophers and men of letters began again to hobnob: the Schlegels, Hölderlin, Novalis, Schleiermacher, Herder, Schelling, Goethe, Schiller—these were the spokesmen, literary and philosophical, for a new life of freedom, spontaneity, and beauty, for a new idealism celebrating the centrality of man's mind as the organizer and determiner of the whole phenomenal world.

No one was more eager to rescue man from that enslavement to utility, that condition wherein "the frontiers of art are contracted as the boundaries of science are enlarged,"[27] than Friedrich Schiller. Very much in the Greek tradition, Schiller tried to see into man's essence and he found that essence, true to his own age, in freedom. But freedom, he went on to say, is less fully manifest in moral earnestness than in aesthetic play:

> ... Man plays only when he is in the full sense of the word a man, and *he is only wholly Man when he is playing.*[28]

For the fullest realization of freedom, for the sublimest kind of play, man must be educated. There is, Schiller wrote,

> an education for health, an education for understanding, an education for morality, and an education for taste and for Beauty.[29]

The surest mark of a people's passing from slavery and animality to full humanity is the development, he said, of "a delight in *appearance,* a disposition toward *ornament* and *play.*"[30] Art, he taught, is a synthesis —Schiller anticipated Hegel in this way of thinking—of the sensuous and the moral. Sensuousness always implies exclusion and partiality. Absolute goodness is too lofty an ideal. "Beauty alone makes all the world happy. . . ."[31]

Like many another poet and philosopher, Schiller neglected to tell us how this aesthetic education is to be accomplished, but he made the no less useful contribution of projecting certain ideals to inspire the workers in the vineyards.

In England Coleridge thrilled to the words of these German romantics and developed his own theories of the human imagination, fancy, and creativity. The human imagination at the height of its powers, Coleridge wrote in a letter, "dissolves, diffuses, dissipates, in order to recreate."[32] So far from being the passive recorder of the outside world, this mind ranges widely over a world it helps to create itself, idealizing, unifying, vitalizing nature. It is in a man's style, the very means by which he formulates his thoughts, that one recognizes the quality and scope of his intelligence, Coleridge said, and this suggests the proper end of education. Wordsworth, Coleridge's pupil in formal philosophy, brought to the Romantic movement a totally different temperament, one which directed him to institute a reform of poetry in the direction of a return to nature, but a nature seen and interpreted, as he insisted, through the language of the common man, rather than through the artificial conceits of neoclassicism.

Very much in this same tradition were the American transcendentalists, all of them concerned with education in a broad sense. Emerson, himself a schoolmaster for a time, spoke and wrote on the subject at some length. At once an individualist ("Self-Reliance") and a pantheist ("The Over-Soul"), Emerson exhorted his fellow-Americans to cultivate the beauty which resides in sensuously perceivable nature, in intellect, and in the moral will; and he saw the educative forces of school, college, and society itself, making "humanly speaking ... the difference between men. ... When a man stupid becomes a man inspired, when one and the same man passes out of a torpid into the perceiving state, leaves the din of trifles, the stupor of the senses, to enter into the quasi-omniscience of high thought,—up and down, around, all limits disappear."[33] Furthermore, though often thought of as ultra-genteel, Emerson complimented his native New England on allowing the poor man, who is forbidden to steal food or clothing, "to put his hand into the pocket of the rich, and say, 'You shall educate me, not as you will, but as I will: not alone in the elements, but, by further provision, in the languages, in sciences, in the useful and in elegant arts.' "[34] And on this note Emerson affords a bridge between Romanticism and the reforming democrats of the age.

For hard on the heels of Romanticism Triumphant, indeed, well before its race was run, there appeared a soberer type of thinker, one who came to ask about the *usefulness* of education, and to heap scorn on that which proved nonutilitarian. Education, said James Mill in the 1824 edition of the *Encyclopedia Britannica,* has as its goal human happiness: ". . . the question whether the people should be educated, is the same with the question of whether they should be happy or miserable" he wrote, and added that the time had come to be egalitarian with respect to intelligence as well as with respect to justice, temperance, and veracity. Happiness for the elder Mill as for his associate Bentham, was the same as goodness, and may be quantitatively analyzed to determine how we ought to act in any given instance. The chief way in which education conduces happiness is by yielding us "a knowledge of the order of those events of nature on which our pleasures and pains depend. . . ."

Increasingly it was asked what school subjects are most closely connected with the business of the pupil's life, and those who put the question were usually prepared to answer in terms of the superior "relevance" of the sciences and technologies. As with many Romantics, from Rousseau to Pestalozzi, though for a different reason, *things* were increasingly contrasted with *words:* The advice was, with ever greater frequency, to decrease the amount of rhetoric and to increase the amount of whatever has to do with a direct understanding and control of our environment.

John Stuart Mill, for all of his devotion to utilitarianism, interpreted utility in a broad sense, telling in his autobiography how he had himself suffered a breakdown from an overemphasis (mainly through the extraordinarily demanding tutelage of his father) upon intellectuality, and came to discover through poetry, especially the poetry of Wordsworth, the feelings he had so studiously neglected and suppressed. Thus poetry was for him, in a strict sense, utilitarian, and consequently justified. But Herbert Spencer, in 1883, answered the question "What Knowledge is of Most Worth?" forthrightly enough: the scientific kind. To the more usual and contemptible question, "What Knowledge brings most prestige?," he said the answer was literature and language, which continue, perversely, to dominate the curriculum of school and university. Consider, he said, what we need to know in order to live, and we can discover five categories of knowledge:

1. What we need to know for direct self-preservation.
2. What we need to know in order to secure the necessaries of life, food, shelter, etc.
3. What we need to know about the rearing and disciplining of offspring.
4. What we need to know in order to maintain social and political relations.

All of these kinds of knowledge are scientific, natural or social.

Only with the fifth and least essential category do we come to the humanities.

5. What we need to know in order to fill out our leisure time interestingly.

This is the area of taste and feeling.[35]

Even history Spencer considered to be nonutilitarian, except for that kind of history he would have called "descriptive sociology."

Spencer's encomium to science stood in severe contrast to John Henry Newman's stately defense of liberal—by which he meant philosophical—education thirty years previously. The highest, noblest, and best education, according to Newman—ultimately, the most useful, too —is not scientific or professional education, but education of the intellect, the cultivation of the ratiocinative powers. His idea of a university was of an institution that was utterly and completely humanistic; from the kind of education he nowhere found but demanded, he expected— everything.

But a University training is the great ordinary means to a great but ordinary end; it aims at raising the intellectual tone of society, at cultivating the public mind, at purifying the national taste, at supplying true principles to popular enthusiasm and fixed aims to popular aspiration, at giving enlargement and sobriety to the ideas of the age, at facilitating the exercise of political power, and refining the intercourse of private life. ∴.. It prepares [a man] to fill any post with credit, and to master any subject with facility. .... He has the repose of a mind which lives in itself, while it lives in the world, and which has resources for its happiness at home when it cannot go abroad. He has a gift which serves him in public, and supports him in retirement, without which good fortune is but vulgar, and with which failure and disappointment have a charm.[36]

Similar in outlook were Thomas and Matthew Arnold, father and son, the former the most renowned public school headmaster of his century, the latter the eminent poet and man of letters who earned his living as a schools inspector. For this eloquent and tireless apostle of Sweetness and Light, education meant gaining a deep understanding of "the best that has been thought and said in the world." Science, he said, is all very well for the few; for the many it has little value. So if we have to choose between an emphasis in the schools upon humane letters and the natural sciences—and he insisted that the choice need not be made in fact—there is far more to be learned about living well from the humanities. Arnold once complained of a student in one of the technical colleges paraphrasing Macbeth's question, "Can'st thou not minister to a mind diseased?" by "Can you not wait upon the lunatic?" and went ahead to comment:

If one is driven to choose, I think I would rather have a young person ignorant about the moon's diameter, but aware that "Can you not wait upon the lunatic?" is bad, than a young person whose education had been such as to manage things the other way around.[37]

His great debating rival T. H. Huxley refused to admit the necessity of deciding between the fields, contenting himself with a strong insistence, in sharp anticipation of the argument of Lord Snow in his famous lecture on "The Two Cultures," that though it is inexcusable for a man of some education to be ignorant of Cromwell and his significance in English history, "it would be as great scandal that [he] should be ignorant of the law of gravitation or of the chemical fact that air is not an element . . . or of the circulation of blood in his own body."[38]

Looking back over the hundred years that separate the Huxley-Arnold debate from the present, one realizes that Huxley won, even decisively, if the verdict is made in terms of outcomes. Not alone in formal curricula, but in the expenditures of money, in the esteem of the public and in a dozen other ways, the natural sciences have more than attained the equal status (with the humanities) that Huxley claimed as their right. Arnold's proclaiming of "high seriousness" as the touchstone of poetic excellence now looks like a last-ditch stand at the genteel tradition (in Santayana's expression), after which to an ever-increasing extent apologists for the humanities have seemed primarily apologetic or even desperate, as in the proclamation of art for art's sake. To be sure, the curricula of Oxbridge in the late nineteenth century, and of all the universities of Britain and America that took their cues therefrom, were still predominantly classical, the prevailing assumption continuing to be that the study of classical language and literature was the best of all possible training for the mind—almost no matter what the mind was afterwards to be devoted to. Besides, there was the wonderfully genteel uniformity of the education of gentlemen; thus, British civil servants, divines, M.P.'s and squires formed a single class by virtue of their classical education, no matter how much the utilitarians scorned its irrelevance to the work which they performed. Yet, the criticism was not to be stilled, and as Western civilization became year by year more technological, and the world of work correspondingly expanded; as the social sciences developed and the findings of sociologists, political scientists, and economists became indispensable to those who would conscientiously deal in public affairs; as the professions of law, medicine, engineering, and education became ever more closely affiliated with the university and began to influence the course of study; and as higher education came to seem, especially in America, the best single promoter of upward mobility; the centrality of the humanities in education and in life appeared more and more dubious. When psychologists questioned and finally discarded the faculty psychology which had buttressed the old curriculum and given schoolmasters reason to believe that getting up

Latin declensions and conjugations strengthened the intellect and made pupils inherently more rational, the study of the classics fell off sharply. Then, too, more and more voices suggested that the study of literature is effete and inconsequential, and that most philosophy and all religion are on a level with astrology and numerology.

Auguste Comte, founder of sociology, developed a positivistic historiography which saw progress as leading always away from myth through metaphysics to science, in every field of learning. Indeed his apotheosis of science seemed to be vindicated by huge advances in mathematics and the sharpening of ever new techniques for empirical investigation, as well as by the growing conviction that nothing—not the soul, religion, the Bible, man's sex life, morals, even dreams—was unamenable to scientific scrutiny. Comte's brand of positivism proved in time simplistic and naive, but gave way to an even more sweeping doctrine which, beginning to take shape in Austria, Germany, England, and elsewhere about the time of the First World War, pre-empted the whole of the cognitive domain for the formal and empirical sciences and reduced the world of value to subjective and therefore inscrutable preference.

The achievements of the mathematicians and scientists, and even more obviously of the technologists who derived from them, were so palpable and impressive, that arts and letters and philosophy (except as it became up-to-date in pragmatism and positivism and analysis) and the historiography of Gibbon and Burckhardt all seemed, to an expanding body of intellectuals, so old-fashioned as to be quaint and even laughable. Psychologists, for instance, began, even before the end of the nineteenth century, insisting that theirs was a discipline quite distinct from philosophy, and very much closer to physiology, medicine, and even physics, than to epistemology, metaphysics, and ethics. Anthropologists and sociologists at about the same time began to accumulate such a large body of data about the differing mores of people as to make cultural relativism seem as well documented as Darwinian evolution or Mendelian genetics. Equally, this same body of intellectuals set aside the conception of man as rational animal that had come down from Aristotle in favor of the class-determined and the Oedipal man revealed by the self-styled scientists, Marx and Freud, both militantly antiphilosophical.

Even as late as the 1950s C. P. Snow could complain that in England humanists still disdained science, loving to quote G. K. Chesterton's "If there's one thing I despise, it's the solar system" and similar sayings, boasting of their ignorance of even the simplest mathematics or of such a fundamental principle as entropy (which Snow compared with being totally unfamiliar with even one Shakespearian play), and of using their prestige to keep huge numbers of schoolboys locked into their own narrow confines. On the other hand, in America the natural sciences had, much earlier, solidly established their place in general education at all levels, from elementary school to college.

A more thorough study of this period could catalogue many rearguard actions (such as that of the so-called neohumanists of the thirties, hearkening back to a happier day before either Rousseau or modern science) and laments (such as that of Joseph Wood Krutch that modern man had been robbed of the ability to write tragedies by being deprived, especially through psychology and the social sciences, of any belief in man's nobility); but these would furnish only additional documentation to what has often seemed a general retreat, at times almost amounting to a rout, of the traditional humanists. As philosophers increasingly decided that mathematical logic was at the very core of their discipline, philology gave way to an empirical and quantitative linguistics; literary critics became ever more infatuated with counting references and word repetitions (even employing computers for their work); and art historians became increasingly dependent upon chemistry. The humanists sincerely flattered the scientists by imitation.

Yet, there were countervailing tendencies, some of which in very recent times seem to cast considerable doubt on that interpretation of history which makes the past hundred years an inexorable advance of science at the expense of the humanistic disciplines. Consider, for instance, the rise in the middle of the nineteenth century of a movement that came to be known as existentialism, which went from Kierkegaard's defense of subjectivism and his attack on the rationalism of Hegel (particularly on Hegel's logic of history that minimized the influence of individuals no matter how "great"), through Nietzsche's celebration of the *uebermensch* who would will his way beyond the strictures of science and rational philosophy, to the twentieth-century philosophers (including some pragmatists and intuitionists) who rediscovered the irreducibility of concrete, individual existence to categories or concepts or laws, no matter how scientific and logical. And over and over again those who have insisted upon the primacy of individuality and existence and perception[39] have proclaimed the primacy of the arts and of aesthetic experience. Henri Bergson in *Laughter,* a fascinating study of the comic spirit, wrote:

> Hence it follows that art always aims at what is *individual.* What the artist fixes on his canvas is something he has seen at a certain spot, on a certain day, at a certain hour, with a colouring that will never be seen again.[40]

And indeed Bergson's book should serve as a reminder that our age, beginning with Santayana's *Sense of Beauty* in 1896, is the great age of aesthetics and certainly one of the great ages of criticism in all the major arts. So to say is not intended to suggest that there is any lack of creative genius in our time that issues in works of art themselves, but is intended rather to suggest that in this age often called "scientific" there has been a vast deal of hard thinking about beauty, the arts, and (more generally) aesthetic experience, as well as about the nature of religious experience, man's fate—and indeed, the whole range of traditional humanistic topics, along with certain new ones. Add to this that in our age there has come to be, through phonograph records and tapes, colored reproductions, paperback books, and films of various kinds, including videotapes, an access to works of art, religion, literature, philosophy, and history unapproached and undreamed of in previous ages. For all the laments about the crassness and materialism and callow practicality of our times, a not inconsiderable share of the gross national product is spent in developed countries upon that which has humanistic value.[41]

It is not uninteresting, either, that there appears in recent years, at least in the United States, a slackening of interest in the natural sciences and technologies on the part of high school and college students, and a turning toward certain of the social sciences and humanities.

Who at the end of World War II could have predicted an efflorescence of interest among youth in poetry and Zen? Who could have expected secular colleges and universities to start adding courses and even departments in religion, or an upturn in the publication of books on theology and mysticism?

Given these unexpected but undisputed facts, it is not surprising that just lately there has also developed a new curiosity about the nature of the humanities, their relations to the sciences, and their place, presently and optimally, in school and college curricula.

4

Some Recent Definitions
of the Humanities

We have briefly traced the history of the humanities, as an area of human
concern, scholarship, and creativity, from the time of the early Greeks,
who of course had no conception of such a field, to the present. We noted
the critical place occupied by the humanists of the Renaissance, and their
fascination with rhetorical-literary analysis, especially of the ancient
writers of Greece and Rome. We noted too the rise of a clearer and
clearer—or at least sharper and sharper—distinction, and sometimes
enmity, between the humanities and the sciences, including in the last
century or more the social with the natural sciences, and the accompa-
nying affiliation of most but not all philosophers and historians with the
scientific "culture." We noted the resurgence of subjectivism with the
existentialists of the nineteenth and twentieth centuries, and the emergence of aesthetics as a subdivision of philosophy, as practitioners and
critics of the several arts came increasingly to see likenesses among
painting, music, poetry, and other fine arts.

Yet from all of this it is still not apparent how the crucial word
should be defined. What is certain is that the most common definition
that has emerged in our time, in both higher and lower education, is
hardly a definition at all but a classification. What are we to mean by "the
humanities"? Oh, the following fields, or even academic departments:
English, Foreign Languages, Philosophy, the Fine (Visual) Arts, Music,
and—in a way—History. Such a classification, even without a specification of the grounds for corralling these fields, may be good enough for
some curricular purposes. But it certainly gives rise to a number of hard
questions, about the exclusions as well as the inclusions, and about what
kind of reasonable definition can be abstracted from the list. Is there
indeed an implicit essence which all the fields share?

Certain it is that there are those who clamor to get in—and to get
out. For instance, the logicians amongst the philosophers are not at all

easy about their being included; nor the philosophers of science, and many of the epistemologists, political philosophers, etc. Probably the majority of historians prefer the company of political scientists, economists, and sociologists to that of the people in English and the arts. There are scholars in both English and foreign languages who in specializing in the linguistic rather than the literary side of their field may think of themselves as employing tough-minded scientific procedures in their investigations, and may liken themselves to anthropologists on the one side, psycho-linguists on another, and to logicians and mathematicians on still another. Gone are the days when one could assume that a linguist is more interested in the language of literature than in the language of technology or science; often it is quite the other way around.

Then, again, why is not religion included? Can it be explained by recent adherence to the principle of the separation of church and state, which effectively excludes most direct religious studies from the curricula of public high schools and colleges? And if music, painting, and sculpture get included, why not the dance, architecture, and the film? Are there not aspects of archaeology, especially classical archaeology, that should be ranked with the humanities?

Yet again, are we quite sure that the musicologist, the composer, and the performer should be lumped together as humanists; or the art historian and the painter? Are the practicing sonneteer and the specialist in the social origins of the Troubadours so sure to share their deepest interests?

It is pretty apparent that the classification, though ready, is rough, and it is but little consolation to remark that there are singular difficulties about whether psychology and physical anthropology should be classified with the biological or the social sciences, or about the enormous range in methodology from mathematical economics to descriptive ethnology.

One interesting suggestion, still on the curricular or at least collegiate-structure level, is that of W. J. Ong when he proposes to replace the humanities with a kind of expanded field of anthropology. Thus, there would be a division between those sciences which have as their central concern, nature; and those sciences—or perhaps better, say, kinds of knowledge—focused on man. The anthropological fold would then encompass literature, education, psychology, philosophy, history, all the social sciences, and linguistics of every sort. Their common thread is their concern, their basic and not just incidental concern, with "man as distinctively man." Ong finds the Renaissance humanists making this distinction in contrast to the Medievalists who lumped science and the humanities together under philosophy.[1]

There probably are some advantages to this new dichotomy between nature and man, but one important disadvantage is that it creates a huge spread in the methods by which knowledge (and other ends) are pursued throughout the anthropological wing. The natural sciences remain fairly closely unified in this way, but the inclusion of the social and behavioral sciences along with the traditional humanities, puts those who are carrying on carefully controlled, objective, publicly verifiable experimental procedures, which yield results expressible in statistical or other quantitative manners, alongside those whose methods are intuitive, subjective, and designed to protect, not exclude, emotional, attitudinal components. It is of course true that in the present scheme of things there are very large differences between the philosopher and historian, and between the literary critic and the theologian, not to mention those who are creating art works; but to widen this range to include the social sciences seems unfortunate, especially when a good part of that which divides scholars —making it difficult for them to share their interests and pool their results—is fundamental difference in methodology.

This is not to deny that there are valuable cross currents between the social sciences and the humanities. Very likely they can often profit mutually by less insistence upon the separateness of the fields. But this is true for the whole of the cognitive enterprise, for that matter, as Einstein recognized when he said that every person tries to fashion for himself

> a simplified and intelligible picture of the world; he then tries to some extent to substitute this cosmos of his for the world of experience, and thus to overcome it. This is what the painter, the poet, the speculative philosopher and the natural scientist do, each in his own fashion.[2]

Another attempt to widen the field of the humanities beyond its usual (though vague and shifting) confines is made by Ralph Barton Perry in

"A Definition of the Humanities." His essay deserves to be quoted at length:

> I define 'the humanities' . . . to embrace whatever influences conduce to freedom. 'The Humanities' is not to be employed as a mere class name for certain divisions of knowledge or parts of scholastic curriculum, or for certain human institutions, activities, and relationships, but to signify a certain condition of freedom which these may serve to create. The meaning of 'the humanities' is relative to the meaning of that condition. The term 'influence' implies that freedom in the sense of my definition is no inborn natural or metaphysical trait, but a possibility of human development which may or may not be realized through growth and interaction with the environment. The degree of its realization will depend on ancestral traits and the accidents of genius, but it lies within the range of those agencies by which men make men, or by which men make themselves, what they are.
>
> But what is meant by freedom? . . . By freedom I mean enlightened choice. I mean the action in which habit, reflex or suggestion are superseded by an individual's fundamental judgments of good and evil; the action whose premises are explicit; the action which proceeds from personal reflection and integration.[3]

Perry goes on to say that it is a historical accident that the humanists of the Renaissance neglected science. Actually, he says, science can be just as humanistic in terms of his criterion, as any other field. "Can be"—that is the key phrase. Any subject can be humanistic or non- (even anti-) humanistic. Science becomes humanistic when its revelation of nature is of a kind to assist men to choose the ends of their action. Furthermore, he says, science becomes humanistic insofar as its pursuit of truth is pure and nonacquisitive, thus illustrating one of the noblest employments of human reason; in this respect, it joins with other fields of endeavor to "unite men and contribute to their common heritage."[4] Yet science is not as easy to humanize as history and philosophy. It is indeed dehumanized to the extent that it is made "highly technical, and encourages the repetition of operations with no sense of their significance. In the interest of technical precision it has become highly abstract. Nature is stripped of its sensuous covering and its qualitative diversity."[5]

It is certainly the case that the sciences can contribute greatly to the attainment of human freedom; the history of any one of the sciences, including mathematics, and most obviously including medicine, could be written in such a way as to demonstrate the magnitude of this contribution. But the "dehumanization" of science in Perry's account is less clear and more dubious. "The repetition of operations with no sense of their significance" would appear to be ineffective procedure, no matter what the ends in view. And why shouldn't the highly abstract, technically precise results of much scientific endeavor vastly conduce to freedom, and even have its ultimate importance understood in these terms, even perhaps by the discoverers. And as to the "sensuous covering" which science does tend to eliminate—is this not now a new criterion, rather than an elaboration of that having to do with freedom? Besides, this can be said of most philosophy and a vast amount of history too, both of which Perry thinks of as central humanistic fields—in the sense of fields which are easy to humanize and hard to dehumanize. It will be useful to follow Perry further as he characterizes these subjects, along with literature.

History, he says,

> is eminently humane in so far as it presents events under the aspect of human purposes and needs. History will have exercised a humanizing influence upon him who through its study has come to participate in the life of the race, and to regard its quarrels as domestic quarrels, and to feel that he is in some sense commissioned to complete the unfulfilled task of his predecessors.[6]

This, we think, could hardly be improved upon as a characterization of how a subject *humanizes*. It shows an approach to history, to its writing, its teaching, and its learning, that makes it something more than a tedious recital of "and thens,"[7] something more than a fanatical attempt to set down the record, for the sake of accuracy alone.

Letters and arts are also intrinsically humane in their content, according to Perry. Art

> presents life concretely, presenting models for admiration or condemnation—for imitation or rejection. It enlarges the range of immediate experience, and communicates it feelingly; it stimulates the imagination and breaks the mold of habit; it expresses the diverse

visions and aspirations of great men; it integrates the different cultural elements of a society or an epoch; it embodies beauty and commends it as an object of disinterested pleasure; at its best, it brings a sense of moral elevation.[8]

So understood, the arts of all media are not wholly self-contained, purely intrinsic in their value, but as lovers of literature, music, painting and the other arts have claimed down through the ages, are able to please *and* instruct. But the instruction, at best, is not obtrusively didactic; it is instead illuminating, mind-and-spirit-expanding—in short, freeing in its effect. And this of course is precisely Perry's criterion of the humane.

Finally, Perry says that philosophy too can become, as the teaching of literature or history so often is, a dull, deadening recital of detail, pedantic and picayune. Or it may be used as propaganda, which by definition binds rather than frees.

But it is difficult so to teach the history of philosophy as to avoid the multiplication and dissemination of intellectual alternatives. It is difficult to teach systematic philosophy without broadening horizons and encouraging the ordering of ideas. Metaphysics raises doubts and excites speculation: it will almost inevitably 'joggle the mind,' to use Emily Dickinson's expression.[9]

Perry is eloquent and convincing in his account of some of the humanizing effects yielded by the study of—anything. Yet his characterization of what it is that constitutes the inner core of the humanistic is not quite convincing, simply because it is so tremendously broad. The removal of an infected appendix may free a man to make wiser decisions by relieving him of the necessity of concentrating on his discomfort. Aeronautics may have a similar effect by speeding him to a great concert or to a philosophical conference. Household appliances may, as the advertisers claim, free the housewife from the drudgery of mindless chores, and help her thus concentrate upon higher matters. Yet, it seems odd to speak of surgery and aeronautics, or other forms of technology, as humanistic. The category gets so big as to lose any real focus. Yet, there is a sense too in which this characterization is at the same time too narrow. It is not *only* because of their liberating effect that history and philosophy and the arts are exemplary fields in their humanism. In fact, from Perry's own examples this is sometimes clear. When he speaks of art as embodying beauty and commends "it as an object of disinterested pleasure" or when he says that "Science becomes humanistic insofar as its pursuit of truth is pure and non-acquisitive . . ." he is describing activities which, though not irrelevant to making enlightened choices or decisions, do not have their whole justification in conducing to that end. The study of music sometimes makes available to the student the exquisite enjoyment of sounds; the study of history may help a person acquire a taste for the contemplation of ages and epochs. These *seem* to be somehow humanistic ends that are not yet wholly swallowed up in their liberalizing effects.

In short, what Perry has admirably succeeded in doing is to characterize and justify the liberal arts—that is, all the studies that *do* free man from the bounds that always threaten to contain his spirit. And though the humanities are a part of the Liberal Arts, they are not the whole of them.

A very different approach to the characterization of the humanities starts from the discovery that man is, in Ernst Cassirer's words, "the symbolizing animal." Between man and things in themselves, there always stands the symbol, the all-pervasive mediator in our dealing with "reality." And the more man develops, the more this is true, which some would interpret as man becoming more *human*—anyway as less and less like his biological relatives.

> No longer can man confront reality immediately. . . . Physical reality seems to recede in proportion as man's symbolic activity advances. . . . He has so enveloped himself in linguistic forms, in artistic images, in mythical symbols or religious rites that he cannot see or know anything except by the interposition of this artificial medium.[10]

From this neo-Kantian position, Cassirer proceeds to conceptualize as symbol systems the great human enterprises which have the names of Myth, Religion, Art, Science, History, and Morality. Each has its own mode of symbolizing, mediating, interpreting reality. It is not that science gives us truth and myth gives us—well, myth, in the popular sense of that word which offers a contrast with fact. Rather, each affords a pair of spectacles with which to see the world—and of course the world thus seen is very different in the one case and in the other. Without *some* spectacles we see nothing, and yet there is no lens adequate for all purposes.

Such a philosophy of symbolic forms, as Cassirer calls the scheme, offers a distinctive and important approach to man's diverse attempts to know his world, and himself as a part thereof. It can be employed also to structure the school or college curriculum.

Perhaps the simplest typology of the modes of symbolism is one that makes a fundamental distinction between cognitive symbols and emotive symbols. Those who employ this distinction typically identify cognitive inquiry with science; or at least for them the sciences afford the paradigm for the meaningful search for and expression of knowledge. Nonscience fields tend to be assimilated by the emotive or affective realm. Such a schematism comes much closer to doing justice to the sciences—though even there, as Michael Polanyi has shown, there remains an ineradicable element of the personal as distinct from the objective and public—than to the nonsciences. Not only is it obviously the case that in fields like literature or musicology there is a vast amount of factual information such as the date of the first publication of "The Rape of the Lock" and the prevailing key signature of Mozart's last symphony, but there is the presence *in* (and not just *about*) literary works of knowledge—albeit mainly of a different kind from that in science. To this subject we will return for a fuller treatment in the next chapter; suffice it to say for the present that though the cognitive-emotive dichotomy had a great vogue in positivistic circles in the thirties and forties, and remains at the heart of a number of works in popular semantics, it has been completely abandoned or rejected by most serious students in favor of a far more complex organization of symbol systems. Let us have a look at one such which was worked out in order to deal with curricular problems: that of Philip Phenix in *Realms of Meaning*.

Phenix grounds his "Philosophy of the Curriculum for General Education" in a statement that "Human beings are essentially creatures who have the power to experience *meanings*. Distinctively human existence consists in the pattern of meanings."[11] He finds six such patterns, modes, or realms of meaning: symbolics, empirics, esthetics, synnoetics, ethics, and synoptics.

Symbolics embraces all the ways in which meaning is symbolized, ranging from informal language to mathematics, but including also gesture, bodily movement, and nonverbal sounds.

Empirics "includes the sciences of the physical world, or living things, and of man."[12]

The remaining four realms may be said to constitute the humanities, and will therefore require a fuller accounting.

The esthetic realm includes the arts in all forms and media, and they are interpreted to be as meaningful, as much concerned with knowledge, as the sciences. (In a broad sense; Phenix realizes of course that "knowledge" is often *defined* so as to belong only in the realm of empirics and of that part of symbolics that is mathematics and symbolic logic.) The great difference is this:

> Knowledge in language is primarily of general patterns of expression, which may be used in a great variety of particular contexts. Knowledge in science is ideally of general laws and theories, connected with observable particulars by way of prediction and verification.
>
> In the esthetic realm, on the other hand, the object of knowledge is the singular particular form. The primary concern is not with types of things—not with kinds and classes of things—but with unique individual objects.[13]

He goes on to say that the meanings contained in the arts are known —to employ Bertrand Russell's well-known distinction—by acquaintance, rather than by description. That is, scientific knowledge tends to be conceptual, mediated by general terms, and to refer to objects and relations quite external to the symbols themselves. Esthetic understanding, on the other hand, is perceptual, immediate. Still again,

> The language of science is discursive, aiming at precise literal descriptions organized according to the principles of ordinary logic and reaching perfection in the formulas of mathematics. The language of art, on the other hand, is nondiscursive, symbolical, and metaphorical, and is organized according to the different logic of presented forms. Furthermore, the language of science is more readily separable from the expressions in which it is employed than is the language of art, where expressive materials and expressive content are virtually inseparable.[14]

Although there are profound differences among the several empirical sciences and among the several esthetic arts, the similarities in patterns of meaning among the sciences and among the arts entitles us and even obliges us to think in terms of the unification which the metaphor "realms" suggests.

With the fourth realm of Phenix we run into the difficulty of a pattern of meaning that has no commonly accepted name, and indeed —the point may be redundant—whose very existence is not commonly acknowledged. The name "synnoetics" signifies the pattern of meanings associated with "relational insight, personal knowledge, or existential awareness . . ."[15] There is no academic field or set of fields whose principal aim is the yielding of synnoetic knowledge, though Phenix finds psychology—he is here thinking of depth psychology and existential psychology—literature, religion, and philosophy the fields in which concern for this sort of understanding is principally centered. Among the key ideas in synnoetics are "freedom," "personal relatedness" (most notably Martin Buber's "I-Thou" bond), "love," "self," "responsibility," and "personal knowledge" (à la Michael Polanyi), as well as those that are most closely associated with existentialism: "anxiety," "absurdity," "guilt," and "time."

Dwelling within the realm of synnoetics has as its end better "direct insight into other beings (or oneself) as concrete wholes existing in relation"—this is in obvious contrast to empirical studies of human beings which tend to fragment persons, deal with them either in isolation or as members of groups, and aim at objective rather than subjective understanding. But Phenix thinks of this mode as contrasted also with art, which he sees as inclining toward the abstract and as being concerned with essences, whereas personal knowledge is concrete and existential. Furthermore, even though a work of art, say a poem, may contribute to one's knowledge of persons in their concrete relatedness, nevertheless, "it is one thing to perceive a poem or a play esthetically, as an objectified abstraction of a type of subjectivity, and another thing to use that esthetic insight synnoetically, as a resource for deepening one's understanding of real existential relations between unique beings."[17]

Now, there is an important connection between synnoetics and the realm of ethics, which has to do with *"right deliberate action,* that is, what a person *ought voluntarily to do."*[18] These two fields are at once "the most essential and the most problematical."[19] There are fewer experts in these than in any of the other realms, and far more conflict of opinion, more uncertainty, more perplexity. Thus they are the realms which schools and colleges are most apt to neglect, as being messy and troublesome—besides where are teachers to be found?—in spite of their constituting the kind of knowledge many, perhaps most, persons are particularly concerned about.

Finally, the sixth realm, synoptics, embraces the major integrative fields, those which bring together meanings from all other fields into comprehensive wholes. There are three sub-realms: history, religion, and philosophy.

"The goal of historical inquiry," Phenix writes, "is to attain an understanding of past human events from the inside. ... Historical understanding thus consists in a re-creation of the past through participation, in thought, in the lives of those who made the past what it was."[20]

Religion is that field which integrates meanings and values (many derived from other fields) characterized by "Ultimacy." Phenix regards religion as characteristically, but not essentially, supernatural.

Philosophy is said to have as its distinctive function "the interpretation of meaning."[21] Each realm is, as has been seen, a pattern of meanings, but philosophy most importantly concerns itself with the meanings of meanings. This function is perhaps clearest in the various "philosophies of—." Thus philosophy of history, philosophy of science, philosophy of religion, philosophy of art, all set out theories to interpret the ways in which meanings are sought in each of the appropriate disciplines.

Phenix's lead has been followed in some detail since his work is the most important and comprehensive yet to appear that deals directly with the curriculum, and in which differentiation of forms of symbolism is taken to be the best means for understanding the pursuit of truth, knowledge, and meaning.

It is not our intent here to scrutinize in detail Phenix's elaborate and impressive scheme, but only to see what it tells us about the humanities. A confession is in order. When we said above, after mentioning symbolics and empirics, "The remaining four realms may be said to constitute the humanities ..." this was *our* grouping, not Phenix's. Although he makes connections between and among realms—as for instance the one already noted between ethics and synnoetics—he does not, in fact, group the last four under any such rubric as "the humanities." Indeed, note what he does do to replace the orthodox trinity of natural sciences, social sciences, and humanities. The first two he fuses as empirical sciences, withdrawing only the mathematics, logic, and linguistics sometimes associated with these sciences, to constitute a separate realm (symbolics). And then he proceeds to chop up—though the metaphor is too violent

—the conventional area of the humanities into realms that are, presumably, as relatively autonomous as any of the others. In such a common expression today as "The Arts and Humanities,"[22] we see a betrayal of a certain uneasiness about subsuming the creative aspects of music, the visual arts, theatre, film, dance, poetry, and fiction under the humanities. However, Phenix is willing enough to put together the scholar and the creator-craftsman in the arts, but to mark them off from the other three realms. Ethics is separated off from its usual place within the commodious halls of philosophy; and philosophy, history, and religion are yoked together somewhat hesitantly, as is evidenced by Phenix's statement "... It might seem better to treat each as a separate realm ... [but] for all their differences, they share the one fundamental purpose of integrative or synoptic understanding."[23] And then he creates, as we have seen, a separate realm of synnoetics to which psychology, philosophy, literature, and religion are the major contributors. It is significant that three of these are from the synoptic and esthetic realms, and indeed the *kind* of psychology he is concerned with is thought by many academic psychologists to have more affinity with philosophy or even literature than with a behavioral science.

Apparently, however, Phenix finds no good reason for putting these last four realms of his under any such grand title as the humanities. And perhaps he is right. If anything is clear by now it is that there is no neat and tidy way of showing that all the knowledge or all the methods or all the values typically contained within those subjects or disciplines commonly labeled "humanistic" are of a certain kind. Two lessons in particular are to be derived from the Phenix classification: (1) it is folly to assume that each of the academic disciplines is an integrated whole; (2) philosophy and history (perhaps religion, too) tend to have a different kind of relationship to the other disciplines than the others do to each other: they exist on a different level—not higher in a value hierarchy, but different. Yet we feel impelled not yet to give up the search for a reasonably adequate way of characterizing all the usual fields and interests and activities called humanities. Meantime, one other systematic attempt to characterize the humanities, to show their distinctive qualities, will be examined,[24] this time briefly: that of R. S. Crane.

Having noted that it is easier and commoner to praise the humanities than to define them, he gives examples down through the ages: The humanities have been recommended or defended (as in Vives) on the ground that they restore man to humanity and raise him toward God, or (as in Sidney) that they lead to the knowledge of a man's self, with the end of a well-doing and not of well-knowing only, or (as in Newman) that they induce a philosophic habit of mind, or (as in Arnold) that they lead to a harmonious expansion and interrelation of all the powers which make the beauty and worth of human nature. Or again, by another line of writers, their peculiar value has been stated in terms not so much of the intrinsic good of the soul as of some external utility: they are those pursuits and studies which better than any others (as in Sir Thomas Elyot) prepare a man to be a prudent, just, and temperate magistrate; or (as in Milton) which fit a man to perform justly, skilfully, and magnanimously all the offices, both private and public, of peace and war; or (as in Mill and many others) which prepare and discipline men best for active life by convincing them that they are men before they are lawyers or physicians or merchants.[25]

He observes that such definitions do not really help much in determining what subjects are and what are not humanistic, any more than a discovery that if, for the Renaissance, humanistic study was pretty much confined to the rhetorical analysis of the classical authors, then, in the eighteenth century everything was included except theology and natural science; or that whereas for T. H. Huxley, the humanities (now sharply distinguished from the sciences, for the purpose of debating curricular priorities) were narrowed in scope to poetry and eloquence, for his opponent, Matthew Arnold, everything was included, literature and science alike, so long as it belonged to the charmed class of "The best that has been thought or said in the world."

Crane goes on to argue for an extension of the proper mission of the humanities beyond grammar, rhetoric, philology, history, and philosophy. The objects of humanistic studies, he says, must also be seen as "great human achievements."

As such they have characteristics and values over and above the common traits of language, over and above the circumstances of their creation, over and above the characters of their creators or the spirit of their age, over and above the specific thoughts or doctrines that can be drawn from them, characteristics and values which appear fully only when they are understood and appreciated as constructions of particular kinds, each with its peculiar complexity or richness.

To study human achievements in this way—poems as poems, histories as histories, philosophical works as philosophical works—and each kind in terms, not of its lowest common denominator in language, thought, or experience, but of the principles by which it is constructed and achieves its distinctive excellence—this, it seems to me, would be to constitute the humanities in a new way and in a form which is more nearly adequate to what the name has always signified.[26]

Crane fully faces up to the fact that his program would necessitate the development of standards and techniques of criticism not now generally available. Of such humanistic arts he would demand both rigor and a willingness to be normative.

Here again, then, is an attempt to characterize the humanities that goes well beyond the conventional grouping of subject matters; indeed Crane makes a point of including among the "great human achievements" works of science as well as of literature, history, and philosophy. The ruling dictum here is of course, Aristotle's ". . . Each art ought to produce, not any chance pleasure, but the pleasure proper to it . . ."[27]

Now, there is surely some good justification for this in the case of the historians of science; and those who (like Crane) are supporters of a Great Books approach to general education typically include Archimedes, Galileo, Newton, Darwin, and Einstein along with Homer, Plato, Dante, Shakespeare, Gibbon, and William James. The works of these men are said to be great in what they tell us about men as well as

about the world. But where Crane goes beyond the usual Great Books approach is in his insistence upon genre definition: "poems as poems, histories as histories, philosophical works as philosophical works—and each in terms . . . of the principles by which it is constructed and achieves its *distinctive excellence.*"[28]

When one thinks of how many great works have been mangled and garbled and reduced by being considered in terms of criteria quite foreign to the intent of their creators: literature considered as history and sociology and biography; philosophy as indicating something about the psychology of its author, or as a revelation of its time; and so on—one sees the virtue in Crane's proposal. He would not, presumably, object to the discovery of the "philosophical content" of a poem, if justice had first been done to the poem not only as an esthetic object, but as the kind of poem it is or tries to be; surely he would not object to analysis of Plato's *Symposium* as a dramatic work, provided one had given it its due as a philosophical dialogue. He would certainly agree that something can be discovered about Samuel Clemens' psychological struggles from *Huckleberry Finn,* and this is legitimate if it is *fully* recognized that the work is a novel.

There are however, some objections to be made against Crane's characterization of the humanities. In the first place, it confines humanistic studies, apparently, to achievements in language: nothing here about music or the visual arts; and such a view unfortunately splits the aesthetic field in such a way as to obscure the exceptionally important relations between the several arts. Secondly, Crane is apparently willing, as some of us are not, to give the humanities to the "scholars" as distinct from the "art creators." Indeed one might say the creators in any field, except insofar as "scholarship" (by which we here mean the study of what has already been achieved) itself has a creative element. We look, rather, for ways of more closely associating the composers with the musicologists, the critics with the poets, the art historians with the painters and sculptors, the historians of philosophy with the practicing philosophers of history or aestheticians. Thirdly, important as genre study is, it has its traps, which Crane seems nowhere to acknowledge. It is an interesting question whether the Book of Job is or is not a tragedy (in the Greek tradition, say); but that surely is only one of the interesting things about the work, some of which have little to do with its classification. Hume thought of himself as a "man of letters" and his works, or some of them, may perhaps be equally well thought of as philosophy or literature; so too with Plutarch, Montaigne, Pascal, Goethe, Emerson, Dostoevsky, and Santayana. In short, some of the very greatest of works seem to be great partly because they transcend genre, and defy the attempts of scholars to pigeon-hole them. Finally, Crane's device for bringing the sciences into the humanistic tent, though nobly-motivated, may have little power in contemporary science, for the reason that increasingly, in both the natural and social sciences, the significant achievements are piecemeal and additive, rather than great comprehensive, integrated wholes. They tend, furthermore, to be the results of teams, rather than of single individuals. And they very strongly tend to such a high degree of technicality as to be beyond the understanding, except in very general ways, of nonscientists—or indeed of nonnuclear physicists, or nonbiochemists, etc. The latter point does not invalidate Crane's scheme, but it does, if it is well taken, mean that there will still be a fairly sharp break between the humanities and the sciences in our own and presumably future times. By this we do not intend to indicate that Crane was trying to assimilate the whole of the natural sciences into the humanities: no, he is distinguishing between the sciences as revelations of nature, and scientific works interpreted as *human* achievements —with only the latter being appropriate objects for humanistic study. But the point is that, seemingly, scientific achievements reveal less and less about their human creators.

5

The Sciences and
the Humanities

In briefly tracing developments in the humanities from the time of the Renaissance, we noted among other things the general affiliation of other aesthetic arts to humane letters, the inexorable rise in prestige and power of the natural (and more recently, the social) sciences, and the uneasy division among philosophers and historians as to their own primary allegiances to one or the other of these two camps. Or is "camps" an unduly militaristic metaphor?

When several years ago Lord Snow told us of "the two cultures," he set off a furious debate. Not only did many persons accuse him of favoring, in his account, either science or the humanities, but some suggested that there were other cultures as well—that of the social and behavioral sciences anyway, with their considerable differences from the natural sciences, and a culture of technology, and perhaps still others. Or, of course, the original dichotomy may be attacked from the other side: it puts asunder what, in a diviner light, is a unified whole.[1]

As long ago as 1943 Herbert Read was saying, "In the end I do not distinguish science and art, except as methods, and I believe that the opposition created between them in the past has been due to a limited view of both activities. Art is the representation, science the explanation —of the same reality."[2]

Coming, unlike Read, out of a strongly scientific education, Michael Polanyi has similarly attacked the separating off of science and the arts. The sciences, he shows in some detail, are saturated, inextricably, with values: they are at the farthest possible point from just collections of facts.

And many of these values are aesthetic in nature: it is not only sonatas and cathedrals and epics that are beautiful: problems can be beautiful; discoveries, inventions, solutions can be beautiful. He says that in fact the word "beauty" is more often employed today by scientists and engineers than by creators in the arts.

He also likens the arts—particularly music—to mathematics, as of course many have done, saying that only he who loves mathematics for its "internal splendors" really understands it.[3]

> Music, like mathematics, dimly echoes past experience. It develops the joy of its understanding into an extensive gamut of feelings, known only to those specially gifted and educated to understand its structure intimately. Mathematics is conceptual music—music is sensuous mathematics.[4]

Bronowski's unification of the arts and sciences centers mainly in the creative act which he says is the "same act in original science and original art."[5]

Neither, he insists, is in any important sense a copying of nature, but a sheerly original act of invention. Furthermore, this likeness continues into appreciation, for the latter is only a kind of repetition of the former: "In the moment of appreciation . . . we re-enact the creative act."[6]

Furthermore, science and art are not even separable with respect to truth. They differ only in that the one appeals to and communicates "facts of the heart" and the other is concerned with exploring the concept in its logical consequences.[7]

From such positions—and today many teachers, often in the interest of larger integrations of subject matter than just humanities, social science, and natural science, deprecate distinctions among these traditional parts of the curriculum—one can be led to speak of the arts *and* the sciences, instead of, in the title of a recent book, *Arts v. Science.*[8]

We would agree that pointing to likenesses and overlaps is interesting and useful, but for some purposes we would resist the collapsing of the old distinction, no matter how noble the motivation for a higher synthesis.

Before proceeding to a detailed contrast, however, a small response to some of the passages just quoted may be useful.

Read's insistence on there being a common reality to which both art and science are answerable is no doubt correct, at least on a certain rendering of "reality"—but this by no means precludes important differences in their respective ways of treating that reality. Indeed, when Read says that art *represents* whereas science *explains*—though we have serious doubts about whether this goes to the heart of the distinction—he is admitting this difference.

One of Bronowski's points is similar: both science and art deal in truth, including that part of truth called "fact," but when he goes on to speak of art's concern with "facts of the heart," he seems to be assuming an important distinction. On his other point, the identity of the "act of creation" in the two fields: we can to a considerable degree assent. That is, in psychological and other descriptions of what it is to create, we do learn of important similarities between the stages of the process and even, no doubt, the feelings of both frustration and satisfaction. Furthermore, there have been careful studies that reveal striking similarities between the personality structure of creators in quite different fields. However, this is a very long way from saying that the interests, attitudes, techniques, materials, forms, and outcomes of scientists and artists are identical. Indeed, a close examination of the phenomenology of the creative act would, we believe, show important differences too.

Polanyi is of course right in mentioning the prevalence of the word "beautiful" in the vocabulary of scientists. In fact, recently it has become one of the most common words of praise in everyday speech, but this is not to say that because "good," "pleasant," "agreeable," "delightful," and many other words have now been replaced in the discourse of relatively inarticulate people by the word "beautiful," there is no important difference between the meaning of the word in the two following contexts:

"Let's go eat a hot dog."
"Beautiful."

"Is his new house well designed?"
"More than that. It's beautiful."

So, too, between the beauty of science and mathematics—which, for instance, has absolutely minimal reference to the sensuous aspects of phenomena—on the one hand, and "beauty" in aesthetic discourse on the other. This is not to say that there are not aesthetic *aspects* of a mathematical theorem or a scientific explanation, but it would be as foolish to reduce either to a "work of art," as to pretend that a concerto and a law of physics have the same sort of explanatory predictive power.

Having noted that even Polanyi, Bronowski, and others admit distinctions as well as admire convergences among the sciences and the humanities, we may proceed further to see whether any headway can be made toward characterizing the humanities by contrasting them with the sciences. However, we will do this not on the assumption that the humanities can be adequately characterized as a kind of residue: everything left over after you have subtracted the sciences.[9] Nor do we do it, either, on the assumption that there is necessarily point-for-point an antithetical contrast between the sciences and the humanities. Rather, the sciences afford a base (not a foil) from which to begin because (1) they are relatively tightly unified in their methods and their ends, and therefore admit of an unusual definiteness of description; (2) some persons to the contrary notwithstanding, the sciences do not and cannot exhaust the whole of man's effective procedures for learning about and dealing with the world in which we live, and if this is so, rival areas need to be examined; (3) in at least *some* respects the contrast between the scientist's way of working and that of certain humanists (using the classification now as the traditional one) appears so stark as to suggest the fruitlessness of trying to assimilate either field to the other, or to ignore the differences in the interest of the "unification of all knowledge" or the "basic identity of all creativity" or some other such ideal of convergence.

We will hypothesize, then, that the sciences are marked by the following characteristics:

1. Scientific works, small or large, tend to get absorbed (though sometimes only after a considerable amount of time) into the scientific body of knowledge or to get excluded from it: in either case, the tendency is to leave the individual work behind as a relic dispensable for scientific purposes. For instance, Bertrand Russell once scoffed at the continued use in some quarters of Euclid's *Elements* in mathematics courses. He said that almost any geometry textbook is better than Euclid's for the purposes of learning geometry: only a humanist would suppose there to be some special virtue about going back to the "original source." The attitude is typical. No chemist feels that he is less of a chemist for not having read Lavoisier: he presumably knows whatever Lavoisier contributed to the science that is true and important; the rest has fallen by the wayside and needs no further attention.

Harold Burstyn, an historian of science, has gone so far as to say:

> The practicing scientist need pay no attention whatever to what actually happened in the past. Whatever of it is usable he has mastered in its modern form; the rest is of purely antiquarian interest. And the more creative a scientist is, the less likely is he to be interested in the past of science.[10]

Alfred North Whitehead made the same point, that science progresses only by forgetting its origins.

2. The sciences have a strong tendency toward generalization, abstraction, and systematic synthesis.[11] One who has not thought long on the subject may be at first surprised, even dismayed, by this claim, either because he associates "abstractness" with vagueness or because he is accustomed to thinking of sciences as rooted in observation of nature—not just armchair theorizing but looking, counting, experimenting, recording instances, etc. But "abstractness" in the present context is illustrated most readily by mathematics: "$2 + 2 = 4$" is more abstract than "two pencils and two pencils make four pencils," in that the numbers apply to anything at all; and $x + y = y + x$ is even more abstract in that *any* numbers at all can be substituted for the letters. For sciences to be empirical (now unlike mathematics) means that they be based in experience, grounded in observation, ultimately always checkable by appropriate use of the senses, etc.; and yet the scientist as scientist is seldom interested in the individual object, except as his observations of it afford him data for describing the nature or behavior of *all such objects.* The botanist examines a tulip minutely in order that he can say something about tulips or the lily family: the death of the original flower is not scientifically poignant. Such sciences as geography and astronomy offer apparent exceptions to this. But note that the geographer, too, readily passes from a description of, say, San Francisco Bay to some generalizations about (1) the tendency of bays in metropolitan areas to be filled in for commercial purposes (2) the function of navigable bays anywhere in the facilitation of commerce, etc. Similarly, the astronomer, though he is interested, perhaps, in our sun, inevitably sees it as belonging to a class of stars, as a member of a subclass of stars of a certain order of magnitude, age, etc.

The high prestige of physics, as the most exemplary of sciences and the science to whose condition all others aspire, arises from the high abstractness of this science, its "possessing" a number of extraordinarily broad, well-founded laws, and hence having immense predictive power. Political science is thought of as one of the least scientific of the sciences because it has not yet been able to develop such laws or such predictive power, but still contents itself, to a considerable degree, with describing individual governments or aspects of governments; still, from the time of Plato and Aristotle, students of government and politics have attempted to establish typologies: democracies, oligarchies, timocracies, tyrannies, etc.

In short, the scientist's way of thinking is strongly "convergent" rather than "divergent."

3. Since we have seen that mathematics is by nature high on the abstraction ladder, it may seem redundant to say that the sciences tend strongly toward quantification and in other employment of mathematics. Yet it is not wholly so. Though quantification is a tool in the process of raising the level of abstraction, there are many purposes served in the sciences by developing ever more precise means of measurement—for example, to help an engineer design bridges. Indeed, so useful has quantification become that the constant search of scientists is for measurable or otherwise quantifiable elements in the object of his investigation. Thus, for the psychologist it is not enough to speak generally about intelligence: since intelligence differs, it must differ in amount, and therefore it is theoretically possible to construct a scale for its distribution. Hence the emergence of the formula $I.Q. = MA/CA$. Oftentimes, the scientific ideal is said to be the construction of a system wherein particular instances can be deduced from laws.

Mathematics has been greatly useful to the sciences in other ways too, including the way of suggesting alternative explanations for phenomena. On the basis of Euclidian geometry, Einstein could not have thought of his relativity explanations: the availability of alternative geometries opened up new possibilities that had not, incidentally, been thought of in the "pure" speculations of its inventors.

4. Scientific investigation tends to intellectualize its procedures as much as possible, discounting, in large measure, the feelings, emotions, attitudes, and most of the values of individual investigations, though obviously the scientist does not set aside such a value as intellectual honesty; indeed, so to do would be self-defeating. The political differences between two zoologists should make no difference in their scientific findings: if they are apparently influenced in such a way by their values, they are held, in so far, to be unscientific. Darwin described how when he discovered in himself a strong interest that his investigations turn out in a certain way, he had to redouble his efforts to verify his findings and his methodological skepticism, lest his conclusions be slanted. A few years ago, Soviet genetics was a disgrace in the scientific world because of the

enforced belief, among its practitioners, in the inheritability of acquired traits—in order that the beneficent influence of the classless society could be vindicated. Although the picture of the scientist as an absolutely cold, unfeeling, disinterested, neutral observer-calculator-theorizer has been overdrawn—as Polanyi and Bronowski, among others, have shown— still, the scientist in his practice does use a variety of means of protecting his methods against the intrusions of feelings and values.[12] In this section we are lumping together traits that might be separated from each other and individually developed: impersonality, the attempt to eliminate feelings from any influence upon findings, and value-neutrality.

5. A characteristic of scientific procedure similar to the above is named by the phrase "public verifiability." The point is that every observation, every experiment, ought to be described in such a way that it can be "replicated" by competent investigators, the assumption being that two independent scientists ought to arrive at the same conclusions if they are conducting identical investigations; if they do not, something is wrong —that is, at least one of them is in error, or their investigations are not after all identical. The scientist cannot entertain the claims of the mystic because such experience is presumably unpredictable. Freud has been criticized for making generalizations[13] about human nature on the basis of his observations of a segment of middle-class Viennese society in the late nineteenth century: some later clinicians claim that their patients do not have the same problems or pattern of development. Similarly, Piaget's account of the development of children's thinking and moral attitudes has been called into question by other investigators of similar problems, and the interpretation made that either his observations were not sufficiently careful, or his sample too limited to bear his conclusions. At the other extreme, it is assumed that Soviet and American astrophysicists and engineers would agree almost completely in their calculations concerning a moon-shot.

6. Partly because of the assumption about public verifiability, and the tendency of scientists to replicate observations and experiments, and to correct each others' accounts, scientific investigation is increasingly thought of as a group endeavor, where members of the group may be widely separated in space and even in time. It is well recognized that large problems admit of parceling out, so that the results may come in piecemeal, and gradually add up to a general solution. It is instructive that increasingly Nobel prizes in the sciences are given not to single

scientists but to two or three persons working as a team, or from their different vantage points making approximately equal contributions to the solution of a major problem.

7. Scientific findings tend to be expressed in what might be called "hard" or "tough" propositions: statements of a kind that are either verifiably true or false. Strenuous efforts are made in scientific writing to eliminate ambiguity, vagueness (hence the importance of quantification), and irrelevancy.

Typically imagery, metaphor, idiosyncratic language, are frowned upon as foreign to the spirit of science itself, though perhaps necessary for purposes of "popularization," that is, explaining science to nonscientists.

These, then, appear to us to be some of the principal characteristics of the scientific enterprise. These characteristics, it should be noted, strongly influence the *selection* of problems for investigation. Thus, the educational psychologist may readily agree that it is less important to know the correlation between ability to remember nonsense syllables and the scores on the Wechsler-Bellevue intelligence scale than to know how to account for the differences in motivation between two groups of students; but they defend their investigation of the former and their neglect of the latter in terms of likely and precise results. They choose problems which apparently admit of solution; they tend to fight shy of those which do not at the present seem to lend themselves to scientific investigation.[14]

The incredibly numerous successes of scientists and technologists in the last hundred years have been recounted so often, and everyone stands so in awe of these accomplishments, that the report and the praise do not have to be repeated here. Suffice it to say that so far as education goes, the kind of snootiness which in the past has characterized many humanists vis-à-vis the scientists has very largely but not entirely disappeared, and for excellent reason. It is hard for us now to imagine that when President Eliot was appointed at Harvard, a number of people expressed indignation because he was only a chemist. Nor do many humanists, at least in America, support a general education that permits the bifurcation into two cultures that C. P. Snow has so tellingly described, such that those with a literary education not only do not know but are rather proud of not knowing any science—even something so fundamental as the second law of thermodynamics.

Indeed, so much has the situation changed that a certain defensiveness is now fairly prevalent among humanistic scholars. Perhaps it is this that accounts for some of them trying to ape the scientists, becoming, for instance, so in love with facts and theories that they forget that in the humanities, whatever be the case elsewhere, merely factual description, categorization, and analysis are means to something else, and not ends. Part of the defensiveness comes from the assurance of progress in the sciences, and the uncertainty of any such thing in arts, letters, and philosophy. But part of it comes too from the considerable amount of uncertainty that obtains as to what the humanities *are.*

Certain persons are hard to classify as between humanists and scientists. There is no law against being both a musician and a physicist. A professional painter may be an accomplished botanist too. A medical doctor may be a fine poet. One who spent his early years in mathematics may become equally proficient in philosophy. As we have already seen, Jacob Bronowski among others has been greatly impressed with similarities between scientists and artists, going so far as to assert a single creative activity, which is displayed alike "in original science and in original art."[15]

And yet there are contrasts too. These can be seen by going again down the list of characteristics of the sciences.

1. If scientists tend to cumulate their findings, keeping what has proved true and assimilatable to the standard body of knowledge and discarding the rest, with relatively little sense of the inviolability of the individual scientific work, there is the opposite humanistic tendency to honor individual human achievements not only for what they tell us (often mistakenly) about the world, but for what they tell us about the age, nation, or person that produced them. Plato's *Phaedrus* is as live today as it was upon its first appearance in the fourth century B.C. Aristophanes' plays compete for a place on the stage with those of Ionesco. Thucydides' *History* is read more widely today than any more recent description of the war between Athens and Sparta. For that matter, historians of science and philosophers of science—in contrast to practicing scientists—are fascinated with the achievements of, say, a Ptolemy, even though his earth-centered astronomy did not survive Copernicus' attack. And they are interested in Harvey's treatise on the circulation of the blood, even though no contemporary medical student would learn his physiology from that source.

Because of this interest in great achievements, a considerable amount of the energy of humanistic scholars goes into (a science-like) textual purification and emendation, so that we may, as nearly as possible, have before us the very work that was created—and this of course applies fully as much to music and painting as to literature. But also humanistic scholarship never tires of new interpretations of human achievements. As T. S. Eliot once said, every time an important new work is created—say in drama—the whole of the *past* has to be recreated to make room in the tradition for this innovation.

There is also that about works in the humanities that is strongly *contextual,* in the sense that they do not tend to yield "results" or "conclusions" that have much value in separation from the whole achievement in which they occur. In a work of physics, a single formula can be extracted and all the rest discarded. Though we quote single lines from the Bible or Shakespeare, we are properly uneasy about such "lifting out of context."

Furthermore, artistic and other humanistic works do not tend to add up in the way scientific works do. They resist synthesis and systematization. To be sure, we hear of schools of art and schools of criticism. The impressionists share a way of looking at and even representing light; the literary neohumanist critics share some philosophical outlooks that tend to make them agree in their literary judgments. But even in these cases there is little that is additive or amenable to system.

2. If scientists have a strong tendency toward abstraction, artists at least (among the humanists) have an equally strong tendency toward concreteness.[16] A painting by Monet of water lillies does not facilitate interest in the family of lillies: it tries to show us how one very particular group of flowers looked on a certain day in a certain season, with the light just so—and furthermore how it looked to a unique person—the artist himself. About some of the great characters in fiction and drama, we have the feeling that they are more particularized than most living persons. Falstaff and Oedipus and Emma Bovary and Alyosha Karamazov cannot be confused with anyone else, living or fictional. The composer, though he may be interested in theoretical acoustics, is much *more* interested in creating a pattern of sounds that is unprecedented and from which nothing can be inferred about other sounds.

The point is sometimes exaggerated. There is also, in many, perhaps most, artists, some drive toward abstractness too. The so-called abstract painter may be trying to show us not how one particular building looked to him, but how buildings look, in an urban scene that might be Paris or New York. In calling his greatest novel *War and Peace,* Tolstoy is doubtless telling us that his is not merely a reporting of some aspects of the Napoleonic invasion of Russia, but an account about wars and their effects on people's behavior. Oedipus is indeed a unique character and yet his name is borrowed to designate a "complex," so well does Sophocles symbolize a common human problem. Perhaps Tchaikovsky in his sixth symphony is trying to write music whose pathos fits not just some particular event but a wide range of events. And so on.

Indeed, there *is* a real tendency toward generalization and abstractness in the arts, but in the works of art counted as great, the particular, the individual, is never discounted in its leading to a higher order abstraction, never *used up* in order to attain a generalization. Those, after all, who are mainly interested in an Oedipus or an Electra *complex* are psychologists, not students of the theater.

However, the situation is somewhat different when we move from creating artists to literary critics and critics of the other arts, to philosophers, to historians. Philosophers, taken as a group, are perhaps not less abstract than scientists. Historians, though they nearly always retain an interest in "exactly what happened," and in a particularity that can never be duplicated, often have the same interest as scientists in pushing toward a theory of what is likely to happen when certain conditions prevail, or to work out à la Hegel or Spengler or Toynbee a *theory* of history. (One can of course argue that such an enterprise belongs more to the philosophy of history than to history itself.) And literary critics, musicologists, and art historians often develop accounts of whole ages, explaining what the spirit of the High Renaissance was, or the principal characteristics of music of the baroque, or the respects in which Ibsen departs from the true tragic genre. Yet in these latter cases too, the critic or art historian typically retains a strong interest in individual works, and may even justify his generalizations by their help in interpreting those specific artifacts.

In any case, with respect to abstractness, though the situation is complex, and varies among humanists (as it does to a degree among scientists); yet it remains true on the whole, that the humanities have a considerably larger place for the concrete and a smaller place for the abstract than do the sciences.

Bronowski doubtless points to something true and important when he says, "The scientist or the artist takes two facts or experiences which are separate; he finds in them a likeness which had not been seen before; and he creates a unity by showing the likeness."[17] For notable instance, the centrality of metaphor to poetry signifies the aesthetic tendency to liken what may seldom or never have appeared similar before. All the same, there is an important difference too between the artistic and the scientific mind. The artist is fascinated by that which was never before on sea or land, in the utterly unique, in exceptions to rules, in the inadequacies of old saws, in the subtle but crucial difference between two shades of green, two tones of voice, two musical keys. Put him in the presence of a collection and he will begin noting the differences—unless the collection is so apparently random as to challenge him to find similarities. Neither artist nor scientist is fully described by the respective epithets "divergent" and "convergent," but they suggest a significant difference.

3. There is but little tendency in the humanities toward quantification or the use of mathematics. Certain exceptions could be noted. There is logic within philosophy, but this is a problem only if one insists that everything that goes on within a certain "humanistic field" is itself humanistic. The same is true with linguistics insofar as this subject is still sometimes included in Departments of English, say.

But musical theory and prosody have a place for measurement, as does the theory of perspective and other aspects of painting and sculpture —to say nothing of the whole engineering side of architecture. Increasingly, literary studies have been conducted by counting occurrences of certain words or images or references. Attempts have been made to determine whether the *Iliad* and *Odyssey* had a common author by computerizing aspects of vocabulary and style in the two works. There was even one attempt (by G. D. Birckhoff) to develop a mathematical formula for the judgment of works of art, whereby merit is said to be represented by the division of the degree of complexity by the degree of order or unity.

Yet with such exceptions, it remains obviously true that humanistic studies are very largely nonmathematical, and indeed typically represent a resistance to converting qualities into quantities. (By contrast, the theoretical physicist warns the beginner not to *picture* subatomic reality, and thus to falsify the mathematical formula.)

4. The impersonality, objectivity, neutrality, and highly intellectual (as opposed to emotional) character of scientific investigation again has some counterpart in the work of historians, philosophers, and the scholars associated with the arts. We resent the historian who puts his thumb on the scale, the philosopher who (like Hegel) is an apologist for his own nation and religion, making all history seem to culminate just there. And many people criticize the critic who works out of a tradition, such as Marxism, that apparently obligates him to make his judgments on the basis of social considerations. For instance, Mao Tse-tung is reported to have said in 1942 in answer to the question of whether Marxism destroys the creative mood in literature: "Yes, it does. It definitely destroys creative moods that are feudal, petty-bourgeois, liberalistic, individualistic, nihilistic, art-for-art's-sake, aristocratic, decadent, or pessimistic, and every other creative mood that is alien to the masses of the people and to the proletariat."[18]

And yet it is normally believed (and we think rightly so) that there is a far greater place for temperamental differences, for the expression of personal preference, for the use of value judgments of many kinds, for the inclusion of feelings, and for subjectivity on the part of humanistic scholars than on the part of scientists. The case of creative artists is of course even more contrastive for, as has famously been said, the art object is always reality seen through the corner of a temperament.

As everyone knows, the artist who suppresses his feelings in his creative act is dooming his work to artistic failure; on the other side, to say of a work of art that it leaves one cold is to condemn it as art. But here too it is easy to exaggerate the difference, as some naive interpreters have done, to make art, by contrast with science, a wholly emotional affair: Scientists think, artists feel—so runs the simple-minded formula. Yet of course the amount of thinking that typically goes into the creation and particularly the revision of a work of art is extensive, hard, and far-ranging.

5. Two cameras of identical make, identically set, and with the same film, set side by side, should take simultaneous pictures that vary only by the minute difference in their placement. Two artists standing side by side will of course paint very different pictures of the same scene—and doubtless would, even if they were identical twins. For the artist *cultivates* the uniqueness of his own outlook. As we say, we may learn to "look through his eyes," but this in no way rules out the equal legitimacy

of a vastly different interpretation by an artist whose eyes we may also look through. Hence there is no question in the creative arts of "public verifiability." Yet, if one is willing to stretch the term a bit, there is a kind of "private verifiability." That is, what the artist does is to present to us, his audience, a kind of hypothesis, an interpretation of some corner of reality. In contemplating his work, we try out this interpretation, in the light of our own perceptual, conceptual, emotional, valuation experience. Our liking or approving his work is in some measure a matter of the "convincingness" of his interpretation, of its fitting in with what we know, affording us a new insight that yet "makes sense." When a work makes novel, interesting, important sense to a number of people, it is praised and becomes famous.

Again the case is somewhat different among the scholars. Although rationality and accuracy are among the criteria employed, few critics and historians expect to command universal agreement, or even believe that such would constitute an ideal end. Histories, even of the long ago, keep having to be rewritten. Somehow the past will not hold still. Two radically different interpretations of the causes of the First World War may still both be very valuable, and neither one obviously superior to the other. Somewhat similarly in philosophy, there is far less contradiction and refutation than many people believe. Theories tend to lose their initial interest and get abandoned in favor of theories that address themselves to a problem at least slightly different. So, except for those who model philosophy very closely on the sciences—apparently a dwindling number—it is not expected that a philosophical treatise will command an assent based upon the assumption that anyone else competently addressing the same problem will come up with the same answer.

6. Humanists, artists, and scholars alike, are notoriously individualistic. Joint authorship of philosophical and historical works is rare, except when there is a clear division of the field, as when one historian handles the age of Jackson, and another the succeeding age. It is very hard to get graduate students in the humanities to work as teams in the way that has become so very common in the sciences. Partly this is because the humanist puts and wants to put part of himself into his work. Anatole France's description of criticism is extreme, but it contains an element of the truth. When I function as a critic of Shakespeare, he said somewhere, it is not so much Shakespeare that I write about as "moi à propos Shakespeare."

7. As to the kind of language used in the sciences and the humanities: the latter field inclines much more strongly to the employment of metaphor, imagery, and ornamentation—in short, to language expressive of feelings and values—than does science. There is a much higher degree of tolerance of ambiguity, and indeed in poetry and some other literary media, there may be an exploitation of "ambiguity" in the sense of deliberately intending the several meanings that may reside in an expression. Though the historian and philosopher and some kinds of critics may pride themselves on their clear, precise, rational styles, others of their fellows may depart considerably from any such canon. The language of poetry, fiction, and drama tends not to be propositional; if it is assertive, it is in a lighter, softer, tenderer way than characterizes the sciences, and as a result the true/false dichotomy does not operate in the same way.[19]

There are important differences, then, between what have been called the humanities and the sciences. If one starts with the fairly well-circumscribed area of the sciences, with their intellectualistic, empirical-mathematical approach, and with their objective of knowledge about all aspects of the world that admit of being formulated in propositions amenable to verification or validation in a strong, public sense (some would say this is what "proposition" *means*), then the question is whether the realm of science exhausts what human beings want and need to know or understand about man and the cosmos in which he dwells. Perhaps the question must be answered differently for different people. Very likely there *are* those whose curiosity is exhausted by the knowledge that is (at least potentially) available through scientific means. Such persons are likely either to dismiss all of the humanities as unimportant, or even iniquitous, or to regard their subject matter as valuable only in a noncognitive way: They might say, for instance, that painting, music, poetry, and philosophy may be pleasant and agreeable, but endeavors that don't *tell* us anything, don't contribute insights, don't help our understanding of—the world. However, a great many of us are not satisfied with this sharp dichotomy between the scientific-cognitive and the nonscientific-emotive, believing rather that there are kinds of knowing, kinds of understanding, kinds of insights different from those available through the means of science, and that these, or some of these (not unfairly to close the door on still other possibilities such as supernatural revelation or ESP) are associated with the arts and humanities.[20] This is not to say that everything valuable about the creation and appreciation of the arts, philosophy, and history must be *cognitive,* even in a broad sense of the word. It may well be, indeed, that the most valuable part of the hearing of music, for instance, is the sensual/emotional experience and not anything to be learned from the sounds. Yet this possibility does not rule out a cognitive component in the experience of any of the humanistic subjects.[21] Indeed, the plain truth is that by far the greatest number of creators in the humanities think of themselves as perceiving and revealing something about reality; and doubtless most persons who prize poems and paintings and historical or philosophical essays do so not purely for mindless amusement, but because of what can be learned from them about what it is like to love or feel grief or experience defeat or just to touch an apple.

There are *many* reasons for likening the sciences and the humanities. If we think of the humanities as saturated with value considerations, we will be ill advised, in the interest of a neat polarity, to see the sciences innocent of values. If the sciences are exceptionally focused on cognition, we should not be insensitive to the humanistic scholar's disinterested pursuit of truth or the poet's claim to be affording insight into an ill-lighted corner of our universe. The descriptions of creative breakthroughs in the two fields sound astonishingly alike. Ofttimes the creative artist, the performer, and the humanistic scholar are heavily dependent upon scientific and technological achievement for their own endeavors; no less often the scientist and mathematician invoke aesthetic criteria in judging their own work. And surely we have reached the point in the development of educational goals of seeing the necessity for both humanistic and scientific understanding in every person, and of ways in which these understandings overlap and even sometimes integrate. And yet. . . .

Like it or not, the humanities and the sciences are now, and have for a long time been, rivals. With some misgivings, we have here undertaken to learn something more about the humanities by contrasting them with the sciences. The following points appear to have emerged:

(1) In several respects philosophy and history—to which could be added, most studies in religion—have more likeness to the sciences than do the aesthetic arts. This in itself confirms two earlier impressions: (a) that at least some of the fields typically listed as belonging to the humani-

ties are conglomerates; and (b) that there is a considerable—for him in search of a definition, a frightening—divergence among the humanities.

(2) On the whole, the sciences are more nearly exclusively cognitive than the humanities, which often concern themselves with sensations, feelings, emotions, attitudes, and values in other ways than as ingredients of knowledge. (3) Insofar as the humanities *are* cognitive, they often employ modes of inquiring, thinking, verifying, and knowing that are specifically and rigorously excluded by scientific method.

Finally, perhaps as an implication of (2) and (3), humanistic products tend to retain their value as individual wholes, to resist being swallowed up in classifications or abstracted from in the interest of higher generalizations, and to bear the stylistic marks of their creators.

6

Toward a New Characterization of the Humanistic

Not all scientists are scientific. Not all humanists are humanistic—not to say humane. Not all that goes on in the science courses and laboratories is in the best traditions of scientific procedure; and much that bears the official label "humanities" has little of the spirit one would like to associate with that enterprise.

There would be nothing peculiar in a student's report that he had got his best insights into the human condition or into the range of human value from a zoology teacher; or that he had best learned how to conduct a rigorous investigation of an empirical problem from a teacher of English; or that he had been inspired to religious enlightenment by an economist. Still, we expect scientists in their professional life and books, magazines, and courses in science, to *be* scientific; and we expect persons identified with religion to *be* religious. So we are entitled to feel disappointment at discrepancies. So too with the humanities.

But we still know rather better—however imperfectly—what it means to be scientific than to be humanistic. It may be that the latter concept is doomed to remain, like many another of noble vintage, vague; but *some* clarification ought to be possible.

The temptation is, of course, to stipulate a definition. Thus, it can be laid down that the one indispensable ingredient of the humanities is a concern for history, or that the only dependable humanistic quality is the aesthetic, but however much one may yearn for such simplicity as a way of cutting through the morass of complexity, the cost is too high: too much gets shut out that way.

Again, as we have seen, the characterization may be so broad and generous as to encompass the sciences and even the technologies. Yet this is to give over the attempt to find anything distinctively humanistic: this is indeed Hegel's night in which all cows are gray.

Another way is to settle on one of the brief definitions already extant, such as those cited in our Introduction. Many of these are admirable, and there is little to be gained by criticizing them or pitting them against each other to try to come out with a winner. But for one who wants a more comprehensive understanding of what it is that makes any claimant to inclusion within the humanities *humanistic,* these are hardly commodious enough accounts.

Perhaps the trouble lies in the very concept of "definition." From the time of Socrates we have sought essences, those characteristics determining membership in a specific class (be it "table," "man," "democracy," or whatever). Essence, necessary and sufficient conditions, genus plus differentia—these ways of defining "definition" are powerful aids to thinking in those circumstances wherein either the definiendum is relatively simple, in the sense of having only a few, clear-cut qualities associated with it, or in which the need for precision is so great as to justify an arbitrariness with respect to criteria. But there are other cases in which the concept is messy, there having grown up around it a number of associations that are neither obviously dispensable or indispensable, and in which it is more important to have a large, general understanding than one sufficiently sharp (though arbitrary) to make definite decisions as to what is in and what is out.

When William James wrote *The Varieties of Religious Experience,* he had come to believe, as a result of looking at a bewildering variety of people's claims to having had a religious experience, that "We call all sorts of things 'religious,' and it is plainly false that there are one or more characteristics to be found in each and every one of them."[1] Yet this did *not* lead him to draw sharp or narrow boundaries, nor did it prevent his continuing an arduous search for the meaning of "religious"!

But no philosopher wholly came to grips with this problem of definition until Ludwig Wittgenstein wrote *Philosophical Investigations.* After considering at length some of the many ways in which people use language, or, as he liked to say, play language games, he imagines the objection: " 'You take the easy way out! You talk about all sorts of language-games, but have nowhere said what the essence of a language-game, and hence of language is: what is common to all these activities, and what makes them into language or parts of language.' " He replies that this is true, that language phenomena do *not* have an essence, a common property, but that they are related in a variety of criss-crossing and overlapping ways.[2] He calls these "family resemblances," for the various ways in which members of a family resemble each other—eye color, body type, features, manner of walking, etc.—criss-cross and overlap, without there being any single characteristic which all members of the family possess.

Looking at the humanities and at putative instances of the humanistic, we find, as William James did about religion and the religious and as Ludwig Wittgenstein did about games and language, nothing in common right across the board, or at least nothing that would not obtain in the case of other, seemingly nonhumanistic objects, events, or processes. But we do find it possible to tease out certain qualities, characteristics, themes, and sets that recur significantly often. These recurrent similarities may be sufficient to indicate that we are in the presence of a "family."

First of all, let us make a three-way distribution of characteristics: *objects, approaches* or *attitudes,* and *effects* (intended or actual).

By "objects" let us mean certain *products,* the human achievements that Crane and many others consider to be the subject matter, the content of traditional humanistic study; equally they can be looked at as the issue of humanistic creativity. These are, most prominently, poems, plays, and prose fiction (including folk tales, legends, and myths); paintings and drawings; statues and relief-sculpture; buildings; compositions for voice and instruments; notated dances; so-called "art films"; dialogues, essays, and treatises in philosophy; historical writings, whether general in scope or in such special areas as science; and prophetic, devotional, theological, inspirational, or interpretive works of religion. But there are many other possibilities—many other actualities: landscapes (planted, not painted), fountains, jewelry, vases, rugs, clothing, furniture, lights, windows, musical-choreographic-dramatic improvisations, and so on. The list is literally infinite, for the excellent reason that, strictly speaking, *anything* can become a humanistic object by virtue of a humanistic approach—just as a humanistic approach tends to be called out in the presence of such kinds of objects as those listed. Still, it is no accident that some kinds of objects are more commonly encountered and addressed in this way than others, since objects differ with respect to their tendency to evoke the sort of response here relevant.

By "approach" we intend an attitude, a way of regarding, a kind of attention, a sort of interest, a mode of perception. The following list of ways of approach is meant to be suggestive, and is known to consist of overlapping rather than exclusive categories: appreciative, empathic, *person*al, imaginative, distancing, and integrative or inclusively relating.

Appreciative

It is a great pity that "appreciation" as in "art appreciation" and "music appreciation" has become a word of sorry repute. Say "appreciation" to a student or teacher and the result is eyes cast to heaven and a groan (possibly silent). Unfortunately, though, the word is indispensable for present purposes: there is no adequate synonym. The word's value lies in its synthesizing these three meanings listed in Webster's Seventh:

a) To evaluate the worth, quality, or significance of;
b) To admire greatly;
c) To judge with heightened perception or understanding: be fully aware of.

Now, characteristic humanistic products contain their creators' appreciation, and evoke in others appreciative attitudes. A very considerable amount of what goes on in philosophy and history may be said to have as one of its principal aims the establishment or the deepening of appreciation for man and his achievements. As Collingwood has said, "The value of history . . . is that it teaches us what man has done and thus what man is." Similarly, a vast amount of philosophy from ancient times to the present has been "anthropological" in the root sense of the term: concerned with man, his nature, his vices and virtues, his ways of thinking and knowing, his place in the cosmos—all these in the interest of evaluating, judging, perceiving, understanding, being fully aware of man. The extent to which literature, and to only a somewhat lesser extent painting and sculpture, contain and elicit appreciations of man needs no demonstration or detailing here. But if we come to appreciate man and human acts and achievements better because of the *content* of philosophic, historical, and aesthetic objects, so are we appreciative of the genius of those who afforded us this increased understanding. That is, we are appreciative both of the Thomas More revealed in the famous portrait, and of Holbein its creator; both of Molly Bloom and of James Joyce; both of Abraham the prophet and of the Old Testament author (add Kierkegaard for good measure) who told us of him so effectively; both of man shown to be one who must die but need not die complainingly, and of Epictetus who conceived this idea; both of Luther struggling to work out his relationship with his father, and of Erik Erikson who not only explained but showed this process.

Yet it is not man alone who is directly the object of humanistic appreciation, and the word "humanistic" must not be allowed to suggest so. Picasso has helped us appreciate the extent to which guitars, grapes, and light rays may be profitably seen as cubes. Debussy has helped us appreciate the sounds of the sea; Robinson Jeffers, rocks and hawks; Brancusi, the act of flight; Thucydides, Pepys, and Camus, the plague; Dante, hell.

The creative artist, historian, philosopher tries to originate an object that will say for himself, and hopefully for others, something about an aspect of the world as it impinges upon a subjectivity. To the extent that he succeeds, he and others will have gained a better appreciation of man and the world. The humanistic scholar has as his aim the dealing with human achievements so as to make them more fully and clearly available; to interpret them; and to relate them to each other, and to the persons, times, and places most relevant to them. This he does both to help others appreciate these achievements themselves, and also through them, the subject matter of the creators.[3]

In speaking thus of appreciations, we have inadvertently slipped over into speaking of effects even more than of approaches, but this was necessary to see what the approach hopes to gain. Still, the gaining of appreciations is apparently dependent to a very considerable extent upon coming to the object with a certain kind of expectation, a certain kind of attention, a certain attitude—which we can only call "appreciative." To come to someone or something in the attitude of appreciation; to set out to try to appreciate; to assume the posture that will tend to understand, extract the value of, enjoy, heighten awareness of, partake in the special quality of the object (and, as already noticed, of the object's creator as well as of what may be symbolized by the object) all of these are prior conditions that most conduce to experiential appreciation. Sometimes we appreciate something almost in spite of ourselves and without half-trying. But more importantly, we *learn* to appreciate; that is, we learn how to approach an object in such a way as to increase the likelihood of our appreciation greatly. Thus, if we put on a record with the intent of really listening, with the hope and expectation of "taking it in," realizing it, getting what it has to offer, responding to it not just casually or incidentally, but as a whole being; then, though we may be disappointed in the results, we have done what we can to have an experience of worth.[4]

Empathic

The word was invented as an "English" equivalent to the German *einfühlung:* feeling-into. The strictest sense of empathy is the kinesthetic: I know what the Greek discus-thrower feels like by mimicking, at least incipiently, his posture. I tense my muscles more or less like his, and that tension is part of my perception. But the word has taken on a more general meaning, such that it applies to all sorts of feelings, and not just those directly associated with the body. Usually two steps are distinguished in empathy; *both* are essential. In the first, we respond to an object, for instance, a painting or a symphony feelingly; then we project our own feelings back into the object in such a way as to regard that feeling as a quality of the object. To approach an object (including, of course, a person) empathically, then, is to be prepared to undergo this double process. Here again subtle learning processes are involved such that in time we may come to be able to be empathic without the least conscious effort.

Creators in the arts—this approach pertains less to the nonaesthetic humanities—learn ways of evoking and facilitating empathy, as when the playwright or the novelist invents a character with whom an audience can "identify," and performers, especially dancers and actors, similarly have their ways of eliciting empathic acts on the part of the audience.

Personal

This word is intended to suggest an approach with respect to persons, but not by any means necessarily in the private-individual way that "personal" normally connotes. The point is that in the case of relations with humanistic products, there is at least one sort of implicit relationship between persons; that is, between me as "consumer" and him as creative artist. The object of his creation and of my attempt at appreciation—painting, book, dance, or whatever—is a mediator between him and me, no matter how anonymous he be and obscure I be. Chances are great that he as creator will not be exclusively interested in what he "has to say" or in the medium in which he is to exercise his craft, but will also be trying to communicate with—someone. Put the other way around, the artist who has a sense of not reaching anyone is normally exceedingly frustrated in his apparent isolation. On the other side of the transaction, I will tend to be somehow conscious of the person behind the creation, of him who has left his entirely distinctive mark on what he has made, and in the case of great works I may feel a bond of exceptional strength between us, for who else can have spoken so piercingly to my condition, and who was better prepared than I to receive the signal he sent out, the cry he uttered, the laugh he let escape.

In the instance of dramatic works, there may be still another kind of *person*al relationship, that between the audience and the persons inside the work, the characters, the human subjects; and again this may be a very intense, if necessarily one-way relationship, as will be testified to by anyone who has developed an especial interest in Becky Sharp, Heathcliff, Hedda Gabler, Isolde, or some other fictional character.

Again, this relationship is facilitated by a certain attitudinal approach. What one must come to realize, and the earlier the better, is that a humanistic product does carry a signature. (An ingenious story known to have issued from a computer or from an accidental striking of keys would be weirdly depersonalized.) But a signature has to be read and responded to—in fact, has to be looked for and made intelligible. Unless one approaches not just words but the Plato, the Jefferson, the Chaucer whose words they are, one has already condemned the words to a muted voice. Another way of putting this same point about the *person*al, is in terms of "expressiveness." Briefly—and more has been written on "expression" in the field of aesthetics than on almost any other topic—this means that one goes to the humanistic product looking for an expression there of its creator; and goes too with the hope that the work will prove expressive of oneself, saying what one somehow had it in himself to say, yet never quite.

Imaginative

Any novel creation is of course imaginative: Hilbert's Undecidability Proof or Heisenberg's Uncertainty Principle, no less than Mozart's Jupiter Symphony or de Chirico's "Nostalgia of the Infinite." However, humanistic works, with great frequency, are imaginative in an additional way: they are imagistic; they will conjure up in the mind that approaches them with appropriate expectation and readiness persons, places, things, and events that occupy their own charmed space and time. One goes or ought to go to many humanistic works—all drama and fiction, most painting, a fair amount of philosophy and religion, and some history, anyway—with an "as if" attitude; prepared to take seriously, but not necessarily literally, what one finds; ready to let the creator have his way, devise and prescribe his own set of rules, phantasize to his heart's content, and ours. Some people cannot endure a story or an account unless they have a certification as to its factuality. This type of insecurity with respect to the imagination is fatal in the realm of the humanities.

Distancing

The successful experience with a humanistic product may be said to be "distanced." The humanistic creator has as one of his challenges and requirements, the attainment of "distance" on his material. The object itself "works" only if it tends to establish "distance" in its beholder. Finally, he who approaches the humanistic product or occasion has, typically, a certain problem to solve, the establishment of "distance."

The point of this "distance" concept, or "psychical distance" as it was called by Edward Bullough, who made the idea famous, is to keep the humanistic experience just far enough away from one's own personal, individual life to be recognized as "arranged for," "special,"—one would say "contrived" except for that suggesting a certain speciousness. But it should not be kept so far away that one's attitude is impersonal, utterly objective, cold, merely analytic. The latter is "over-distanced." Rushing onto the stage to save the damsel from the villainous clutch is "under-distanced." What in any given case constitutes appropriate distance cannot, of course, be specified in advance or by rule. It varies with many circumstances. But this ability is highly developed in some, largely missing in others. An element of "formalism" compensates for the tendency to underdistance, but a concentration upon form alone moves an experience toward colder intellectual scrutiny. William James put the point brilliantly, though we would not confine the case to "belief" merely:

> The greatest proof that a man is *sui compos* is his ability to suspend belief in presence of an emotionally exciting idea. To give this power is the highest result of education. In untutored minds the power does not exist.[5]

James is of course in turn echoing Coleridge's famous formula for reading poetry: "The willing suspension of disbelief."

Integrative or Inclusively Relating

The final point is most important of all—and the most ill-named. But the attitude or approach we are after here is that of commitment of an exceptionally large part of oneself to the experience. The temptation is to say "one's whole self," but that is to say too much, as will appear in the final chapter. Nevertheless, the truly dedicated creative artist approaches this limit. Joseph Conrad's advice was, "To the destructive element, commit yourself." Only the artist or philosopher who is willing to run great risks, risks with his very sanity, his grip on reality, plays for the greatest stakes.

The psychoanalytic tradition has discovered a great deal about this sort of risk-taking; the revelations of Freud about the dream life of all men were themselves unsettling, stoutly resisted, and denounced. Yet the artist disregards the realm of the unconscious, stays cosily in his sunlit parlor in order to concoct—trivia. Or as Jung has said, whatever the powers of the intellect, and they are huge, they do not exhaust those of the whole personality. As the intellect tries to deal with some aspects of experience, it produces, he said, "mere concepts, a *flatus vocis* with no weight or substance." Outside of its own field, intellect is "a great cheat and illusionist . . ."[6]

In the ranks of philosophers, some of the most rational of minds, some who were most devoted to getting rid of fuzziness and uncertainty, and establishing life on an absolutely secure base, had also a mystical streak in them, or some other commerce with the dark and irrational side: Plato, Spinoza, Hegel, Whitehead, James, Heidegger, Wittgenstein, perhaps even Kant—to say nothing of those admittedly outside the camp of the rational or scientific: Plotinus, Boehme, Schopenhauer, Kierkegaard, Bergson.

Of course, the attitude of the partaker, the observer, is less sweeping, less intense than that of the creator scaling the cliffs and plunging into the seas. All the same, the greatest rewards are reserved for that person alone who is willing to engage a very large part of himself in the humanistic experience, even though it derive from or center upon somebody else's product. It is easier to approach a metaphysical, religious, or artistic work as analyst, highly distanced critic, or uninvolved historian than to let those attitudes inform the deeper-running stream of feeling; but only the more complex, the more inclusive attitude suffices for the authentic humanistic experience.

Once again, the point can be made by contrast with the scientific sort of attitude, which is severely, austerely cognitive. The humanistic attitude—we are not saying it is better or worse, but different—is not in this way austere, though it is not anticognitive. It tries to be at once responsive to the sensuous, emotional, moral, and spiritual, as well as cognitive aspects of the products it addresses itself to and of the process in which it participates.

We have spoken, then, of typical kinds of genres of humanistic products, admitting that it is possible for any object to be addressed humanistically, and to have values we associate with the humanities. We have spoken too of aspects of the humanistic approach, attitudes which tend to yield certain rewards; here our emphasis has been upon the beholder, the audience, the enjoyer, but we have not entirely neglected the creator and the performer. There remain the effects, the results, the values; here, though we have indulged in some anticipations, we have reserved for chapters on "value" and on "humanistic teaching goals" the main effort of explication.

Still, we already have enough characteristics before us to be able to see likenesses among the several best-reputed members of the humanistic family; these characteristics in turn allow us to recognize kin in products and processes that turn up with different names, like archaeology, astronomy, mathematics, and psychology. Mathematicians, for instance, once they get beyond the rudiments of their subject, are forever invoking aesthetic criteria in the judgment of proofs, even though mathematics tends to be exceptionally highly distanced and nonsensuous. In the case of psychology: a great deal here depends upon which "kind" of psychology one has in view. The stimulus-response, or the operant conditioning sorts would seem to have few of the humanistic qualities. But it is not entirely an accident that there is a school of thought *called* "humanistic psychology," and one has not to read far into the works of Maslow, Rogers, Rollo May, Erich Fromm, Viktor Frankl, Bruner, Gordon Allport, Jung, and some of the Gestaltists to understand why, even apart from the fact that they are intelligible to the statistically illiterate, they are more widely read by "official" humanists than are Hull and Spence. Jung, for instance, has said that "In psychology one possesses nothing unless one has experienced it in reality." This in our terms means a much lower distance than that normally associated with the sciences. He speaks of knowing things not just intellectually, which is too often not much more than verbal knowledge, but of knowing "the substance of the thing from inside."[7] Such a characterization goes far to bringing this kind of psychology into the family.

At the same time, our characteristics quickly reveal that either certain whole fields often listed with the humanities are going to have to be taken as "first cousins once removed," that is, as somewhat peripheral members of the core group, or are going to have to be shown to be conglomerates, such that some of their subfields are very much more humanistic than others. Philosophy is here a good example, for logic and the philosophy of science seldom yield humanistic products. But this is true of the linguistics component of "English" and other language departments, too. (Some such carving is possible in the case of each of the usual humanities fields.) Or again, as in the case of psychology, certain ways of conceiving of a field will be the key to whether it belongs in or out of the family. Some there are who see history as almost entirely factual, or see it (as did Herbert Spencer) as a kind of descriptive sociology, the more scientific the better. Still others see it as having its closest affiliation with political science and economics. Such sorts of historians are only with great uneasiness yoked with the humanists. Some of these same attitudes toward history may characterize historians of literature, philosophy, art, architecture, music, or any other field, with the same results. Some members of departments of literature, the visual arts, and music are so taken up with textual problems as again to have few interests in whole humanistic products or in the cultivation in themselves or others of the approaches that yield humanistic experiences. In philosophy the positivists—unless like Wittgenstein they "recanted"—have had little affiliation with the humanities; and so, too, have others who have seen philosophy as a very severely cognitive, tough-minded discipline, with little room for the speculative, the imaginative, the dramatic, and the personal.

So, it turns out not to be possible to say, without many qualifications, that such and such is the certified list of *the* humanities. At the same time, the qualifications are not infinite or infinitely confusing, and they deserve to be made in the interest of what will then be, for certain curricular purposes, fruitful groupings.

One approach to this problem of academic classification popular in

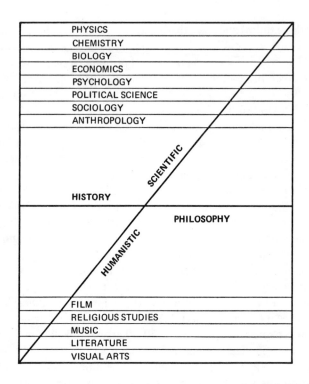

recent years, is that which bears the name, "Structure of Knowledge." Without going at all deeply into this matter, which is peripheral to our present interests, the following two charts are meant to be suggestive. It is to be noted that in one, history and philosophy are pulled out of the usual tri-partite scheme and made to serve a synoptic function. In the other, they are ranged with the humanities, but only slightly more so than with another division.

We have not, then, come up with a tight, neat definition of "humanities" or "humanistic," but we have tried to arrive at a general characterization by designating typical humanistic products or objects, and typical humanistic approaches or attitudes (whether as creator or beholder) to these or other products. Added to the list of predominantly or optimally humanistic fields of study and creative endeavor, these resemblances give us a picture of a family. In the final chapters we will come to a larger consideration of the effects which humanistic education tries to achieve.

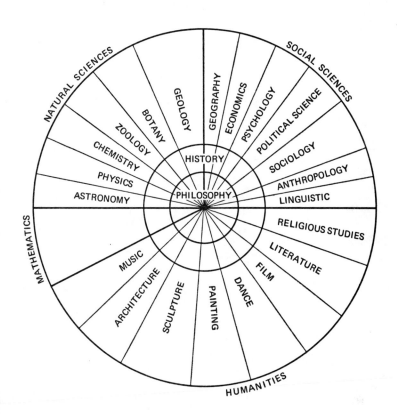

7

Humanists and Their Vices

In characterizing the humanities in terms of certain family resemblances, we have taken no pains to hide our admiration of, and fondness for, humanists and humanistic qualities. However, admiration is not idolatry; fear of the sin of misdirected idolatry may have been partly responsible for the Catholic Church's having long ago established the custom, in the proposal of a candidate for canonization, of appointing a scholar to dig up and express the worst that can be said about the putative saint.

It is time now to play the devil's advocate with respect to the esteemed humanities, even though they are by no means under consideration for collective sainthood. We will save further encomia in order to concentrate for a brief while—in a kind of interpolated coda—on certain characteristic vices of practitioners in the humanities.

The Renaissance humanist directed many of his shafts at the medieval logician or metaphysician, that is to say, at the abstruse categorizer, the arid speculator. Rabelais praised learning, but heaped scorn on pedantry. Montaigne had fun with the two travelers who felt they had fully described themselves when one said, "He is a grammarian and I am a logician."[1]

Today it is the scientist who is often caricatured, though uneasily and ambivalently, by humanists. Current stereotypes of the scientist, dating at least from Mary Shelley's Frankenstein, show a gimlet-eyed, nerveless, unfeeling and even unscrupulous deviser of magic; or a reductionist, a "nothing-but-er," a thinker who dismisses as contemptible or unreal anything that eludes his formulas; or as a super-mechanic, lacking in the cultural graces and human compassion. But the devoteé of the humanities is not entitled to his sometime complacency with respect to the image *he* casts: he needs to be aware of how unattractive he appears to some—and not without reason.

Renaissance humanism left the whole western world in its profound debt by its restoration of the marvels of the Graeco-Roman civilization, but as often happens in history, a great achievement got solidified into a dogma: for centuries, untold numbers of schoolboys were required to give over an incredibly large portion of their time and energy to the study of Latin, and to a lesser extent, Greek, on the assumption that even if they did not spend the rest of their lives happily and profitably reading Virgil and Cicero, they would at least toughen and sharpen their minds by memorizing the rules of grammar. It is hard to say which part of this assumption is more ill-grounded.

Down through the centuries, voices were raised against the tyranny of the classical languages and literature, but the efforts were futile, so strong a grip did the classicists have upon the curriculum, and so firm a hold did they have upon the criteria of intellectual attainment. John Locke, writing in 1693, was typical of many would-be reformers:

> When I consider what ado is made about a little Latin and Greek, how many years are spent in it, and what a noise and business it makes to no purpose, I can hardly forbear thinking, that the parents of children still live in fear of the schoolmaster's rod, which they look on as the only instrument of education; as if a language or two were its whole business.[2]

When in the nineteenth century, apologists for the natural sciences began to assert more boldly the virtues of their subjects, they had to establish their *bona fides* by having demonstrated their ability to parse Latin, to translate Livy, and to write verses in a language that no one any longer spoke. It was much to T. H. Huxley's credit and credibility, as a spokesman for the natural sciences, that his own classical training was above reproach.

Entrenched classicism is, of course, no longer a power, but the vice of which it is only a special case still looms large in academe: the worship of the past. A great many students get the idea from their teachers and textbooks that history stopped some while ago; all that goes on today is something very dubious and frilly called "current events." The course in Western Civilization or in Great Books stops at the safe distance of the first World War or William James. In American Literature pupils are often led to suppose that today's writers are but pygmies when compared with the giants of the past, Washington Irving and Henry Wadsworth Longfellow. Young poets are often cast down when they find that their eminent professors of poetry have apparently read nothing that has appeared during the last thirty years. Art historians in the schools and colleges sometimes mention the great Armory exhibit as if it were the very latest and most daring event imaginable: its date was 1913. From many music courses one would get the impression that Debussy was the last composer worthy of notice, though the Stravinsky of "The Firebird" vintage (1910) is sometimes tremblingly mentioned.

The present (or even the recent past) is, we are continually told, so messy, so unclassifiable; it is, by definition, without perspective. To get involved with it is to be pulled and tugged by forces we know not how to analyze or evaluate. Take, for instance, the notorious difficulty of defending (or even attacking) a judgment about a new work of art. Who knows but what we—or worse still, Informed Opinion—may reverse our initial opinion?

One does not relish new evidence of one's fallibility. With respect to the brand new, the maturest teacher may privately confess himself no better off—and possibly in some ways even worse off—than the veriest novice among his students. It is a state of mind sufficiently uncomfortable to promote a retreat to more familiar heights. The necessity of preserving a reputation for expertness may be the single largest reason for fleeing the present for the past.

A closely-related vice is that of historicism, the inveterate practice of getting to and dealing with a subject, be it ever so urgently contemporary, through an account of its origins and history. Is not the book in hand a case in point? What does it do when approaching the present state of the humanities but retreat immediately to the ancient Greeks and solemnly march down through the centuries? The scholar has been likened to the matador, who, before making his decisive thrust, takes one step back. But having taken one, or two, steps back, the scholar may find that safer ground more to his liking, so that the thrust into the present never gets made.

It is no wonder that today a new and vigorous anti-history movement is afoot among young people, which, when combined with mere indifference to the charms of history, makes the job of the history teacher frustrating. History is today often seen as the opiate of the scholar and of those whom he can corrupt. "When we would strike a blow for peace or freedom," the activist now complains, "you teachers give us a lecture on the history of peace movements, or freedom as an eighteenth century ideal." For all of their own master's historicity, young Marxists often see the academic infatuation with the past as a cop-out, and in this they are joined by activists and reformers of many other persuasions. Yet existentialists, just as much as political radicals, attack historical scholarship: the notion of being determined or even rough-hewn by the past is anathema to those who assert their indetermination by anything but their own unique wills.

Finally, with respect to the vice of over-fond dwelling on the past, we must recognize and acknowledge yet another caricature, that of the absent-minded professor. Mircea Eliade, perhaps the world's foremost historian of religion, tells the story of an old professor in Berlin, Theodore Mommsen. The time was the 1890's, and Mommsen was getting on in years.

In his very first lecture, the eminent classical historian told about Athens in the time of Socrates, tracing on the blackboard a map of the city and locating (without benefit of a single note) all the more important buildings, wells, groves, and temples.

> Awed by Mommsen's amazing display of erudition, memory, and literary insight, my professor . . . then noticed that an elderly valet had come forward, took Mommsen's arm and gently guided him out. At this point another student still present explained that the famous historian did not know how to go home alone.[3]

In short, the man who knew every nook and cranny of ancient Athens could not, unaided, find his way around in his own city. Eliade told the story not to heap scorn on the old scholar; he was obviously charmed by this discrepancy, as many other humanists would be. Yet, in another way, it is symptomatic of what is wrong with many humanists: knowledgeable about the past, they are inept in the present. It makes but a dubious justification for studying history.

It must not be thought, however, that historicism and worship of the past exhaust the rings of hell reserved for sinning humanists. An even larger category than those so far visited, is that of academicism, by which we understand excessive devotion to study, to books, to reflection, to analysis, to explanation, to conceptualization. There comes a time to leave off talk about art in order to enjoy, to appreciate, and even, perhaps to create it. Let us glance at some four kinds of attack on academic humanities.

First, altogether too often humanists forget the ends in their preoccupation with means. Sometimes for them background is given, not to help in the grasp of what, presumably, is in the center of the stage, but as its own excuse for being. In plotting the structure of a symphony or a play, they may seem to have forgotten the work of art as an immediate source of satisfaction. It is not at all uncommon for students to gain the strong impression that their teacher secretly does not really enjoy the works that he praises and explains—even that he thinks their enjoyment is somehow irrelevant. A recent "framework" for a statewide program in music went on at length about skills of performance and abilities to listen and discriminate, but somehow neglected to mention the deep satisfaction to be taken in playing and hearing music. Since Freud's early works, we have known that forgetting is selective and significant: this case is no exception, for the teacher and the theoretician can and do forget sometimes the culminating aesthetic or other humanistic experience in their deep concern for testable achievement or scholarly attainment.

Theorizing is also sometimes a substitute for creation of a more direct kind. The sculptor struggling to achieve precisely the texture he wants on a certain plane may grow understandably impatient with the academic commentator. "Roll up your sleeves," he says, testily," and get your hands dirty. Stop talking." Often the purely verbal and analytic humanist may not do credit to the satisfaction of dancing, acting, painting, designing, or singing; he may in subtle ways disparage performance by novices and thus rob them of pleasure thereby, and even of the special kind of understanding that comes (or *can* come) from overt participation. Similarly, there is something to be learned about painting that cannot be learned as long as one fails to take up a brush, and the academic substitution of words for paints may actually inhibit the appreciation that is presumably the goal.

He who talks and writes about the arts and other humanities—there is a difference too between doing history and doing the theory of history, between writing philosophy and writing accounts of philosophies—may only be sparing himself the pains of creativity. Is it not easier, especially if one's college and graduate training have been appropriately rigorous, to deal with a subject at one remove, to concentrate on its history or its structure, perhaps to compare and contrast schools of thought or representative achievements, than to immerse oneself in the "destructive element," to run the psychic dangers of commitment to creation? And yet are not the rewards of schools and colleges most commonly given those who take the safe, scholarly course?

Talk about the humanities may also screen out the feelings, sensuous or emotional, that have so often been celebrated as the very core of aesthetic, religious, and other kinds of deeply imaginative experience. Spinoza may be taken as the purest prototype of the intellectual who, though himself a deeply feeling man, required himself to subjugate passion to the "active" role of thought. Only this way, he taught, could a man escape "passivity," the surrender of the self to the play of forces from outside. The desperate need for control, for self-sufficiency, for protection, may be behind the academic's comfort in substituting ideas for feelings. The point here is not so much that this in itself is bad, as that what starts as a game may become an ingrained habit, so that the torments of an Anna Karenina, the self-destroying compulsiveness of a Don Giovanni, the serenity of Bellini's St Francis may be noticed, analyzed, and accounted for without ever having been felt.

John Holt recently had this to say:

> The humanities have become increasingly a little bunch of things that in certain contexts we talk about because it makes us feel good to so do. Meanwhile we go on dealing with one another in a very different sort of way. This gulf is dreadful.[4]

Faced with war, disease, poverty, and racial strife, the humanist may seem very inhumane if he wags a finger at those who noisily cry out for action and with a contented sigh shuts the door of his study or studio. Less urgently, but perhaps even more pervasively, the problem of impersonality, the interposing of mechanisms between persons and between persons and nature, may seem to go almost wholly unrecognized by the academic humanist in his zeal to add an intellectual footnote to his studies. Then, when the academic goes on to defend himself by saying that students are in school to study, not to conduct social reforms, he may be further alienating those already convinced that study is more an escape from, than a preparation for, fruitful action.

The charge that humanists and the humanities are infected with a snobbish elitism is directed beyond the groves of Academe. If one thing more than another distinguishes humanists from other sorts of intellectuals, it is the consistency and fervor of their dedication to *the best*. If in the search for novelty, or anyway publishability, humanistic scholars have often been tempted into the byways of obscurity and mediocrity in the works and creators they have studied, hardly any of them are deficient in their praise of Aeschylus, Shakespeare, and Goethe; Plato, Spinoza, and Kant; Thucydides, Tacitus, and Gibbon; Bach, Mozart, and Beethoven; Michelangelo, El Greco, and Cezanne. The enduring masterworks, the great books, the canon of eminent achievement: these are his stock in trade, and the emporium has a distinguished clientèle. A young professor in an esteemed liberal arts college has recently put the humanist's defense of his high standards in this way: ". . . The culture that he represents is in some significant sense better than the culture of the typical American. . . . To read Milton or Dante is more rewarding than to read the works of any living author."[5]

Humanists have long been used to encountering resistance to their suasions to seek the best, but not until recently have the resistances become boldly articulate. "I prefer *bad* books, third-rate authors, corny music, high camp," is something now asserted by persons who have in fact read widely and developed "cultural tastes." The reasons for this reverse snobbishness are doubtless complicated, but they at least include a feeling of distaste for the established and dogmatic snobbishness of the self-styled spokesman for the humanistic tradition.[6] Very often in trumpeting the greatness of Milton or Brahms, he has hardly been at pains to hide his contempt for those whose heroes are less lofty. As we have seen, he has often saved himself the difficulty of evaluating present achievements by taking refuge in the well-documented reputations, and he has defended his actions as those which exhaust respectability. He has insisted on education as an elaborate and long initiation rite, so that no one still young or for other reasons ignorant of the great moments in history is deemed entitled to either judgment or appreciation.[7]

With the strongest sense of defending the truth and the light, eminent literary scholars have denounced the attempts of publishers and curriculum guiders to choose stories that will speak to the present condition of children who come from bookless homes, as a betrayal of our cultural heritage, and have insisted that it is Chaucer, Shakespeare, Milton, and Wordsworth or nothing; that if students don't in fact like to read the sermons of Jonathan Edwards or accustom their ears to the eighteenth century concerto grosso, they *ought* to do so, and teachers ought to make them conscious of their duty. Such priggishness has helped beget a counter-attack that ends by denouncing the heritage as utterly irrelevant, boring, and even corrupting. What sorrier commentary could there be on the failure of masterpieces to humanize than the snobbism of some of their handmaidens? Yet these very scholars know chapter and verse about the pedantry of the French Academy when faced with the Impressionists and the pity of Schubert's not being able to earn a decent living by his music.

In their zeal to separate themselves from the hoi-polloi, some critics and artists have retreated into pure formalism and the denial that true art has any legitimate or important connection with real life. A Clive Bell may insist that there is nothing worth attending to in a painting but its lines, colors, and masses: all representation is irrelevant or worse.[8] An Eduard Hanslick may hold that musical emotion is strictly *sui generis*, and that therefore it is nonsense to talk of pathetic symphonies or militant marches, or tunes that bespeak love.[9] Ortega y Gasset may go so far as to demand a *dehumanization* of art, saying with approval that "modern paintings and sculptures betray a loathing of living forms or forms of living things," and that "The poet begins where the man ends. The man's lot is to live his human life, the poet's to invent what is nonexistent. . . ." In short, "life is one thing, art is another."[10]

Similarly, it has become common for historians and philosophers to admit—even to take pride in—the "purity" of their products and processes. The question, "What lessons are to be learned from history?" is then regarded as hopelessly naive: "None at all," is the smirking answer. History is its own excuse for being.[11] Philosophy perhaps even more so, not merely in its metaphysical and logical modes, but in ethics and aesthetics as well, so that it is commonly said that no connection is asserted between the ability to carry out an expert analysis of "duty" and —doing one's duty. Furthermore, ethics has to do with the former, exclusively, just as aesthetics has to do wholly with straightening out the "grammar" of critical statements and not with improving the aesthetic quality of human lives. That religious studies can be similarly "dehumanized" is no new discovery but constituted the substance of many a complaint in the Renaissance and Reformation about medieval scholasticism.

The aesthetic dimension of life, like the scholarly, can be overvalued. As Kierkegaard taught, love itself and not merely the anguish of broken romance, can be poetized out of existence. Or to go back farther in history, Augustine deplored the time in his life when his education had taught him to weep for the fate of Dido but to be oblivious of the woes of live men and women. The love of beauty can become effeteness, and in sinking that low, can do a disservice to the whole cause of improving the face of the world. Worse yet, it can serve as a mask of wanton and perverse cruelty. George Steiner has reminded us that there are known to have been Nazi prison administrators who adjusted their record players by light filtered through shades of human skin—and then settled back to exult in the masses of Johann Sebastian Bach.[12]

Admittedly, this is an extreme if chilling example, so we end with the more moderate, more characteristic vice. Again, Steiner is spokesman for a plausible charge. Taking issue with Matthew Arnold and F. R. Leavis, he wonders whether the humanities *do* humanize. Perhaps, indeed, he says, such concentration on a written text, as is usually associated with humanistic study may even blunt our moral responses.

> Because we are trained to give psychological and moral credence to the imaginary, to the character in a play or a novel, to the condition of spirit we gather from a poem, we may find it more difficult to identify with the real world, to take the world of actual experience to heart.[13]

The humanities have, then, their shadow side; not all here is sweetness and light. The teacher who would *be* humanistic and promote humanistic qualities by way of the humanities should be, more than anybody else, alert to the dangers of counter-productiveness.

8

The Humane, the Humanitarian, and the Humanistic

Some persons may have read this far in the book in a growing sense of amazement and disbelief. It is as if a book on Hamlet, chapter after chapter discussed Ophelia, Gertrude, Rosencrantz, Guildenstern, with scarcely a mention of the Prince of Denmark. What! A book on humanistic education without an indictment of our corrupt society or a plea to close the generation gap, without a discussion of alienated, dissentient youth and the real reasons for dropping out and the popularity of drugs? Without so much as a mention of encounter groups, sensitivity training, and gestalt therapy, and no more than a glancing notice of self-actualization? Without an indictment of racism, sexism, punitiveness, mistrust, and parochial devotion to middle-class morality?

It is perfectly true that today many educators rally to a cause they call "HUMANISTIC" with very different interests from those we have in this work emphasized. For instance, a recent book entitled *Toward a Humanistic Curriculum* says very near its beginning, "The humanistic school will not abandon its abiding concern for each child in its custody." Such a concern for children means, among other things, "helping them to find in the curriculum a place where they can be comfortable, successful, and secure."[1]

Another book, *Humanizing the School,* finds that schools have been clear about the necessity for punctuality and neatness and about the penalties for cheating, swearing, and wearing hair and skirts of disapproved length; but have been lax about cultivating respect for all persons, regardless of race, economic condition, or customary modes of behavior.[2]

A recent article entitled "Humanizing Teacher Education" tells us that it is time for schools to go beyond their concern for more facts and a faster reading rate, and to help young people

> develop compassion, concern for others, faith in themselves, the
> ability to think critically, the ability to love, the ability to cooperate

with others, the ability to maintain good health, and, above all, the ability to remain open to other people and new experiences. This is *humanistic* education.[3]

Still another new book is in large part based on the following contention:

A humanistic approach to the education and socialization of the young is one that attempts to analyze the dysfunctions of institutional repression of human needs, desires, and curiosity. It is a view that does not distrust all because a few may take advantage of permissive attitudes in disapproved ways. . . .[4]

The *Journal of Humanistic Psychology* is the organ of a school of psychology that sets itself over against mechanistic (or, in William James' term, "brass-instrument") psychology, rat psychology, S-R psychology, behavioristic or operant conditioning psychology, and other schools that pride themselves on a rigorously scientific, experimental, usually very quantitative, approach to the field of human behavior. Sometimes humanistic psychologists also contrast themselves with the orthodox psychoanalytic tradition, though they themselves run heavily toward clinical and personality theory. The theories and practices of Abraham Maslow, Carl Rogers, Rollo May, Arthur Combs, Viktor Frankl, Erich Fromm, Fritz Perls, and, to an extent, Carl Jung, are often favorably invoked by the humanistic psychologists, as well as many of the tenets of existential, phenomenological, and gestalt psychologies. The application of central precepts of this approach to education theory results in the popularization of such ideas as Development of a Positive Self-Concept, Training of Affect, Education of the Emotions, Nondirective Therapy, Interpersonal Communication, Self-Actualization, the Fully-Functioning Personality, as well as certain terms that no school can claim as its own but which in this group receive particular emphasis, such as "acceptance," "trust," and "love."

Yet already there is a discernible spread in the uses of the term "humanistic" among those educators and psychologists just mentioned, ranging along a continuum from individualistic psychology and ethics, where the emphasis is put upon helping one person at a time achieve a sane, positive, self- and other-loving being (with society being tacitly assumed to be only a function of single selves), to the more sociological and political way of thinking about and reforming institutions (such as schools and school systems), communities, and whole nations and societies.

These other "humanistic" educators and psychologists obviously may, but need not, see the study of the humanities as helpful in their cause. They may even see the humanities as all too characteristically elitist, as symbolic of the inequities of society, or even as an opiate of the people. Furthermore they *may* be uninterested in religion, philosophy, history, or the arts and the kinds of values mainly associated with such endeavors. Contrariwise, the devotee of the humanities *may* be himself aristocratic, snobbish, even tyrannical.

Before dealing further with the relation between these ways of using the term "humanistic" and the characterization arrived at in Chapter 5, let us look briefly at two other uses.

To many intellectuals, "humanistic" refers specifically to a way of thinking discussed in the chapter on historical background, to the Renaissance Humanist and his descendants—that is, to those who rediscovered the great values of Greek and Roman literature, ethics, criticism, history, and rhetoric, and who exalted the study of these subjects above the great medieval preoccupation with theology, metaphysics, and logic. This use of the term is still common in Europe, but to most persons of the Anglo-American countries humanities has a far broader meaning, so broad that it is possible (however regrettable) for a person to be wholly unacquainted with the ancient world and still be a profound creator and scholar in the field of the humanities. For us, *The Humanities* has to do mainly with creation, appreciation, and study of aesthetic, philosophical, religious, and historical processes and works in such a way as to participate in their full human meaningfulness.

Religious humanism is espoused by those who believe that the supernatural aspects of most orthodox religions are superfluous or even iniquitous. It puts emphasis upon the ethical parts of religious practices and maintains that no divine sanction is needed or justified for the good life. The roots of such religious beliefs can be traced to Greek Epicureanism in ancient times and to various reformers within the Judeo-Christian tradition, including some who stopped considerably short of a nontheistic position, such as early leaders in the Unitarian movement. But religious humanism has few important ties with Renaissance humanism, except insofar as both may be said to exalt the place and achievements of mortal men and to minimize theology; virtually all Renaissance humanists were theists, and some were exceptionally devout Christians. Similarly today, there is no inconsistency in being at once a religious humanist and completely uninterested in the humanities side of the curriculum or in being, like B. F. Skinner, a humanist in religion and the very *bete noire* of humanistic psychologists; nor is there any inconsistency, of course, in having an exceptional devotion to philosophy, history, arts, letters, *and*—some form of god-centered religion.

At this point a proposal. Realizing how hard it is to reform a language, and therefore without being sanguine about the likelihood that the following glossary will get wide adoption, we would like to offer the following assignment of names to positions:

> *Religious humanism* names nontheistic religious groups and beliefs.
> *Renaissance humanism* names the kind of study and curriculum which puts great emphasis upon the rhetorical arts and upon classical authors.
> *Humanitarianism* names a kind of social and political reformism. The Humanitarian is he who is typically committed to reduce the amount and degree of hunger, sickness, enslavement, ignorance, poverty, lack of opportunity, and feeling of oppression among people (or a certain group of people), and to increase the general access to the goods of life. He is, in short, eager to ameliorate man's deplorable lot. The adjectival form of the word is of course humanitarian.
> *Humanistic psychology* can remain as it is without serious confusion.

This then leaves the cluster *Humanities, Humanistic, Humanist* to apply to what we have mainly devoted ourselves to in the present work.

However, even if this exercise in semantics should prove acceptable, no one in his right mind would believe that the major problems are thereby solved. What these *are* can best be attacked, perhaps, by introducing yet another term, this time the cognate, *Humane.*

The adjective "humane" when applied to a person—curiously "The Humane Society" has to do with kindness toward animals—connotes a compassionate, sympathetic, caring, concerned being. A less common but ancient and respectable use of the word, as in "the humane arts" or "humane learning," signifies an unusual degree of refinement, elegance, and enlightenment; highly civilized, cultivated, cultured.

On the first and commonest meaning, many of those who today criticize the schools for demeaning the young (like Friedenberg), for destroying the values and even lives of black children (like Kozol), for being hypocritical and insensitive (like Kohl), or for making the child's life "absurd" (like Goodman) may be said to bespeak humane criteria both for their indictments and for their affirmative programs,[5] which range from neighborhood governance of the school to Ivan Illich's proposal to "de-school."[6] Once again, it needs to be said that (1) those who think along these lines, whether activist humanitarians or more individualistic emphasizers of compassion, are not logically bound to have any particular interest in the humanities, and some in fact do not; (2) not infrequently, our kind of humanists are relatively apolitical or politically conservative, or are quite impatient with "permissiveness," "egalitarianism," and much else that they call sentimental and romantic.

Nevertheless, we would now like to explore the possibility of a nonfortuitous connection between the two meanings of "humane," or, putting it another way, between the ethical ideal of compassion and the humanities.

We hear a great deal today about the necessity for children to develop a "positive self-concept" in order that learning proceed—and the evidence is clear that this is indeed essential, for the schools are crowded with children whose seeming inability to learn or to even try to learn has probably little or nothing to do with a deficiency of constitutionally-based and native intelligence, but a great deal to do with a deep-seated lack of confidence in themselves to master even the most elementary intellectual skills. It is unquestionably true that such self-doubt often has to do with a strongly implanted sense of racial inferiority, and it is a major scandal that this basic fact has, until very recently, received little more than token acknowledgement. Recent emphases upon the positive achievements of Black, Chicano (and other Latin), Native American, and Oriental writers, artists, dancers, musicians, story tellers, and craftsmen of various sorts may indeed help to dispel the notion that Anglo/Caucasians have a monopoly, by achievement or ability, on humanistic or any other sort of success.

Still another step in a forward direction lies in the development of what might be called a "positive species-concept." We know and need to know a great deal about human iniquity and inconsequentiality. We are quick to agree with Pascal that man is a reed, but sometimes turn away without hearing his addition—"a thinking reed." Man may be a clod, but a clod odd in its ability to say, "I exist." But one of the great messages that the humanities bring us is that man is capable of rising to supreme heights. We may learn from Sophocles and Dostoevsky of man's capacity for error and suffering, from Saints Paul and Augustine of his talent for sin, from Hogarth and Daumier of his brutishness, from Beethoven and Tchaikovsky of the pitifulness of his lot. But what shines through all these sad tales is the now-credible greatness of their creators. Plato and Chaucer, Cezanne and Stravinsky existed and they were men. We, too, are men. We remember Hamlet's saying, "What a piece of work is man! How noble in reason!" and we remember his going on to say in chilling antithesis, "Man delights not me. ..." But Shakespeare rose above his character's misanthropy: it is the poet who shows us what man can become.

In the interest of fairness, one might at this point object that the finest achievements of scientists and mathematicians no less than of the artists and philosophers exalt the place of man, and this is true. But one of the great differences between achievements in the sciences and in the humanities is that whereas in the former the particular self of the creator tends to drop out of view, unless specifically made visible by a humanistic historian, we have a sense of communicating through plays and symphonies and philosophical dialogues and paintings with the person who made them. We may know nothing about Homer apart from the *Iliad* and *Odyssey,* but through the poems we are better in touch with Homer than with most of our live acquaintances.

Furthermore, in the case of at least some of the humanities, especially literature, religion, and the value-centered parts of philosophy, there are still closer ties with sympathy, compassion, and human concern. Any reading of the world's great poetry and prose requires a capacity for *imagining* oneself in the depths and heights of the human condition, for empathizing with the dilemmas and the resolutions of men and women, for sympathizing with pain and suffering, and for sharing in triumph and joy. No person can be said to have understood Oedipus unless he knows from inside what it feels like to *have to know,* even with the realization that the knowledge will be unbearable. No person can be said truly to have read *King Lear* unless he has felt what it is like to *become* capable—as Lear until late in his life was not—of a tragic fate. The understanding of Kant's dictum, "Treat man always as an end, never as a means only," requires more than a *conceptual* grasp of the words. And for a weighing of Jesus' beatitudes it is necessary that one internalize what such virtues as meekness and humility are. To be sure, it is possible to be a competent musician or a keen interpreter of sculpture, or an able critic of architecture without much development of one's capacities for human compassion and concern, but the connection between Bach's "St. Matthew Passion" or Michelangelo's "Pieta" or the Cathedral at Amiens, and the heart of Christianity is not accidental. He who *has* the sensitivity to weep for the bereft Dido *can* care about real human bereavement, and he who develops in his ability to feel his way into a fictional or philosophically hypothetical ethical problem is capable of applying such sympathetic understanding to live situations.

There is also that about the great achievements in the humanities that invites a *feeling* response that is often both sensuous and emotional. One may get excited by a mathematical theorem or a chemical formula, but the excitement is, so to speak, gravy, and gravy, notoriously, spots the purity of the cloth. The feeling response to a cathedral, to a religious ritual, to a literary or musical work, however, is not only legitimate but important. A work of art that is unmoving is, in so far, a failure as a work of art.

Humanistic works also tend to invoke a richly valuative response in us. If we are constantly required to keep cool and neutral about descriptions of the natural and social scientists, we need to be helped to become deeply subjective, in important ways, in the presence of works of art and of much philosophy and religion.

In the humanities, then, we involve a large portion of our selves, responding as valuing, feeling, personal being, as well as inquirers and knowers.

Now, all this suggests some respects in which teaching/learning in the humanities ought properly to assist the development of our full humaneness. For instance, experience in the humanities ought to assist us in the regarding of other human beings as *thou*s, to use Martin Buber's profound distinction, and not mere, impersonal, objective, thing-like *it*s. And it ought to teach us to find live connections between things that both common sense and logical analysis require us to distinguish.[7]

Still, not only humanitarians, but many others of a humane bent, look upon almost any form of dehumanization with horror, equating art or literature that has lost its direct connection with human life with indifference to human welfare and perhaps even with impersonal, unfeeling cruelty: that is, with *inhuman* attitudes. Just recently, even within the ranks of creative artists and advanced critics, there may be seen a swing back toward low distance and away from formalism, stylization, severe elegance, and dehumanization. For instance, the so-called "New Criticism" which largely dominated the scene of literary criticism for twenty years or more, stressing as it did the virtual anonymity of the artist and therefore the illegitimacy of most references to his personal life, preferring irony and paradox to the warmer sentiments, and insisting upon close formal analysis of prose and poetry has in recent times been severely challenged by those who with W. J. Ong would have us communicate with the artist himself, as a person, through his work. Ours is a day of "confessional" poetry, and of the insistence upon the uniqueness of each poetic "voice." Painting and sculpture have to a considerable extent again become figurative rather than abstractly expressionistic, and a great deal of music has veered away from the severe rule-domination of a Schoenberg once again toward recognizable tunes and infectious rhythms, and even stories or programs. But especially in film and theater can we see the attempt to reinstate low-distanced art, and even to prove legitimate that kind of art which a short while ago would have appeared far below the distance limit.

Some have set out to reform that about the theater that separates audience from stage and actors. The separation, it is argued, is artificial, stultifying, antisocial. The great opportunity that the theater has—unlike some other art forms—is to promote a sense of community. Consequently, groups like "The Living Theater" have put on plays in which the actors, often unclothed, have circulated in the audience, crawled over laps, and in general so acted as to interfere with the tradition of theater as a spectator sport.

Similarly, as everyone not hopelessly isolated from reality knows, films from every part of the western world have turned far away from previous inhibitions about nudity and sex play, homosexual and autosexual as well as heterosexual, and deliberately set out to be maximally erotic. Again, this is a direct attack, *inter alia,* on the long-reigning idea that aesthetic value requires a considerable distance; perhaps it is even an attack upon there being much of a distinction between the aesthetic and the sensual (as Brecht's is an attack upon the distinction between the aesthetic and the political.)

The particular relevance of all this to the present discussion is that to many in our time, much of traditional art has seemed not only stuffy, but puritanical in a body-hating, eros-shunning way, and has thus denied, or scorned, or at least underplayed the most intimate of human relations; or has been socially neutral, apolitical, and therefore trivial. For art to be fully humane, the argument goes—to say nothing of humanitarian—it must foster loving and sensual human relations, effectively oppose tyranny, poverty, and war, and even more generally enhance the sense of belonging to a community of fellow human beings. When the arts fail to accomplish such ends, they are accused not merely of having missed valuable opportunities, but even of supporting the entrenched forces of antihumanitarian divisiveness.

Still another cognate of *Humanities* is—*Human.* Does it make any more than emptily rhetorical sense to say that cultivation of the humanities makes for one's becoming more human? The answer must be Yes. In this way.

"Becoming human" or "Becoming more fully human" are phrases that suggest humanness as an ideal. In some important senses, one is not human simply by virtue of having two legs, an upright posture, a body relatively hairless, and a convoluted brain. The life described by Hobbes as the state of nature—poor, nasty, solitary, brutish, and short—is an animalistic, not a human condition. One wants various comforts, but even more one wants certain refinements—if that word can be stripped of its effete overtones—in one's environment. And in the aesthetic experience, creative or appreciative, one is afforded a kind of model of what living can be: a sense of cohesiveness of parts, a meaningfulness that pervades the whole process, a realization of values that are inherent and not merely postponed. "Not the fruit of experience, but experience itself, is the end," as Walter Pater has famously said.

A counted number of pulses only is given to us of a variegated dramatic life. How may we see in them all that is to be seen in them by the finest senses? How shall we pass most swiftly from point to point, and be present always at the focus where the greatest number of vital forces unite in their purest energy?

To burn always with this hard, gemlike flame, to maintain this ecstasy, is success in life. . . . Not to discriminate every moment some passionate attitude in those about us, and in the brilliancy of their gifts some tragic dividing of forces on their ways is, on this short day of frost and sun, to sleep before evening.[8]

But curiously Pater in this famous passage is talking not specifically about art, but about philosophy, whose service toward the human spirit, he says, "is to rouse, to startle it into sharp and eager observation." It is a service, more broadly of all the humanistic studies: to help us live better, more humanly.

If, as some philosophers from the time of the Greeks onward seem to have believed, the only distinctive and important human quality is rationality, then one can cultivate his humanness as much or better through the sciences and mathematics. But it is as much a part of being human to be sensitive in feelings and to respond to humor as to be rational. And this is precisely what is so characteristic of *human* humanistic products, that they draw on a large range of human potentiality of response: with them before us, we are stimulated emotionally and sensuously; we laugh, cry, feel reverent and irreverent, erotic and pious, profound and playful—all distinctively human responses. So, if being "more human" is to mean something like the cultivation of a larger spectrum of capacities unique to humanity, then the humanities can legitimately be praised for their contribution to our humanness.

So far in speaking of the ways in which the humanities can, and sometimes do, contribute toward the development of humaneness and humanness, we have been mainly concentrating attention upon the individual human being. But questions can and must be asked about man as social animal too. Today, more than for a long time, we are seeing and understanding how life can hardly rise above subhuman levels when one's home and neighborhood are bleak and graceless, when one's place of work appeals—perhaps as the work itself does—only as something to flee from; and when the dark and menacing streets one walks are bare of aught but trash. Air and water pollution are not new problems, but we have, or are developing, a newly-sharpened consciousness of them. Today there is more disapproval, perhaps, of litter, of the beer can in the tide pool or the potato-chip bag on the mountain trail. Today we are beginning to realize that cities need not be ugly—no, nor even suburbs. Occasionally, town councils will now spend the money to bury telephone wires, or put the noise of a rapid transit system underground, use the power of zoning laws and building codes to obscure junk heaps, forbid the encroachment of rootbeer stands and dry-cleaning shops into residential areas, and even to block the erection of particularly offensive eyesores among properly zoned buildings.[9]

We are at last beginning to realize that our defenseless ears—we can often avert our gaze but not our hearing—need to be protected against unmuffled engines of the air or road, of cruising sound trucks and walking transistor radios, of neurotic barking dogs and department store Muzak.

But even worse than visual and auditory blemishes are the obscenities—we are beginning to see a more important use for this epithet than as a puritanical tongue-clucking against nudity and sex—of war and other preventable violence, of malnutrition and benighted ignorance, and even more generally of lives stripped of spontaneous joy and robbed of impulsive pleasure. Herbert Marcuse has been a sharp-eyed critic of the pervading ugliness and soddenness of so much of modern life. Whether or not one agrees with his indictment of capitalism, his statement that "The new sensibility has become a political factor" can hardly be gainsaid.

The new sensibility, which expresses the ascent of the life instincts over aggressiveness and guilt, would foster, on a social scale, the vital need for the abolition of injustice and misery, and would shape the further evolution of the "standard of living." The life instincts would find rational expression (sublimation) in planning the distribution of the socially necessary labor time within and among the various branches of production, thus setting priorities of goals and choices: not only what to produce but also the "form" of the product. The liberated consciousness would promote the development of a science and technology free to discover and realize the possibilities of things and men in the protection and gratification of life, playing with the potentialities of form and matter for the attainment of this goal. Technique would then tend to become art, and art would tend to form reality: the opposition between imagination and reason, higher and lower faculties, poetic and scientific thought, would be invalidated. Emergence of a new Reality Principle: under which a new sensibility and a desublimated scientific intelligence would combine in the creation of an *aesthetic ethos.*

The term "aesthetic," in its dual connotation of "pertaining to the senses" and "pertaining to art," may serve to designate the quality of the productive-creative process in an environment of freedom. . . . This would be the sensibility of men and women who do not have to be ashamed of themselves any more because they have overcome their sense of guilt. . . .[10]

He likes to foresee a time when "the aesthetic dimension can serve as a sort of gauge for a free society. A universe of human relationships no longer mediated by the market, no longer based on competitive exploitation or terror, demands a sensitivity freed from the repressive satisfactions of the unfree societies; a sensitivity receptive to forms and modes of reality which thus far have been projected only by the aesthetic imagination."

It does not insist on a daily bath or shower for people whose cleaning practices involve systematic torture, slaughtering, poisoning; nor does it insist on clean clothes for men who are professionally engaged in dirty deals. But it does insist on cleaning the earth from the very material garbage produced by the spirit of capitalism and from this spirit itself. And it insists on freedom as a biological necessity: being physically incapable of tolerating any repression other than that required for the protection and amelioration of life.[11]

Marcuse sees contemporary art as basically revolutionary. "Non-objective, abstract painting and sculpture, stream-of-consciousness and formalist literature, twelve-tone composition, blues and jazz: these are not merely new modes of perception reorienting and intensifying the old ones; they rather dissolve the very structure of perception in order to make room—for what? The new object of art is not yet "given,' but the familiar object has become impossible, false."[12] He speaks of the "internal ambivalence of art: to indict that which is, and to 'cancel the indictment' in the aesthetic form, redeeming the suffering, the crime."[13]

Bertolt Brecht mounted a brilliant attack upon the whole idea of the theater as an isolated, self-sufficient institution. True to his Marxian commitments, he held that art is (or must be if it is not simply to underwrite the status quo) an instrument for the improvement of society. But the very notion of a well-made play, of a final act that solves the problems of the first and brings down the curtain on a cozy equilibrium is inimical to art as a revolutionary tool. In his own plays—and his theory argued that other playwrights should follow suit—he deliberately left issues unresolved, saying that the solutions after all occur not in the theater, but in the street. The problems he dealt with were of course political and economic—for him these are the *real* problems—and about the best the playwright and actors can do is to ready an audience for action, to show them some of what is wrong, and to send them out the exits with a deep sense of a reform to be accomplished. Yet, for all of this being heretical doctrine in the history of aesthetics and dramaturgy, Brecht became, and remains, one of the most popular dramatists of the twentieth century.

Not all art, any more than all history or philosophy, is thus "indictive," or even critical in its form or content, of the life current within it; but a very great deal is, and today there is probably more than ever before. Nowhere is the new social criticism more evident than in the popular arts, which in other times have so frequently been predominantly escapist and emptily sentimental. When one considers the amount of music, drawing, film, poetry, and stories that is presently satirical or otherwise protesting, especially against war, racism, technology, and institutional (or just adult) repressiveness, it becomes evident that the art forms are being employed to express massive dissatisfaction, a phenomenon that some people continue to find unlikely in an affluent society. Although superficially the much-publicized "juvenile hedonism" of our time seems at odds with political activism—it is often pointed out that historically, revolutionaries have been singularly Spartan, almost puritanical in their private lives, shunning any sensual distractions from their Cause—since the "Establishment" has come to be identified with the work-ethic and with systematic opposition to the impulsive, passional life, a great many of today's youth are at once politicized and hedonistic, even finding in obscenity, nudity, drugs, and the highly visible freedom of communal and street life effective weapons against the entrenched morality of their elders.

Certainly it is not surprising that the same students who have become highly critical of "irrelevant" education should be critical of "irrelevant" humanistic products, whether aesthetic works, religion, philosophy, or history. When philosophy has appeared to be little more than linguistic ruminations and logic-chopping, when history has seemed a romantic dream about the long ago and far away, when religion has stuck close to its Marxist characterization as "opiate of the masses," and when the arts and criticism have been excessively pure in their aestheticism, they have appeared to a great many hedonistic/activist youths as either superfluous or inimical.

Yet sometimes this criticism too has been overdrawn. Robert Coles, whose *Children of Crisis* remains perhaps the best account of the forces in the South blocking integrated schools, brings the testimony of a humanistic psychologist and psychiatrist to support humanistic studies and products. He has said, "I think that more than anything else I have learned to *know* what social scientists know, but *see* what a Eudora Welty, a Flannery O'Connor, a Richard Wright, a Robert Penn Warren, a Walker Percy demand and suggest and hint and urge one like me to see."[14] He goes on to rebut the position of the narrow-minded wielders of the "irrelevant" club:

> I hear from some that Henry James or T. S. Eliot is reactionary; or Carson McCullers merely odd in a clever and powerful way. If you would know America, take courses in "race relations" and political theory. Know the social system, the power structure, the latent this and the unconscious that. And know the facts, man, the facts—who owns what and who is bigger than whom. Yet I believe I find the whole world in the letters of Van Gogh, not to mention his paintings; in a story by Flannery O'Connor; in one of Eliot's quartets; in a "decadent" novel by that great, curious, stubborn, long-winded, ambitious, shrewd observer and artist Henry James. I believe that ghetto children and suburban children can learn the most important "facts" that can possibly be learned from Rembrandt's "Life of Christ," from his canvasses and from the Scripture that he brings alive: how long man has suffered and how much man can do to redeem himself, to win a little ground from life's built-in ironies, ambiguities, and terrors—enemies far stronger than particular men or even social systems.
>
> Finally, I believe that we can actively struggle with the world, but also sit back and wonder at things, understand them and be amused or scornful at how "it all" works out, comes to pass, whatever.[15]

Such words are sound and reassuring, especially since they come from one who is outside the official humanistic establishment. All the same, it cannot be doubted that humanists, both amateur and professional, have often been conservative and even timid. James Ackerman has distinguished two styles within the humanities. "Objective analysis," the prevailing establishment style, that emphasizes craft, scholarship, objectivity; and "The Engaged Style" which

> is individualist, vigorous in its opposition to prevailing systems and to the power that Objective Analysis has given to those who practice it. Its strength is a strength of antithesis, calling to attention the values that were considered irrelevant and damaging to the method of the opposition. In the form of student activism, it is beginning to make itself felt as a force in education through criticism of administrative regulations, of the academic authority and standards of faculties, and of curricula and teaching that lack "relevance" to contemporary life and issues. Its intellectual fuel is said to be provided by a variety of writers including Hermann Hesse, Herbert Marcuse, Norman Brown, Marshall McLuhan, Che Guevara, and the spokesmen of the black revolution. . . .[16]

The Engaged Style is not only typically directed to either existentialist or activist expression, but is more likely to be openly emotional rather than carefully rational in its manner.

In our time, when there is abroad so much concern with the great social problems of war and peace, crime and lawfulness, poverty and abundance, education and ignorance, equality and discrimination, alienation and community, it is not surprising that a great many humanistic creators, critics, and teachers are concerning themselves with such problems. As citizens and moral agents, they doubtless have a duty to do so, but more specifically as humanists no such duty can be foisted upon them: their duty is to their own feelings and interests: anything else is a fake. Stuart Hampshire has expressed this point with perspicacity, warning of the danger of exaggerating conscious intention in creative writing,

> as if a scholar or writer ought to be clear in his own mind that his work has a contemporary social relevance, if he is not to be irresponsible. I doubt whether this is how the imagination works, or can work, whether in literature, history, or philosophy.[17]

We are more likely to *find* relevance (or not) in our own work, retrospectively.

It is harder for historians and novelists and ethicists not to be concerned with man and man's condition than for painters and composers; but in all branches of the humanities, some creators will be and others not, or at least not directly. Some who are will be deeply humane persons and will produce works which, like Beethoven's Ninth Symphony, Picasso's "Guernica," Tolstoy's *War and Peace,* Jesus' "Sermon on the Mount," and Spinoza's *Ethic,* tend to beget humaneness in those who experience them. Others, some of whom may be characterized by such qualities as pessimism, vanity, waspishness, and even misanthropy, will compose works like Voltaire's *Candide,* Schopenhauer's *Essays,* Spengler's *Decline of the West,* or Daumier's caricatures, which perhaps increase one's understanding but not love of man: indeed, writers like Genet and Celine might conceivably influence a reader to become less humane than he was before.

And still other creative humanists, like many distinguished spirits who have gone before them, will be more interested in nature or supernature than man. Humanists are notoriously individualistic, which means they are notoriously hard to generalize about. If it is asked whether they are humanitarian or even humane, the only truthful answer is: sometimes —and in some respects.

And as to education: if we had to choose between the virtues of compassion or humane awareness of other persons, on the one hand, and sensitivity to musical form or an ability to get proper distance on a play, on the other, most of us would choose in behalf of the ethical. But the idea of having to choose is absurd. Not all the value of the humanities is ethical—no apology need be made for sheer enjoyment of a story or a song—but it is still better if the school can at one and the same time help its pupils (and its teachers) develop their humaneness and their humanistic capacities. The latter *can,* indeed, with astuteness, be *one* means toward the former.

9

Value and the Humanities

"The humanities approach leads the student to think about *values*,"[1] states the New York State Education Department's report on the humanities. In agreeing wholeheartedly, we would only add the cautionary note: Or if it does not, something is wrong—for instance, some deep-seated fear of the shifting sands of valuation—of committing a "value judgment."

We have looked briefly at the ethical concerns (and sometimes lack of concern) of humanists, both personal and social. But ethics may be regarded as a species of value study. We turn now to the larger field.

"Value" is a commodious concept, so commodious indeed that only relatively recently in the history of thought has it been fully recognized that the goodness of God and the child's fondness for a toy, the lasting happiness to which men have aspired and the ephemeral lust of a day-dreaming boy, the beauty of the Taj Mahal and the glitter of a bauble, are all accommodatable within its range of meaning.[2]

The biggest, most pervasive, most widely applicable concepts are notoriously hard to define. What is Being? Volumes have been written to answer the question from the time of the pre-Socratics to the present-day Heideggers and Jasperses, but how can such an illimitable idea be caught inside a ring of words? But then are there any aspects of Being which are utterly and necessarily and eternally valueless? Some thinkers have said that such cavernous ideas as Being and Value must be left undefined: perhaps one has a kind of intuitive sense of their meaning, but finds it impossible to say exactly what that meaning is. Yet, others have found that all attributions of value—"This is good," "That has worth," "The other is valuable," etc.—at least implicitly associate having value with a psychological or physiological state of an organism. (There have of course been metaphysicians who treat the universe itself as an organism.) Thus, perhaps value is invariably associated with pleasure. Or with a reduction of tension, a restoration of equilibrium. Or with interest. Or gratification, satisfaction, consummation. Sometimes *value* has been thought to be an objective quality of entities or events. Sometimes it has been thought to be a purely subjective phenomenon, in recognition of the ancient adage that one man's meat (value) is another man's poison (dis-value). Sometimes an intermediate position has been taken and will be taken here, namely: that something's having value means that it is disposed to satisfy or gratify an interest, need, desire, or aspiration, or reward attention, or at the very least to forestall pain, or the frustration of a desire. Such an account recognizes that values do not float in a vacuum, but attach as characteristics to things and events; it also recognizes that values are *for* persons (or other organisms) as well as *of* things, and therefore can and do vary as valuers vary in what they want and prize.

Typically, values are ascribed or attributed to aspects of our world. If I call something valuable or worthwhile, I may mean for myself alone, for certain others, or for everybody—and if I do not specify for whom the value presumably exists, I can legitimately be asked to be more precise. Also, it is usually not enough to talk of value in general: we want to know what kind of value, or valuable in what respect. Furthermore, a value ascription may need to be clarified as to its presumed time of existence. What presently has value for me may not continue to be valuable, just as things which I once prized I now scorn or have grown indifferent to; but sometimes there are reasons for believing that a value will last a longer or shorter time. But reasons or no, I or anyone may be wrong in attributing value to something. We have implicitly already recognized some four common ways in which such an error can be made:

1. Pretty obviously, anyone may make a mistake in supposing that a given object or event will, when it is secured or experienced, be found good, satisfying, rewarding. (I worked and saved to buy it, but I'm disappointed.) Or I may wrongly believe or say that something has value for other persons. (I thought Jack would like that, but he didn't.)

2. I may believe that the value of an object is of one kind when it is really (for somebody) valuable in a different respect. (Whereas Mary really prizes a book for its moral uplift, I thought she prized it for its style.)

3. I may wrongly suppose that because I know you once liked something, you continue to do so, or that what is presently prized will continue to be so. (At the time, I said that this is music not for the day but for the centuries, and already it has been forgotten.)

4. I may mistake something's value (for someone) relative to something else. (I thought she cared enough for the necklace to offer a reward.)

So much has been written and said about the fallibility of value judgments that one may get the notion that it is possible to be wrong but not right; yet this is obviously absurd. Most of the time we are right in our everyday appraisals. The apple looks good to eat and it proves to be so. A swim in the pool seems a refreshing prospect, and so it turns out to be. I think my friend would enjoy a certain new film; I recommend it, and indeed he confirms my judgment. I think the mayor has done a sufficiently good job in office to deserve my vote again, and he continues to function satisfactorily. I remember having enjoyed the view of the coastline from a certain point; I revisit it, and find it is still beautiful. Furthermore, it will be noticed even from this list of homely examples that one typically makes value judgments not arbitrarily but on the basis of some evidence. And, as in every aspect of human behavior, one *learns.* The child is especially in need of various kinds of teaching, because his experience has been insufficient for him to make reliable judgments: he cannot tell a good apple from a bad by merely looking, or whether he will need a coat outside, or what a fair price is for the toy. On the opposite end of the continuum of experience, there exist the apple sorter, the physician, the professional toy buyer. But also the film critic, the political scientist, the tea taster, the psychotherapist—and thousands of other "experts"—by which is meant not persons who make no mistakes, but persons whose experience or training has equipped them to make fewer mistakes than others in certain sorts of value judgments, and who therefore are in a position to guide relevant choices of the less experienced or in other ways less knowledgeable.

Decisions are registrations of preferences or predictions that this rather than that will (for someone or some group) prove to be especially valuable. Some decisions are short-range, others are longer. When one orders from the menu, his "feedback" will soon come, and he will register some degree of satisfaction or disappointment. But to set out on a diet is usually to commit oneself to a longer delay before results can be known. The undertaking of a new career or a marriage is evidently still longer-range and in other ways complicated. The hard decisions are the ones that involve many different factors, and in which there are competing values, good and bad. No one is given a moment's hesitation when there is a simple choice between the good and the bad, value and disvalue, pleasure and pain. Our hesitations are produced by our being presented with incompatible goods and with such mixtures of likely values that it is hard to sort them out, as when one has enough money to buy a new car or to take a three week trip to Europe, but not both.

Values, then, differ in preferability. One has to say that they differ in value; though this sounds suspiciously circular, it is in fact only a recognition that values are more and less, greater and smaller. One measure of value is the intensity of the pleasure which is its typical accompaniment.[3] Generally, as between competing pleasures, we prefer the more intense. However, as philosophers at least from the time of the ancient Epicureans have insisted, intense pleasures are often accompanied or followed by pains that tend to cancel out the pleasures. So this is another respect in which pleasures differ: their "purity" with respect to admixture with pain. Values also differ with respect to duration. The fleeting satisfaction is by no means necessarily without intensity and it may be relatively free of disvalue, but precisely in being fleeting it may compete ill with those that promise to be longer lasting. The completely rational person would make no distinction between those values that are realizable now or soon and those that are remote, but in fact nearly everybody discounts that which is remote in time. Still another respect in which values differ from each other is in depleteability. Thus, if there is but one banana for two hungry men, a bite for one is deprivation for the other. But if (well fed) they discover a sunset, the satisfaction of the one takes nothing away from the other: on the contrary, such satisfactions may well enhance each other. Yet, after all this has been said, there appears still another respect in which values differ, a way different from the (theoretically) quantifiable dimensions so far mentioned. There are occasions when we speak of values as being relatively deep and profound or as shallow and superficial, in ways that transcend intensity, duration, and so on. Perhaps this has to do with the *comprehensiveness* of value for a given personality. That is, we may prefer one value to another in that it seems to involve more of our ourselves, to take in more ground, to be richer, more encompassing. Possibly this can be thought of as the *integrative* character of value in recognition of the fact that some of the satisfactions we encounter seem to be picked up and dropped, or, if kept, done so by agglomeration. In contrast are those cases in which the values we experience are fused, integrated into the whole self, or even function as integrators themselves.

Another way of putting this latter difficult but important point, is that many, if not all, of us desire a superordinate value that is the value of *harmony,* a patterning of the constituent values of our personality. Negatively, there is the not unusual case of the person who enjoys a value-rich life, one of many separate and diverse satisfactions, but who seems finally to lack wholeness, roundedness, completeness, focus. Such a person will experience a frustration that may be the more puzzling the more he obviously has, in the commonsensical expression, "so much to live for," "so many things going for him."

Frustrations, real or anticipated, large or small, appear to be the great negative drive of all of us. Instinctually or through acquired taste we have the complex of drives and wants, interests and desires, ideals and aspirations that makes us the particular personalities we are. (Consider how when asked to describe someone in other than physical ways, we tell what he is interested in and what his tastes are.) But each of these thrusts or instances of will can be blocked, denied, frustrated. Threatened with frustration, we use our wits to circumvent the difficulty: this is the problem-solving characteristic of animals so celebrated by John Dewey among others. Perhaps *all* deliberate human acts can be described in these or similar terms: the return to equilibrium, tension-reduction, etc. From of old, men have known the basic strategies of avoiding or overcoming frustration: (1) discovering more efficient means of reaching a goal; (2) finding a substitute satisfaction; and (3) extinguishing the desire. But such an account can only by awkward stretching cover another part of man's quest for a better life: the deliberate acquisition of new desires and aspirations. Aristotle long ago realized the absurdity of taking the sleeper as one's ideal of the happy man. Sleep as a relief from suffering is rightly prized, but there are values that lie beyond relief. Imagine a parent so deeply frustrated in love that he determined to protect his child against such suffering by preventing the child from developing the capacity to love. (Unfortunately, the case is all too easily imaginable.) But often this is precisely the respect in which one's own life is less than ideal: not the overabundance of frustrations, but the underabundance of interests. We shall return to this matter, but only after some consideration of certain kinds of value.

The most familiar distinction among kinds of values centers upon the proximity or remoteness of the actual experience of value. Generally speaking, the value which an instrument has is not immediately and directly realized. We may be willing to pay two dollars for a screwdriver so that we may tighten a loose bolt in the handle of our car door and thus forestall its falling off and perhaps getting lost. It would be rare indeed that the possession, the employment, the contemplation of the screwdriver would itself afford satisfaction, though it is not hard to imagine a skilled workman taking such immediate pleasure in a well-balanced hammer or a glistening new saw. Better yet, consider how a single thing may afford both direct and indirect, immediate and mediate, satisfaction. The question "Why are you eating that candy?" may elicit bewilderment, because the answer is so obvious: "I like candy. I like the taste of it. I enjoy the sensation it produces in my mouth." But there is another possibility: "I'm feeling a little let down and I thought it would raise my blood sugar, give me a bit of energy." Here the satisfaction, if it occurs at all, is delayed. Indeed, in some cases, the actual *realization* of the value, the rewarding experience, may be separated from the original act by months or even years. The value, then, that things have may be *instrumental,* if their "pay-off" in satisfaction is remote, or *inherent,* if they directly and proximately afford satisfaction.[4]

Another distinction among values, like the previous one useful though not absolute, is between those that are overt and those that reside in the imagination. The value of an aspirin tablet is in relieving a head-ache; of a pencil, in facilitating note-taking; of a map, in locating the right road—and so with most of the things which we think of as having value at all. But part of the value that many things have is anticipatory or reminiscent. Part of the fun of going on a trip is in the planning, the looking through travel folders, and the comparing of rival routes. The pleasure of a party does not stop with the closing of a door, but lingers in the recalling of this or that conversation or other incident. Everyone dreams, asleep and awake, and such fantasy can be enjoyable. Or consider the question, "Why do you keep up your life insurance payments?" The most obvious answer is in terms of the ultimate value to the beneficiaries, but there is also a value to him who pays the premiums—necessarily a value in the imagination and not in "reality."

We will mention here only one more way of distinguishing kinds of values, and that is into large categories that correspond to the principal kinds of human drives and wants. This classification of De Witt Parker's is interesting, though of course debatable: it will at least afford an illustration of our point.[5]

Self-preservation or health
Comfort and sensuous pleasure
Ambition
Workmanship
Love (including sexual, parental, filial, friendship, etc.)
Knowledge
Play
Art
Religion

This or some other such list of the great, abiding, universal desires and interests of mankind gives us a sense of the variety of human values—and therefore of the possibility, perhaps even the great likelihood, that in *some* respects the life of each of us is deficient. With this exceptionally brief (and of course far too simple) account of the nature of value, generally, we are ready to explore the particular values that may be attributed to the humanities. Let us take as our launching question: "Why teach literature in the schools?"[6] (Music, the visual arts, dance, film, theater, history, and philosophy could be substituted for literature, *mutatis mutandis.*) The most general answer that can be provided is perhaps this: to facilitate access to the *values* of literature. But this obviously only redirects the inquiry into what those values are.

How, in what respects, can a story, a play, a poem be said to be good, to have value? The most obvious answer is that any one of them can be immediately enjoyable. If someone says, "That was a good story," he is understood to be reporting a gratifying reading experience; if pressed, he might specify something about the plot, the suspense, the characters, the vividness of the writing, or some other such element of the story that afforded particular pleasure. But in any case, the story has worth inherently: it is a pleasure to read it. Now, to the avid fiction reader, there is no problem here at all. On Monday he draws five novels from the library and the following Monday he is there to return them and take five more. Such reading is a big part of his life. To him the worth of at least some of the books he reads is beyond dispute. He may or may not be critically sophisticated, but he relishes the reading.

In a way, that's the end of the matter. In a way, it's silly to ask for a justification of pleasure, or—again more broadly—satisfaction. The pleasure of reading, of listening to a piece of music, of taking a stroll in the cool of the evening, of playing a game of tennis, of eating strawberry shortcake, of talking with an old friend, is its own excuse for being: it needs no accounting for. Such a situation becomes problematical only if such questions as these occur: Why is it that when so many people enjoy dancing, I don't? Or, Am I getting all I could get out of the music I listen to? Or, Does a novel have any value beyond the immediate pleasure it affords—is it perhaps good instrumentally as well as inherently? And this is the great point: he who raises no such questions as these is doomed to remain confined within the narrow cell of What He Happens to Like. Of course a small child enjoys banging a drum and blowing on a horn, drawing and painting, making up stories, working with clay; of course he likes to listen to songs and marches, to see pretty pictures, to hear a story read aloud. *Of course,* this spontaneous, childlike delight is the starting place and remains the core of the more mature aesthetic experience. But the maturation of our capacity for full aesthetic appreciation is an intricate learning process. For this process even to begin, it is necessary to ask oneself: What am I missing? What is there in art that eludes me because I have not yet learned how to look and listen and read. What is there in the best humanistic works that might fulfill a deeper need than the pleasuring of an idle moment?

We have seen how inextricably values of all sorts are connected with desires, interests, needs, purposes. Generally, we think of these as pre-existent states of the organism, which then something partly or wholly satisfies, with resultant value. But we have not so far done justice to that about the prized object which arouses the very desire that it satisfies. Yet this condition is notably illustrated by works of art. Consider how much of music consists in building tensions, uneasinesses, yearnings; how much we are made to want the culminations, the closures, which the resolution of chords or the final cadences afford. Consider how much Shakespeare makes us want Hamlet to kill the king before the long-delayed event occurs. Or consider the ways in which Donne persuades us to share the near-frantic yearning for grace in his poem:

Batter my heart, three personed God; for you
As Yet but knock, breathe, shine, and seek to mend;
That I may rise and stand, o'erthrow me and bend

Your force to break, blow, burn and make me new.
I, like an usurped town, to another due,
Labour to admit you, but Oh, to no end;
Reason, your viceroy in me, me should defend,
But is captived and proves weak or untrue.
Yet dearly I love you and would be loved fain,
But am betrothed unto your enemy:
Divorce me, untie or break that knot again,
Take me to you, imprison me, for I
Except you enthrall me, never shall be free,
Nor ever chaste, except you ravish me.

Donne's achievement may be thought the more remarkable by the reader for whom such religious feelings are strange; but this is precisely the wondrous power of art: to extend indefinitely the range of one's interests and desires, beyond what "real life" has stimulated. A person unused to the intricacies of metaphysical poetry may of course *not* have his interests stirred, to say nothing of satisfied, by such a poem. But as we shall have to say, over and over again, only the very simplest humanistic values are available without effort. When such desires become very strong and the consummation is unusually full, the aesthetic experience may give us a touchstone of intensely realized value.[7]

Maslow has written at length about "peak experiences," those moments that occur in the lives of many not particularly extraordinary people that yet afford a glimpse of what is experienced somewhat more commonly by the so called "self-actualizing" types. The experience seems to occur most commonly when one is deeply in love or in the love a mother has for a newborn infant; after it has occurred, it serves as a kind of ideal of what life can be like at its best, its most intense.

In studying "self-actualizing people," Maslow discovered in them "simultaneously the ability to abstract without giving up concreteness and the ability to be concrete without giving up abstractness."[8] And in turn it appears to be a recurring characteristic of "peak experiences" that they collapse the difference between abstract and concrete.

They collapse the distinction, also, between part and whole, between self and other, mine and thine. The person in a peak-experience feels exalted, possessed of grace and confidence, integrated, powerful. He seems to others open, spontaneous, natural, trusting, and happy.[9]

Maslow strongly suggests that the *having* of peak-experiences tends to be productive to the type of personality that does have peak-experiences, and to be therapeutic with respect to the blocks and inhibitions and deterrents which negate such attainment. The key word in existentialist ethics is employed here: a person becomes authentic.

Now, there is a close affinity between this sense of authenticity, of realization of one's most nearly primal self, and aesthetic experience, at least when it becomes intense.

> Expression and communication in the peak-experiences tend often to become poetic, mythical and rhapsodic, as if this were the natural kind of language to express such states of being. . . . More authentic persons may, by that very fact, become more like poets, artists, musicians, prophets, etc.[10]

Then Maslow engagingly quotes Shelley: "Poetry is the record of the best and happiest moments of the happiest and best minds." Perhaps Shelley says here rather too much—perhaps that was Shelley's habit. Nevertheless, what he says is important, for everyone who cares much for literature or any of the arts knows something of the exaltation of spirit that happens—surely not frequently, but far *more* frequently than in most other sorts of experience—in the presence of great aesthetic expressions. At these moments of joy—and it is not necessary yet again to explain that joy is consonant with the tragic emotions—one has a feeling that may be described as (1) intense, (2) highly meaningful, and perhaps even revelatory, (3) integrated, and (4) consummatory. (Other concepts could be helpfully involved, but we will make do with four.)

The intensity may be of the kind that attends the drama of fictional events, when one discovers in himself as reader a strong fear or a strong hope that the letter will come or that the child will live, a strong aversion to or a strong affection for a villain or hero, a strong sense of doom or of expectation. The intensity may be in the feelings attendant upon the recognition scene or in the sudden realization of how it all *must* turn out. Or it may be the intensity of delight in a turn of phrase or the swing of a line, the subtlety of a musical variation, or the dancer's exit leap.

Aestheticians have often contrasted, and properly, the kind of intensity characteristic of emotions in the presence of a work of art with those encountered in a nonaesthetic context. Doubtless, the victories and defeats, the realizations of love and of betrayal, the horrors of brutality and the serenity of release from pain are all *stronger* upon real-life occasions than they can ever be in the realm of imagination, but only the writers of movie advertisements suppose that aesthetic values are measured in decibels or in watts. Aesthetic intensity is marked by a kind of purity, if that word can be used without invoking the ultra-precious, super-refined, hyper-isolated characteristic of art-for-art's sake.

The quality of integration which characterizes the best art has been described at tiresome length in terms of the inseparability of form and content; yet no understanding of aesthetic quality is possible without a clear view of the cohesive, centripetal forces operative. The total absence of any feeling of irrelevance; rather the recognition that everything conspires to a single though perhaps exceptionally complex end—these are further glosses on the integrity and integralness of the experience of beauty.

The concept "consummatory" signifies not only an ending but a completion, a bringing about of fruition and fructification, of fulfillment of promise and expectation. Here we may return to Maslow's description of peak-experiences, which he describes as "catharsis, culmination, climax, consummation. . . ." He borrows "closure" from the Gestaltists, and the paradigm of complete orgasm from Wilhelm Reich, and offers a contrast with "the partially emptied breast or prostate gland, with the incomplete bowel movement, with not being able to weep away grief, with the partial satiation of hunger in the dieter, with the kitchen that never gets fully clean, with coitus reservatus, with the anger which must remain unexpressed, with the athlete who has had no exercise, with not being able to straighten the crooked picture on the wall, with having to swallow stupidity, inefficiency or injustice, etc."[11]

If what was named "exaltation of spirit," with these just-described aspects, is a state one may associate with the supreme works of art, religion, philosophy, we may continue to recommend such works and such preparation as may be necessary for full access to the works, both for the intrinsic satisfaction of having such experience, and for the effect upon the spirit of being thus exalted. In such realizations, one may reasonably think, there is an overcoming of the alienation and a gaining of the self-identity about which we hear so much today.

To say that works of art and other humanistic products are often celebrations of peak-experiences (on the part of their creator) is by no means to say that they *commonly* produce peak-experiences in the appreciator. But he who has never become truly enraptured by music, never felt pulled into a painting and made to live inside its colors and shapes, never become so caught up with the destiny of a character as to dread his defeat and devoutly to wish his ultimate victory, deserves to feel cheated. Something has gone wrong in his education.

Yet it might be asked: When these rapturous moments occur, what *is* their value. The readiest answer is, of course, that their value is in themselves. As described, they are occasions of great intrinsic value. They are not so much valuable experiences as experiences of value, and value of a particularly exalted kind. But they are more, too. They are part of what makes life itself worthwhile. Only part, for no one lives just for peak-experiences. (Perhaps anyone who did would not live long.) On the other hand, a life largely or entirely devoid of such would be a life hard to praise. But such experiences also afford us instances of realized value against which to judge other aspects of life. He who has known peak-experiences cannot but be aware of the unsatisfactoriness of a life deprived of them, and in this dissatisfaction may be the beginning of improvement.

If now we hearken back to the earlier distinction between overt and imaginative occasions of value, it will be apparent that the arts, and the humanities more generally, operate principally within the realm of the imagination. Suppose the school were thought of as an instrumentality for obliterating the imagination which children bring to kindergarten. The pre-school child lives, if his environment is not too uncooperative, in a world of play, a world of make-believe, a world of the as-if. Universally, the invitation, "Let's play like. . . ." is the child's way of establishing a little community of fantasy. So huge is this world that nearly everything else—washings, and meals, and the odd chore—may seem only interruptions. But gradually, let us say, the school manages to change this. Only gradually at first, for kindergarten is still mostly play —educative play, teachers will hasten to say, but play all the same. Step by step "work" replaces "play." And work is, is it not, the real world, the world of literalness, definiteness, fixity? In the totally "successful" case, then, the school will, by graduation time, have produced a well-adjusted worker, a literal-minded, nondreaming, and above all efficient operator in the real environment.

The indictment is of course unfair, though there may be moments when one shudderingly fears that something very like this process really takes place. In any case, older boys and girls, and even more particularly, adults, do seem to have become, by whatever means, literalists, without the capacity for spontaneous delight in the world's body, beings strapped to the way things are, unable to transcend to rival schemes whose only deficiency is in not existing. To the extent that this is the case, education in the humanities has failed. Not that other disciplines too cannot contribute to the cause, but the humanities above all are—properly conceived and properly taught—liberators of the human imagination. And the value of a liberated imagination is again both in its own exercise and in what may thereby be accomplished in the way of better formulated ideals for living.

However, to imagine is not yet to express; and unexpressed imagination often gives us the feeling of incompleteness. The great artist is precisely the one who combines richness of imagination with mastery of the techniques of expression.

Expression has its roots in, but goes beyond, the spontaneous overflow of feeling. The involuntary "ouch" is a betrayal of, but not yet an expression of, feeling—or if one prefers, is only a very rudimentary expression. From a Grünewald, a Beethoven, a Dostoevsky, we learn a great deal, however, about what pain is, how pain feels: and we learn it not just from the outside, but inwardly, by being inside, imaginatively *having* the pain. In the having, we also reflect upon and contemplate the fact and form of that pain. It is precisely that which successful expression allows. To express a feeling then (which is by no means to rule out ideas) is more than just giving vent to it, indicating its presence: it is to delineate it, to give it an adequate form and embodiment, and thereby to make it poignantly accessible both to him who originated it (for it is a very different thing simply to be the possessor of the pain and to take it in, to comprehend it) and to others. Works of art are among the most successful recorders and stimuli of notable feelings. Through learning to get at works of art, to appreciate them, we gain access to celebrations of human feeling, and thus broaden our life space. We increase our sensibility, that is, our openness to emotional impressions and to the delicacy of feelings.

But we are not entirely dependent on others' expressions, others' achievements, which vicariously serve our own expressive needs; no, to some extent we need also to express more directly what we have felt and imagined, and here again the child gives us our clearest clue to the nature of direct expressiveness. He makes up stories, he fashions ad lib dramas, he dances, sings, makes rhythmic bangs, draws, and in a variety of other ways "objectifies" or externalizes his feelings, creating a new entity that bespeaks how he feels, and allowing others of us to know something about him we might not otherwise have been privy to.

In other words, expression names a fundamental human need. The corresponding frustration is the feeling of being bottled up, contained, cramped, stifled, unreleased. We see this frustration in others when we witness a radical separation of someone's overt acts from what we presume to be his inner feelings. We experience it in ourselves when we feel deprived of access to our own feelings, when we are unable to say *how* we feel, when we feel at a loss to articulate (through not necessarily in words) the inward state.

But through our own and others' expressions, we come to know, at least to know better, ourselves and other persons, and such knowledge is indispensable to improvement of what must be called, lamely enough, interpersonal relationships.[12] William James once praised philosophy for its helping us to become better companions. He meant, not just less taciturn, but more open persons, persons with better understanding of ourselves and more empathy for the condition of our fellows. So it is with all humanistic achievements. Certainly not all the literary sophistication, musical sensitivity, or artistic creativity in the world can guarantee that any man will be humane in his dealings with his fellow men—as we have noticed—but it may assist him in overcoming one sort of human deficiency that militates against humanitarian conduct: and that is crassness with respect to feelings.

Finally (in this partial listing of humanistic values), there are important ways in which the arts and the other humanities help us realize our pervasive desire to be free. Ralph Barton Perry, who it will be remembered defines the humanities in terms of their conduciveness to freedom, makes this point well:

The content of literature and of the arts is intrinsically humane. It presents life concretely, presenting models for admiration or condemnation—for imitation or rejection. It enlarges the range of immediate experience, and communicates its feelings; it stimulates the imagination and breaks the moulds of habit; it expresses the diverse visions and aspirations of great men; it integrates the different cultural elements of a society or an epoch; it embodies beauty and commends it as an object of disinterested pleasure; at its best, it brings a sense of moral elevation.[13]

History and philosophy, too, greatly enlarge the human outlook, decreasing our parochialism and ethnocentrism, giving us glimpses of other times and other places, and of some of the grander visions great minds have attained to.

Thus, once again we see that the best humanistic achievements not only afford immediate gratification, but are also instrumental to the attainment of longer-range goals.

THE TEACHING OF VALUES

We who are teachers, realizing that education means change (of certain kinds) and that children need, in the interest of developing their capacity for and likelihood of living well, to improve their taste, raise the level of their aspirations, and more generally, to improve the value scheme by which they live, are eager to help provide an education that makes a valuable contribution to life. Not just facts and theories, we say, but values too must be part of the content of education. Yet at the same time we have an abhorrence of indoctrination, or at least say we do. Is there some sort of contradiction here?

In any discussion of indoctrination, somebody is almost sure to make the point that everyone indoctrinates, that it is impossible for the teacher *not* to indoctrinate. Sometimes such a point is made in behalf of legitimizing a certain kind of indoctrination that has been frowned upon. Sometimes it is made simply to suggest that it is futile to talk about any such philosophical subjects as "indoctrination" anyway: we all are indoctrinators, so why make a fuss?

The first usage is well illustrated by the following passage from *The Catholic Way in Education:*

> Children are indoctrinated with the multiplication table; they are indoctrinated with love of country; they are indoctrinated with the principles of chemistry and physics and mathematics and biology, and nobody finds fault with indoctrination in these fields. ... The Catholic educator makes no apology for indoctrinating his students in (more) essential matters.[14]

Here apparently "indoctrination" is equivalent to any teaching that such and such is true, mathematics or theology, patriotism or chemistry. But though the Merriam-Webster dictionary supports such a position by making in its first definition *indoctrinate* synonymous with *teach* or *instruct,* this is in fact a much wider meaning than most people intend when they criticize indoctrination. The second dictionary definition is "to imbue with a usu. partisan or sectarian opinion, point of view, or principle." (*Seventh New Collegiate Dictionary*) It is notable that there are two principal marks of indoctrination, one methodological, the other substantive. Look at the word "imbue." This suggests a kind of teaching that specifically sets out to penetrate the learner's mind, to implant something there, even to taint it. But it still might be possible to imbue certain values without yet being an indoctrinator: for instance, the value of truth or honesty. For these are not "partisan or sectarian" values. In other words, indoctrination implies that the doctrines that are promulgated are controverted ones, ones on which informed opinions genuinely differ, and therefore ones which cannot be supported by clear evidence. This rules out the possibility of indoctrinating chemical and mathematical truths. But, once again, we do not speak of indoctrination when controversial matters are *raised* in class, or presented in a certain detached way, or when the student is encouraged to think his way through the problems involved, but only when the teacher (or other authority figure) is implanting his beliefs or values. Thus, it is perfectly consistent to be *against* indoctrination and *for* various kinds of instruction.

The other notion that we are all indoctrinators (so why fuss about it?) is somewhat more subtle. It says, perhaps, that nobody is completely neutral, everybody has values, and that it is impossible not to influence other people. And surely this is all true. But saying that we are all indoctrinators is rather like saying that we are all selfish—another position popular among barroom philosophers. If we are all selfish, then some other word has to be invoked to distinguish between the person whose "selfishness" is mainly manifested by helping other people, and him who continually ignores the interests of others. So with indoctrination: there is an important difference between the teacher whose dogmatic beliefs he is trying to propagate by any means available to him, and the teacher who genuinely respects the rights of his students to differ, and encourages the development in them of their powers of criticism and rational examination.

Yet we have grown increasingly aware in recent years of how certain value commitments can unconsciously dominate the lives and behavior of any one of us, not excluding the very rational, emancipated, tolerant person who prides himself on his having risen above ethnocentrism and parochialism. Two examples are especially telling. One is suggested by the term "middle-class," the other by "racist." A great many persons of "liberal" views harbor strong prejudices against any more than slight departures from prevailing standards of clothes, hair style, and attitudes toward work. Similarly a great many persons, including those of "humanitarian" character, secretly believe that members of their own race are, intellectually, morally, aesthetically, at least slightly superior to others. Such beliefs may be elaborately masked. Often the prejudice emerges primarily in the form of "forgetting" about ethnic minorities, when it is assumed that "everybody" acts in such and such a way. Thus, it *now* seems curious that for generations makers of textbooks for elementary school children assumed that their clientele was white and suburban, living in pleasant houses with both parents, and possessed of a new car with which to visit the grandparents' farm on weekends.

When one of us uncovers any such prejudice, or comes to realize that he has been masking a value commitment, it becomes harder to be sure that there are not others in us (to say nothing of our fellows!) still covered and masked. In fact, we have to admit, if we think about the matter at all, that every person has unexamined, unacknowledged values that not only strongly affect his behavior but that are potentially and actually influences on the lives of others.[15]

Such a realization can be particularly distressing to the conscientious teacher. Let us say that he does not believe in indoctrination, does not want to be an indoctrinator. Is he now learning that he is helpless in this respect, since everyone is in fact prejudiced and everyone by means ranging from subtle to blatant manipulates others in accordance with his own values?

Some who have answered affirmatively to this question have tried to minimize the harm they do by an elaborate program of "neutralization." Typically this takes the form of a self-conscious eschewal of "value judgments." No assertion is commoner among educated people in our time than, "I'm not making a value judgment"; no accusation commoner than "*That's* a value judgment." "Perhaps," such a person says, "I can't altogether overcome my prejudices, but I can seriously reduce the number of value judgments I make, and thereby minimize the extent of my indoctrinating." The position is surely not a stupid one. Think, for instance, how important we have recently come to recognize being "non-judgmental" is for the teacher or the counselor confronted by pupils with very different home backgrounds than the one he knows, or with a different accent from his own, or with a different-colored skin. Many other examples could be given of how a teacher may become less damaging, and more effective, by recognizing his own latent tendency to "put down" his pupils when they do not meet his own irrational, perhaps subconsciously made, expectations, and to "accept" them as they are.

And yet a good deal of harm can come, too, from foreswearing the dealing in values. The teacher who gives the appearance of being neutral on virtually every subject sometimes seems to his pupils as pusillanimous, indeed the Mr. Milquetoast that is the schoolteacher's caricature. In standing for nothing, he seems oddly ineffectual: one whose word is scarcely to be taken seriously, even on a factual matter. But above all, he opts thus out of the value decisions which his pupils must, willy nilly, face. There is a middle ground between the teacher making the decisions *for* his pupils, trying to impose his judgment upon them, and simply taking no position at all.

The indoctrinator is, more than anything else, he who substitutes propaganda for educating. By its very nature, educating entails understanding. Opinions can be proclaimed, beliefs induced, values influenced —all without educating. It is only when opinions are given in a reasoned way, when beliefs are proposed on the basis of their supporting evidence, and when values are intelligently and feelingly assessed, that influence is educative. Generally speaking, the teacher can take one step away from indoctrination by the openness with which he declares his value commitments. But a further step involves the equipping of the students with some of the means of evaluating the teacher's and others' position. Among much else, this requires the offering of meaningful options, other real possibilities.

Suppose the teacher is particularly fond of Mozart, or Sousa, or the Beatles—or all three. How fatuous it would be for him to pretend otherwise. Of *course* he is interested in influencing his students to share his tastes—and if he were not, it is hard to imagine how he could succeed in teaching much of anything. But he wants to develop new Mozart lovers (say) who love the master "for the right reasons," where a wrong reason is that the teacher does; and where another wrong reason is that the students are given no other options, no one else to prefer Mozart to.

But for all his enthusiasm and articulateness in defense of his favorite, the teacher has ultimately to face the possibility that his students will not share his taste. He surely does not want them, if he is a genuine educator, to *say* that they love Mozart, when in fact they do not. For it *is* a matter of fact, that one does or does not have a certain liking, a certain enjoyment, a certain realized value.

Yet often enough when the students do not learn to share the teacher's taste, go on preferring their peer group's momentary favorite, or learn to like someone new, they may yet have learned something even more important from their teacher: of how important music can be; of how good it is to be enthusiastic about some composer, or some sort of music, or some particular composition; and of how tastes can develop concomitant with better understanding. Ultimately, what the teacher does who (without indoctrinating, without attempting to *impose* his values on others) tells his own preferences, displays them, and gives reasons for them, is to offer his students a new possibility for value. He presents, as it were, a hypothesis, saying, "It is my belief that if you will do the following things (for example, listen carefully and repeatedly, notice certain things about what the composer is doing, etc.), you will be rewarded with a good musical experience. I may be wrong (that is, you may do what I suggest is necessary and not get the reward), but there is a considerable amount of evidence that people who do take these pains tend to acquire a new taste; furthermore, I believe that you will, if the end is obtained, agree that the price paid in energy and time was fair for what was obtained.[16] Still, there is no *obligation* on you to share my tastes—people can honestly differ about such things—but it is probable that you will not be able to tell without going to some trouble." Perhaps the effective and open (nonindoctrinating) teacher does at least one other thing: shows that his own tastes and judgments are not settled once and for all. Perhaps he will even find ways of making himself susceptible to the persuasion of his students.

Humanistic products are a rich locus of values—of almost every imaginable kind. They are, furthermore, signposts to values that are to be found elsewhere, as when from a philosophical essay or a short story we may learn something of the value of love and of friendship, the better to realize such values in our own lives. In addition, the very approaches and attitudes by which we learn (frequently through the offices of a sensitive teacher) to discover the values in distinctive human achievements can serve us well not only on a single occasion but in other very similar contexts (as, for instance, when we successfully approach an interesting building, and in realizing its multiple architectural qualities, we become the better equipped to approach another building). We may also find that we can carry aspects of one approach to different kinds of experience (as when it occurs to us that the attention to the relation between form and function in architecture applies, *mutatis mutandis,* in other such cases as automobiles, silverware, and even expository style).

Perhaps the temptation of the teacher is to take all this for granted, or to assume that students will make these connections and transfers easily, or even automatically. But so much teaching fails at this very crucial point, the point of *showing how* to go beyond the work and occasion at hand to other works and other occasions that may, on superficial observation, appear to be totally different. The admonition is: Connect, Relate, Carry over—in the interest, of course, of more valuable life.

10

Humanistic Teaching

A Famous Man was on campus for a day. In the afternoon, he had spoken to a hundred students sitting on the floor in the lounge of a dormitory, telling why he thought the present school system was obsolete, urging us to de-school, at least after the elementary grades. The college experience, he said, was particularly vapid, utterly removed from reality, a waste of money and energy. But, one student said hopefully, maybe the trouble is with the teaching. What we need is better teaching, better teachers, especially of the humanities. The Famous Man hooted. He was himself something of a poet, a man of letters, knowledgeable about music, philosophy, architecture, history, and he was there to testify that the humanities could *not* be taught. The sciences, yes, and various vocational skills. But the humanities, no. Here, everyone was on his own, and teaching was superfluous, or worse. Many heads nodded in agreement.[1]

It is a thing one says—it is widely believed—that the humanities *cannot* be taught. But what does this *mean*? Surely a good teacher can teach a child to read music or to understand the rhythms and rhymes of poetry. History teachers seem to have no greater difficulty teaching about the causes of the American Revolution than biologists have in teaching genetics.

One person can show another how to draw a box so that the sides seem to recede from the front. The different points of view between Plato and Aristotle on the nature of art can be communicated and learned. The difference between the C and B scale can be demonstrated and mastered. Are these not instances of teaching the humanities? But no one denies this, so there must be something else in the mind of those who say that the humanities cannot be taught (only "caught," as a cliché has it).

141

THE SCIENCE IN THE HUMANITIES

Of course *facts* can be taught. But, in the case of the humanities, it is
said, unlike the sciences, the facts (the rational subject matter) are relatively unimportant. What really matters is what the student himself
brings to the subject. He cannot get it from another, not even from an
"expert."[2] If it's a matter of writing poetry, a teacher may provide an
occasion or a nudge; but the student has to do the writing. If it's a matter
of teaching a student the beauty of Beethoven's Pathetique Sonata, either
the student likes it or he doesn't. He's under no obligation, no matter
how learned the professor be. Taste cannot be compelled. Suppose in
spite of a teacher's best efforts, the student ends a unit as he began it,
thinking that the History of the Holy Roman Empire is dull? Logic can
be taught as rules, but not the belief that logic is important. The teacher
may believe that the existence of God can be proved, but what if the
student rejects this proof and remains an agnostic?

Let us speak of those assertions which typically occur in humanistic
subjects—whether in research or teaching—that are amenable to empirical verification as belonging to the scientific part of the field. Perhaps the
most obvious examples of such assertions are the historical ones.

Take "History" itself, that is, the subject that, with usual emphasis
upon political and somewhat more broadly "social" events, tells "what
happened"—and why. Every school child knows that there is a vast
amount of history to learn—facts to memorize. The Spartans defeated
the Athenians in the Peloponnesian War. Henry VIII disestablished the
Roman Catholic Church in England. Napoleon proclaimed himself Emperor. Lincoln freed the slaves of America in 1861. Russian Czardom
was replaced by Soviet Communism in 1917. A world-wide economic
depression occurred in the early 1930s. And so on. The last example of
a fact indicates that not only single events but also generalizations may
be empirically verified. Thus, it is no less true that the sixteenth century
was an age of exploration than that Balboa discovered the Pacific Ocean.

A good bit of the scientific part of philosophy, religion, and the arts
is of course historical. There are the biographical facts about Aristotle,
Virgil, Leonardo da Vinci, Purcell, Rodin, Frank Lloyd Wright. There
are many facts about the publication of literal, philosophical, and musical works, as well as works of criticism. There are indisputable (but of
course also many disputable) assertions about influences, such as that of

Hume and Rousseau on Kant, Haydn on Mozart, Communism on Brecht, etc.

And, to mention but one additional type of prominent fact: there is a science of each of the artistic media. Consider the vast amount which the student of music must learn about the several scales, rhythmic patterns, timbres, and so on. The science of prosody is not without its complexities. Or better, yet, think of how much the architect must *know* about the whole engineering side of his profession—in order to practice.

Which in turn makes the bridge between science and technology, if the latter name may be applied to all the things, creative and analytic alike, that one may *do* with the arts. There is a substantial amount of knowing *how* in addition to the knowing *that*. The performing arts offer the most obvious examples, but it is not at all uncommon for a child to have an impulse to write a poem or paint a picture, and realize that he does not know how to set about it: for instance, how to get on paper the color he has in mind, or how to achieve certain rhythmic effects.

Now, the teaching of the science of the humanities appears to be little different from teaching the science of the sciences, and hardly less essential. Similarly, a good bit of the research that goes on among literary scholars, musicologists, art historians, and philosophers, is aimed at establishing historical truths, restoring faithful texts, analyzing meanings, and in other ways adding to a body of knowledge. The wonder is that this emphasis upon empirical truth by humanistic scholars is not more widely recognized. Surely most school children must intuitively feel the similarity between memorizing kinds of Greek columns and kinds of rock, between distinguishing democracy from monarchy and lyric from narrative verse, or between defining "momentum" and defining "sonata-allegro form." Certainly, examinations in humanistic subjects are typically no less factual in manner than those in other subjects.

Thus, whatever be the preconceptions about humanistic studies, in practice they are so fact-ridden, so dominated by a scientific approach, that the real difficulty is in getting teachers and scholars to attend to anything else.

Take *appreciation,* which we have shown to be of central importance to the humanities. Every teacher of the humanities has had some occasion to bemoan, what his observations often tell him, that students don't change their tastes as a result of their tutelage. They learn about Schubert and Mendelssohn, but they listen to and play the kind of music "popular" at their time. They may be able to demonstrate their knowledge of Shakespeare and his times, but they sell their volume of the plays to a second-hand book store, and go on reading (reading?) *Playboy.* But what is harder for these teachers to admit is that the reason may lie, in part, in their own teaching. Several typical reasons may be adduced:

1. They teach facts to the virtual exclusion of attention to enjoyment. Perhaps the assumption is that since students do not usually know about the history of, say, nineteenth century painting, this ignorance is the principal bar to their looking-with-linking upon the best works of this period; and therefore, an acquaintance with the emergence of impressionism and a familiarity with the life of Monet will promote aesthetic enjoyment. Doubtless this does sometimes happen, perhaps especially with the more daring kinds of art and the more colorful personalities (for example, Gauguin), but surely with far less frequency than could be hoped.

2. Teachers are often uneasy about any but factual instruction. For one thing they may be challenged about a value ascription or a risky interpretation, and not be able to defend themselves. Furthermore, they may feel that there is something subprofessional about dealing in mere opinion or judgment: it is as if they are earning their salary if and only if they are transmitting knowledge. Furthermore, they may fear becoming indoctrinators, *imposing* their own preferences on pupils, rather than being impartial purveyors of truth—the commonest ideal for the profession.

3. Besides, how does one really measure pupil progress apart from ability to report facts or quasi-facts? How does one grade except on the basis of the amount of information learned? (And one *must* grade.)

4. Then too (perhaps) do not the sciences owe their prestige to their emphasis upon fact, evidence, indeed proof? Is not the invidious distinction between the sciences and the humanities rooted in the notorious addiction of humanistic teachers to impression, opinion, and preference?

5. Anyhow, appreciation cannot really be taught at all, merely hoped for. You teach what you *can* teach and test for, and hope that appreciation will emerge as a by-product.

All this suggests that the humanistic teacher needs to develop what Keats called "negative capability:" "that is, when a man is capable of being in uncertainties, mysteries, doubts, without any irritable reaching after fact and reason."³ Information, facts, knowledge, skills—all these are important, even indispensable to the study of and the teaching of the humanities. But their value lies in what they contribute to heightened appreciation, better access to beauty, new insight of a kind that eludes the grasp of science.

TEACHING AS MOTIVATING

How very gratifying it is to the literature teacher when one of his new students indicates that he loves poetry, reads and writes it on his own, quite apart from school assignments, and is eager to learn more, read more, enjoy more. The student in the music class who is rapidly building his own diversified record collection, the art student who never misses an opportunity to visit a gallery or museum, the student of history who sincerely requests of his teacher suggestions for going beyond the class lesson, so keen is his interest: these are the students that in some measure compensate for those characterized by indifference, boredom, a readiness to be distracted, an unwillingness to do anything more than the absolute minimum that is required—if that.

Of course any subject can be interesting—*is* interesting to some. Doubtless there will always be those who love mathematics and hate biology, are fascinated by home economics and bored by literature, or the other way around. But it is unreasonable to think, as we do, that all or very nearly all persons "ought" to like some stories and pictures and songs. Perhaps music is the paradigm case. It is rare to find a person who hates or is indifferent to music. Obviously he may hate to practice his violin, or be unable to concentrate on a Handel Concerto Grosso; but chances are that there is *some* music he enjoys, at least upon occasion, and if only as an accompaniment to dancing or marching. There is, to be sure, a wide range of enjoyment, not to say appreciation. Some persons are content to hear music only rarely; others feel genuinely deprived if they are out of the sound of their favorite kind of music for more than a short time. And yet one does not often encounter a person who feels about all music the way a large number of persons feel about all mathematics, all chemistry, all history, and all religious and philosophical works. Probably not a large number, but some persons, feel largely indifferent (or even more negative than that) to poems and plays and stories, and also to paintings, drawings, sculptured works. Somehow these attitudes seem more unfortunate than similarly rejective attitudes towards mathematics and science and other nonaesthetic achievements. Is this anything more than partisanship?

Yet consider that in some important sense the creator of an aesthetic work depends for his success upon his ability to arouse the interest of his audience. Henry James says in his "Notes on the Novel" that the one indispensable requirement of fiction is that it be interesting. No novel is of course interesting to everybody, but each case of lack of interest represents a failure—on somebody's part. The author of a work on thermodynamics would doubtless be gratified by an unexpectedly large sale, but he scarcely expects or even hopes to appeal to any but those who are already in need of the information and theory that he has to disseminate.

Realistically one has to admit that just as there are a few whose ears are of such unalloyed tin that music is forever going to elude (and therefore fail to interest) them, so too there are some who doubtless are constitutionally, or by very deep-seated psychological make-up, destined not to enjoy or appreciate the visual arts, dance, film, or any form of literature. For instance, there are some persons who have such a minimal capacity or taste for make-believe that they are hopelessly put off by all that does not at least pretend to be a factual account of the way things literally are: for such, the novel will of course remain a closed book. But this must be a small group: generally speaking, one can assume about a person, especially a young person, that he enjoys a good story; finds some sort of picture, photograph, drawing, or painting, agreeable to look upon; and, on some occasion, likes to hear music. Then the teacher's task becomes that of building on whatever foundation already exists, of broadening and deepening the student's taste. Oftentimes this task consists in the first place of cultivating an initial tolerance, a bare willingness to attend to a kind of art work with which the student is unfamiliar or to which he is indifferent or even hostile. No experienced teacher is likely to minimize the extent of latent or even active hostility in students to that which they identify as straight, square, stuffy, old-fashioned, uptight, classical, or more generally as in some way identified with a generation not their own. The recent popularity of such artists as Aubrey Beardsley, Gustav Mahler, and Hermann Hesse proves that such prejudice is not unassailable; still, it is a long step from Rock to Bach,[3] from Rod McKuen to Milton, from "Hair" to "Antony and Cleopatra," especially when a liking, not to say a preference, for the latter in the several pairs is taken to be a rejection of youth culture.

Yes, a big part of the humanistic teacher's job is to get his students interested, interested enough to pursue the subject on their own, seek out and enjoy instances of beauty or other human worth beyond assignments and teacher-direction. The teacher who discovers that a student, following a demonstration of Stravinsky, goes out and buys an album of "The Rite of Spring," his first acquisition of music outside Rock and Country classification—is he not entitled to a whoop of success? But suppose a teacher learns that some of his students were not even sufficiently interested in the "Hamlet" begun in class to finish the fifth act on their own. Someone has failed.

How many kinds of motivation in the humanities can be distinguished? Here is the start of a list:

1. to learn more about,
2. to experience more broadly,
3. to repeat experiences,
4. to internalize an expression of a feeling or an insight, to apply it to oneself,
5. to have an experience so as to *savor* the feeling,
6. to intensify one's sensations,
7. to compare one work with other works, one experience with other experiences, particularly with respect to *form,*
8. to sense relevance to one's own life in that which at first seemed merely remote and alien,
9. to deepen one's sense of human potentiality through a deeper realization of human actuality,
10. to create, on one's own.

BEYOND MOTIVATION: THE DEEPER EXPERIENCE

The achievement of motivating a student to experience a kind of humanistic product that he had hitherto rejected or ignored, even (with a measure of luck added to pedagogic skill) to fire his interest, to register an initial liking, may easily be so gratifying to the teacher that he is content to rest there. Yet this is only the beginning, as the presence of the new student in class who is already interested and strongly motivated to pursue his humanistic interest indicates.

In general, the next steps are either in the direction of broadening or deepening. The former is of course the easier. The student who has read and enjoyed Plato's "Apology" is ready to move to the "Eurthyphro," the "Protagoras," and the "Republic." The student who has discovered in Ravel's "Bolero" as least one engaging musical work in an idiom he had previously rejected, may be leadable to Debussy's "La Mer," Stravinsky's "Firebird," or even Beethoven's Seventh Symphony. To have found one's way into the world of painting by way of Gauguin is to be a latent admirer of Rousseau la Douanier and of Cezanne. But there comes a time when what the student needs is not just more and ever more, but to linger upon what he has acquired an initial familiarity with in order to explore more fully its form and content. There will always be a large place for those works which we experience with pleasure but care nothing about revisiting; yet we save our greatest admiration for the works which give us, both on first and even on subsequent experiencings, the sense of having unfathomable depths, or at least a complexity such that we continually experience in their presence novelty and further insight. These are the humanistic achievements that most appropriately invite analysis.

Nor is analysis to be reserved for the particularly difficult, intricate, or large-scale work. It has been said that (the character) Hamlet has been more written upon than all but Jesus, Napoleon, and perhaps two or three other historical personages, but the idiot Benjy in *The Sound and The Fury* may deserve pondering upon too. Some scholars have specialized not in Milton but in *Paradise Lost;* if one could hardly devote a life to the study of a brief lyric, still a Shakespearian sonnet or an ode of Keats may reveal complexities that elude the first few readings. Students who have only heard and never reflected upon music are susceptible to surprise upon learning that even the most familiar popular song has a structure.

Properly introduced and exemplified, humanistic analysis may quickly exhibit its contribution to understanding appreciation,[4] yet the unlearned are typically suspicious of analysis as merely ingenious, affected, or pedantic. The student who has been shown that Henry James is particularly addicted to the use of periodic sentences may feel no more helped by this knowledge than by remotely tangential biographical information unless the analyst goes on to establish its relevance to the reading experience. For many a teacher, analysis as an end in itself is more comfortable and self-saving than that kind of experience which involves one in a commitment of his emotional resources, and may therefore in his own practice substitute peripheral intellectuality for aesthetic appreciation.

Desmond McCarthy once explained how he went about his work as drama critic: "I let the play wash over me and then examine the markings in the sand." It is no bad advice to the humanities teacher too: Begin with the direct experience itself, and then proceed to analysis. To which we would add: Then let the play (or whatever) wash over the class again, ending always with the experience of the work itself.

The Turner landscape is not, after all, a chart which schematizes the principal masses of the painting; but the analytic sketch may be a great advantage in the more penetrating look at the painter's achievement. After the themes have been identified and perhaps even memorized, they need to be returned to their setting. First and last the master work is a gestalt and needs to be experienced as such.

The humanities teacher, then, is one who, not content with arousing interest in important human products, helps students deepen their appreciation by both analysis and synthesis. There even comes a time when the teacher's most appropriate role is that of "resource person," for students may be "institutionalized" by the overly-aggressive, constantly-active teacher: the student needs to learn independence, but the most impressive teacher overtly may in fact be one who is deepening his students' reliance upon him to interest them, to sustain their interest, to conduct analyses, to prescribe next steps, etc.

But one interesting question has to do with the teacher's role as "depreciator." Sometimes teachers, like certain reviewers and critics, give the impression that so sophisticated are they, so lofty are their standards, that no work quite measures up. What of the film critic, say, who obviously knows a great deal about that medium and has had an extremely wide experience, but who seems never to enjoy himself in the theater? To the extent that he is influential does he not seem to be lessening the amount of satisfaction his readers take in film-viewing? Do not some teachers succeed mainly in ridiculing their students' present likings, making them ashamed of their own taste, or perhaps encouraging them to see an unbridgeable gulf between generations, so that the judgments of teachers and critics can be safely ignored or even despised, except for prudential purposes? Or still again, may not the result be the stimulation of a cynical attitude toward sophistication in the humanities: there are the things one really likes and then there are the things one knows are "proper" and of high repute; hence the expectation that anything that is *approved* by the professionals will almost certainly be dull and boring?

It would seem that the good teacher respects the taste of his students, accepts their opinions as at least sincere; one likes what one likes, and it is doubtless better at least to be open about it. Nevertheless, a great many people have such excessively narrow expectations or demands that their experience is seriously confined and cramped. ("I only like movies about young people," "Rock music is our music; other kinds are *theirs*," "Hesse is the only novelist I can stand," "Western philosophy is so rational and shallow; if you want to understand how things really are, you have to learn yoga and zen and things like that.") Furthermore, to have deep likings, enjoyments, and appreciations, it may be necessary to be *somewhat* hierarchical, to see that some works are ephemeral, superficial, monotonous, glib—however pleasant at first.

Therefore, it would appear legitimate and even important to help students become discriminating, liking some things much more than others—not necessarily duplicating the preferences of the teacher—and becoming increasingly able to assign reasons for greater and lesser likings.

This is not to say that beauty and simplicity are incompatible. What could be more beautiful than "Greensleeves?" How could the intense blue of a summer sky be improved upon? Burn's simple song "My luv is like a red red rose" may be said to be perfect. Chartres Cathedral is not necessarily any more beautiful than a simple adobe house in a Mexican desert. But we tend to reserve the term "great" for a work of considerable proportions and a high order of complexity. It is this sort of art that particularly needs to be *taught* to be fully enjoyed.

BASIC LITERACY IN THE ARTS AND HUMANITIES

Teachers of art and music have typically been far more interested in skills than in appreciation, or perhaps it is better to say that they have been convinced that the best way toward appreciation is through learning to *do,* to perform, rather than by a more direct route. Certain it is that to understand the difficulty of painting or of playing a musical instrument, nothing substitutes for trying one's hand at the art. Furthermore, acquiring at least a minimal skill does tend to teach a better awareness of formal components of works of art; after one has mixed colors on a palette, one probably *sees* the colors of a finished painting more adequately, and so too, *mutatis mutandis,* with the other arts.

Still, the civilized world is full of living, breathing testimonials to the fact that there is no automatic passage from skill to appreciation. Many a student has learned to play the piano a bit without learning to enjoy the performances of even Richter or Gieseking. Many a Sunday painter would not walk across the street to the Louvre or the Metropolitan Museum of Art.

As in the case of all other kinds of transfer of training, learning is facilitated by focused teaching and not by the taking for granted that one value follows from another and different value. The piano student who is also taught to listen to models of playing and taught to listen to the differences—in other ways than just in level of difficulty and in technique —of the things played, has a leg up toward scaling the wall of appreciation as compared with the student who is given no opportunity to play an instrument at all. (However, this is not to deny that there are persons who love to listen to music and yet remain almost totally ignorant of it.)

Indeed, it seems a modest and reasonable goal to expect minimal "literacy" in the major humanistic disciplines by the time a student finishes secondary school. The following list is meant to be suggestive, letting a single subject serve as illustration.

He should be able to sight-read a simple tune by voice and one instrument.

He should be able to carry a "harmony" part.

He should know the structure of such forms as the three-part song, sonata, allegro, and rondo.

He should be acquainted with the distinctive styles of at least half a dozen of the major composers.

He should be able to recognize several musical works by composer's name, form, and period.

Such a student may be said to be literate in music. He is prepared to go on to cultivate and deepen his appreciation of the art. But go on he must. These achievements are the barest beginning. To know "how to read" is not in itself to know how to read in such a way as to understand and thrill to *Moby Dick* or "The Rhyme of the Ancient Mariner." To recognize the recurrence of a musical theme is not in itself to be able to sense and feel a tightening and unifying of our aesthetic experience by means of this reminder of what has gone before.

Some, however, would insist on adding at least one item to the list: he should be able to *compose* and notate a tune and a simple accompaniment or other harmonization. That is, some would insist that in all the arts, a demonstrated ability to create, as distinct from performing what another has created, is essential. Those who are entirely ignorant of music may insist that this is far too difficult a skill to require universally, but hardly anyone who is not entirely ignorant of this art will agree. It is probably no more difficult to learn to write music than to paint a landscape or write a poem or model a vase.

Today few educators can be content with a school program that does not (or at least that does not even pretend to) foster creativity. Without having any monopoly on creativity, the arts offer one of the most attractive means of learning to create. Here the obvious model is the visual arts. Imagine a child who has never drawn with pencil and crayon! Yet somehow this dearly loved activity tends to drop away for all but a small handful of people. Generally speaking, the schools have not yet learned to sustain, much less to develop, the almost universal creativity of young children as artists. But a child almost always finds a piano keyboard or a harmonica irresistible, too, and his efforts with these instruments are no less crudely creative than the child with finger paints or crayons: a starting place, if only there were teachers to follow through! Children also, with few exceptions, like to make up stories and to take pictures with a camera. They like to compose verses and dance in unconventional ways—until they acquire cramping inhibitions. But specifically teaching creativity can furnish an antidote to conventionalism, conformism, routine thinking, feeling, and acting. What better paradigms of the free employment of the imagination than through the achievements of the greatest artists? What better illustration of the painfulness of self-imposed novelty than through the efforts to paint, compose, write, choreograph?

The point applies fully as well to history and philosophy. Philosophizing is already a common requirement of philosophy students (even, increasingly in high school), but how seldom, unfortunately, are they asked to be historians. Yet what better way to discover how history works, how interpretations have to be made, often with too little evidence for security, and how fascinating the problems can be?

AFFECTIVE TEACHING

However it be with the sciences and technologies, a purely intellectual experience with a humanistic product must be called stunted, abridged, incomplete. That is, a humanistic experience involves the feelings.

Two kinds of feelings may be distinguished for our purposes: sensuous and emotional. Sensuous feelings are those which are directly and obviously associated with the body and its sense organs. (The sensual may be thought of as a subdivision of the sensuous, having particularly to do with pleasures that are principally tactile and gustatory.) The emotional feelings—or just emotions—are difficult to define helpfully, so let it be said here only that they are exemplified by fear, pity, joy, and jealousy.

Works of art, or more broadly, objects of aesthetic attention and value, tend to inspire feelings of both sorts. One may debate about the aesthetic value of mathematics or of nonsensory mystical experiences, but generally speaking we expect aesthetic appreciation to be in part directed toward sounds, colors, shapes, and to an extent odors, tastes, and textures, either experienced directly through the bodily senses or imagined.

Again, whether emotions are or are not invariable accompaniments of the aesthetic experience, they are certainly very commonly present, as witness our tendency to speak of how our heart pounded as we approached the climax of a mystery thriller, how our heart ached at the plight of the bereaved lover, how exciting the music became, how peaceful was the painting of the autumn trees, and how awesome the cathedral's nave.

The case for the prevalence of feelings is harder to make out for history and philosophy. Certainly sensory feelings are seldom more than negligible in the products of these two fields, and certainly historical and philosophical writing can be and often is heavily intellectual and (what is by no means the same thing) dry. Furthermore, the two subjects are often taught so as to inspire little or no feeling; furthermore, many teachers would reject, even with disdain, the supposition that their teaching *ought* to involve either the expression or the arousal of feelings of any sort.

Nevertheless, there are times in the writing and teaching of history and philosophy where the attempt to exclude emotions would be almost as artificial, with results almost as sterile, as a similar attempt in poetry or music. (It is to be noted here that the writing of history and philosophy are likened to the writing of poetry and the composing of music; literary criticism and musicology would then have as their analogs history of philosophy and historical theory.)

Part of history is chronicle: this happened and then this, and at the same time elsewhere that other thing was happening. Another part of history is the attempt to connect these happenings by means of causal (or at least *influential*) interpretation. But still another part consists in trying to imagine what it was like to live through these events and to be part of causes and effects. Luther broke with Roman Catholicism: the events can be traced, one by one. But there was the rage and anguish that were his as he nailed his theses to the cathedral door. And that is no less a part of history—it may indeed be a more important and surely for most of us a far more interesting part of history—than the recounting of the overt events themselves. History consists in considerable part in decisions, and decisions can be looked at either from outside or inside. To neglect how it felt to make a momentous decision is to settle for a severely austere and dry history, even though one can be more "objective"—perhaps by definition—about outer than about inner happenings.

Collingwood likens the historian and the novelist in a number of respects. Each paints a picture that is

> partly a narrative of events, partly a description of situations, exhibition of motives, analysis of characters. Each aims at making his picture a coherent whole, where every character and every situation is so bound up with the rest that this character in this situation cannot but act in this way. . . .[5]

The greatness of Gibbon as historian obviously does not consist in his having known more about what happened to the Roman empire than other historians: certainly many of his successors have appropriately corrected his account in many ways. His greatness consists in his ability to imagine and to make us, his readers, imagine what it was like to decline and fall.

But let us take an example from Thucydides. In describing the plague in Athens, 430 B.C., he began by telling how the victims were so "overwhelmed by their sufferings that they sank into apathy," but went on to give a detailed account of the symptoms, the violent fever that made one want to plunge into icy water (but those who did got no relief), the inflammation of the eyes, the pustules on the skin, the coughs, the violent but ineffectual retching, the insomnia. And he ends his account by a consideration of the moral effects of the disease, giving rise, as it did, to every antisocial tendency imaginable:

> The subterfuges and restraints with which certain kinds of behavior had formerly been hedged about were relaxed by the spectacle of the rapid transitions of fortune. The well-to-do were cut off in the twinkling of an eye and people hitherto penniless were suddenly endowed with their possessions. The inevitable moral was to spend quickly and to spend on pleasure, if life and wealth were things of a day. The will to persevere in the recognized paths of honor disappeared in the uncertainty whether death would not intervene before the goal were attained, and the place of honor and welfare was usurped by the pleasure of the moment and everything that contributed to it. The fear of God and the ordinance of Man ceased to exercise their inhibitions. Since death descended alike upon the just and the unjust, there seemed nothing to choose between piety and irreligion; and criminals no longer expected to live to be convicted and sentenced, or, rather they felt that the extreme penalty was already suspended over their heads and that life should be made to yield some enjoyment before the blow descended.[6]

This is great history precisely because it conveys the horror and the hopelessness of a plague that contributed greatly to the subsequent defeat of Athens in the Peloponnesian War.

It would be easy to illustrate the place of emotion in philosophy by citing Thucydides' contemporary, Plato, but lest it be supposed that the Greeks had a monopoly on such writing, we skip down the centuries to Hobbes, finding in him a famous passage (not unlike the quotation from

Thucydides, but having to do not with an actual event but with the general causes of certain events; hence, philosophy, not history). It is his account of the causes of quarrels among men, which he attributes to competition, diffidence, and glory:

> The first, maketh men invaded for gain; the second, for safety; the third, for reputation. The first use violences, to make themselves masters of other men's persons, wives, children, and cattle; the second, to defend them; the third, for trifles, as a word, a smile, a different opinion. . . .
>
> Hereby it is manifest, that during the time men live without a common power to keep them all in awe, they are in that condition which is called war; and such a war, as is of every man, against every man . . .
>
> In such condition, there is no place for industry; because the fruit thereof is uncertain: and consequently no culture of the earth; no navigation, nor use of the commodities that may be imported by sea; no commodious building; no instruments of moving, and removing, such things as require force; no knowledge of the face of the earth; no account of time; no arts; no letters; no society; and which is worst of all, continual fear, and danger of violent death; and the life of man, solitary, poor, nasty, brutish, and short.[7]

Here is philosophical writing that not only announces a theory about human society, but makes us vividly realize what it would be like to be in a "state of nature."

But these examples of vividly humanistic writing by a great historian and a great philosopher suggest ways of humanistically teaching history and philosophy, even when the texts at hand are far more abstract, prosaic, and spare. It then becomes the teacher's job to make the period or the idea come alive, be vibrant, and rich.

For ten years now, or more, we have been told that the modern school, particularly the secondary school, is overextended, that in trying to do so much it has done disgustingly little, that its real area of competence is with respect to the intellect, the cognitive powers, rationality, and—beyond such powers and processes—a body of knowledge.

Yet almost at the precise moment when in the interest of greater rigor and increased rationality it was proved that even quite sophisticated mathematics could be learned much earlier than had been supposed, and that science is such a demanding study that there is little or no time for such frills as music, art, and drama, the news began to be leaked that a large proportion of the school population was dropping out before these wonderful aids to rationality could have their effect. Even intelligent, middle-class children from suburbia were bored with school and persisted only because, for some unclear reason, it had become necessary to go to university. A shocking number of students who have proved that they *can* do science, are saying that in fact they do not *want* to do it, but would rather concern themselves with some kind of tender-minded humanistic subject. Student dissidence, whether of the "activist" or the "hippie" variety—if these shorthand terms can be given a broad connotation—is challenging schools and colleges and universities to rediscover some extra-cognitive dimensions to learning, if only in the interest of better motivation toward the traditional studies. Grouping or streaming according to achievement criteria have been rather thoroughly debunked. Some have begun to speak of grouping according to emotional, attitudinal criteria: perhaps compatibility between teacher and students is important, for all of its commonsensicalness.

In any case, nothing is now more apparent than that we still know very little that can fit comfortably under the rubric "education of the emotions." Yet, for the most tentative of beginnings, we may think first of what the need is. If education is change, development, increment, clarification, arousal (as in the case of interests), then what is it about students' emotional natures that seems to require education?

There are perhaps many sorts of lack or aberration that may be ascribed to the emotional side of any given person's being, but as a start we would mention apathy, narrowness of range, and stereotype, all possibly characteristic of a sizable segment of school or college population, indeed maybe not less characteristic than better-known deficiencies on the more purely intellective side. (One speaks of "sides" in this context with appropriate diffidence: great mischief can be occasioned by any rigid separation.)

Apathy is intended in an etymologically exact way. A fair number of persons of all ages impress their fellows as "sleepy," low-keyed, relatively unconcerned, hard to interest. One has the impression of their almost being under sedation, of their getting little out of life because of not being fully alive.

"Narrowness of emotion" characterizes that person who has some strong feelings, but who emotionally has a great many blank spots. Capable of being exercised about a case of apparent injustice in school discipline, a certain student may seem oddly quiescent respecting many other events that his fellows find equally dramatic; another may be responsive to romantic or sexual matters but to hardly anything else. In such instances, one is impressed not so much with sheer impoverishment, as in the case of apathy, but with serious underdevelopment of any but a few of the feeling centers of the self.

Stereotyped or stock responses are typified by the person who is utterly predictable, whose responses are undiscriminative with respect to the peculiarities of a given situation. In recent years both philosophical existentialists and social psychologists have helped us understand the particular iniquities of certain widely prevalent "self-images," so that a person may be fixed and utterly stalled by a conception of himself which seems dictated by his membership in a class, such as the female, colored, stupid, poor—but also the intellectual, conservative, rebellious. This deficiency is not confined to such self-typing: it extends also to persons who have developed habits of reacting to a number of stimuli in a push-button way.

If these may be taken as a (relatively crude and of course incomplete) classification of emotional deficiencies that is far from uncommon in almost any group of persons, the question can of course still be raised as to the relevance of education to them. Some may maintain that these are or tend to be constitutional characteristics, or anyway so deep-seated as not to respond to the kind of education that may be conducted in ordinary school rooms. Others may say that even if education could be effective in such ways, it is inappropriate for it to try, since it is the cognitive and not the emotional domain that is proper for formal education. It must be granted that the latter type of argument may at times be valuable, polemically, as a corrective to an educational practice that has become so diffuse and unfocused as to be ineffective in almost every way. But the embracing of certain goals in the emotional domain need not militate against the maintaining of rigorous intellectual standards. As to the reputed ineffectiveness of "regular" teaching in emotional ways —well, of course there are pathological cases suitable only for professional therapy, but we are not thinking of these. Many students and teachers can testify in their own cases to big differences having been made by someone else's intervention, in the development of the feeling portions of the self.

Theoretically, we see no reason why any subject matter area should by its nature be out of bounds to emotional education. Probably more depends upon the teacher and his attitudes and approaches than what, particularly, he teaches, but the field that offers especially rich opportunities in this respect is the humanities. Yet a hyper-scholarly approach to the humanities may be inimical to this function, and so may one that is hyper-aesthetical. For instance, the notion that a response in being aesthetic must be severely formal, scouting those emotions that relate to "real life," is a kind of preciosity one should hope safely buried in anthologies of criticism and aesthetics.

The arts, sensitively, warmly, personally approached may be a powerful educator of our emotions. They may help awaken in us a general vibrancy of feeling that has lain dormant. They may greatly extend the range of our responses by carrying us (in comparative safety) beyond the confines which our own life at least seems bound to. And they may reveal to us—by inviting our participation in—novel emotional experiences, which in some cases the author may even pit (e.g., satirically) against stereotypy.

Are many teachers of the humanities afraid of inviting—much less encouraging and facilitating—revelations of emotional response to works of art? Probably. Partly this may be so because of the difficulty of establishing a special openness in the classroom situation, of removing existent inhibitions. Probably, too, most of us teachers are afraid of being *personal,* of falling away from our role of the slightly aloof, authoritative, rational mentor and judge.[8]

LECTURE, DISCUSSION, DIALOGUE

We either smile or shudder at the pictures of classrooms in the Middle Ages or the early Renaissance: the teacher at an upraised lectern reading from a text to the scholars huddled below him transcribing at a furious pace his words into their notes: that is, they reproduced the book, along with interlarded commentaries of the master. Although such "teaching" has not entirely disappeared, a more typical picture today would be of a "learning resources center" with pupils working together in small groups or individually, some reading, some writing, some talking, some looking at slides and listening to tapes, with the teacher moving easily around the area, explaining, recommending another book, perhaps occasionally pulling the group back together for a report by a member of the group or a brief talk by a visitor.

Today we prize versatility in teachers. An important part of their training consists in acquiring a *repertory* of pedagogic skills and techniques, along with the development of some sense of how appropriately to vary procedure with shifting goals and class needs. Seldom would they be encouraged to read aloud from a book in order that the pupils reproduce the book in their own notes, but they might well employ a games approach to learning, or a simulation technique, perhaps with the aid of a computer, or a role-playing process to help students identify with persons in situations importantly different from their own. And, with the growing recognition that a heterogeneous mixture of students can still be taught effectively by individualization of instruction, today's teacher finds it necessary to learn how to serve as tutor, consultant, reference librarian, and much else.

Still, there remains an important place in most classrooms for both lecture and discussion. In recent years it has been popular to disparage lecturing as dull, teacher-centered, overly-intellectual, conducive to passivity, and above all as unnecessary—a hold-over from pre-Copernican times. Critics who speak so must have been exceptionally unlucky in their draw of lectures, for lecturing can be stimulating, emotional, and evocative of intense thought and imagination. The skillful lecturer motivates students to go beyond what he says, to read and think beyond where he takes them, to argue with and try to refute his opinions and judgments. He offers a model of how to relate and integrate ideas, how to think on his feet, how to dream up examples, illustrations, and applications of theories, how to organize an explanation or an explication, and how one can be excited by the subject matter at hand. Few kinds of teaching can be more infectious than that of an enthusiastic, keyed-up, articulate lecturer. No further developments in duplicating machines will succeed in making the lecture obsolete.[9]

Still, we think that for most teachers in the humanities, skill in discussion-leading is of even greater importance, for the well-conducted discussion may succeed where no other procedure can in really involving students, including some who had no original intent of being involved at all, in the consideration of a problem, a theme, an aesthetic object, a book. Too many teachers still confuse discussion with recitation, that is, the eliciting of right-or-wrong answers to set questions, surely one of the most mechanical, rote-memory chores imaginable. With great regularity the best questions a discussion leader can ask—and as a rule-of-thumb, his mode will be 90 percent interrogative—are the kind to which he has no final and definitive answer. Thus he is joining the students in the inquiry, himself searching and not merely conducting others in the search.

The word, of course, is *dialogue,* which, like "creativity," "revolutionary," "authentic," "appreciation," and (sic) "humanistic" has been over- and mis-used in recent times, but is finally indispensable. In the classroom (or other learning environment), "dialogue" remains the best name for the description of teaching/learning that transcends mere transmission and recitation and busy work. Real dialogue, properly so-called, is not to be confused with simple "taking-turns" conversation, but signifies a coming together of selves, a meeting of minds, a joining of issues, a feeling rapport, an engagement of human beings. If only the word could be severed from the implication of belligerency, the word "confrontation" would be yet another synonym for dialogue.

Martin Buber has distinguished genuine dialogue from two specious pretenders: (1) disguised monologue, which has only to be named to be recognized for what it is, and (2) technical dialogue, which is characterized as "prompted solely by the need of objective understanding." Genuine dialogue may even be silent, provided only that "each of the participants really has in mind the other or others in their present and particular being and turns to them with the intention of establishing a living, mutual relation between himself and them."[10]

In another place Buber distinguishes three chief forms of the dialogical relation: (1) "disputation between two men" who though very different from each other recognize each other's "full legitimacy." (2) the relation of education, in which the real teacher continually experiences the pupil "from the other side."[11] (3) The final form of dialogical relation is friendship, "a concrete and mutual experience of inclusion."[12]

Now, the reason why there is something peculiarly appropriate and right about dialogical discussion in the humanities is that, as we have seen, *persons* (not just people) are central to their subject matter, at the heart of their concern, and dialogue is a relating of persons, such that the procedure of teaching/learning now becomes singularly consonant with what the process is all about. Here, if ever, the medium is the message.

THE TEACHER AS A PERSON

Note at least three ways of answering the question to the teacher, "What do you teach?" (1) Music (or English, or whatever). (2) My students. (3) Myself.

The last answer is unusual, too unusual. It is also ambiguous. It may mean that when one teaches, really teaches, one himself learns. But the meaning we are presently after is the same as Anatole France's, in his famous description of literary criticism: that it is primarily about the critic, always *moi,* à propos Shakespeare, à propos Racine, etc. Or as Montaigne said of his essays: Their subject is myself.

Of course it is not necessary to be autobiographical, or even to use the first person singular pronoun, to teach oneself. It is necessary only to *be.*

Some teachers say, in effect, Be like me, do as your teacher does, think as your teacher does, share my tastes, give right answers the way I do. But even a modest, self-effacing, self-deprecating teacher presents to his students a model. He presents himself for his values, his sense of what is important and what not important, the admirable and the unadmirable, the right and the wrong. He lets students see him solving problems, lets them see how he *goes about* solving problems.

This is unavoidable. Suppose the teacher says to himself, "I must be neutral at all costs. I must be very careful not to indoctrinate my students. I must not give them the impression that I know all the answers —or even *any* of them, for sure. I do not want to be dogmatic. I hate authoritarianism. I must always be tentative and guarded and tell them that there is another side than mine." And let us suppose that he is very conscientious in following out this program. Then, at the very least, he teaches neutrality; he teaches them that he values cautiousness, tentativeness, perhaps even indecisiveness.

This is not to say that all teaching is indoctrination. No, as we have seen, *indoctrination* implies the deliberate infecting of others with one's own values in the absence of rational justification. A good teacher in the democratic tradition will try to provide his students with means for combating indoctrination, including his own. At the same time, he will realize that he cannot in any case be purely neutral—and still teach. Furthermore, he may very well teach less effectively than he should if he presents to his students the model of the perfect academic hedger, the one who always says, "But on the other hand. . . ." Today more than ever before, students *want* to know where their teacher stands, tend to resent him if he pretends to stand nowhere.

Today we know that a lot of teaching is subliminal. Doubtless, in spite of their protestations to the contrary, English teachers often communicate their own distaste for *The Scarlet Letter* and *Silas Marner;* what comes across from the music teacher may be, "I really hate music"; the art teacher's real message may be, "I wish to God I were anywhere else than here."

Worse yet, teachers may all too easily and all too often convey to students that for all of their protestations and professions of humanistic ideals, they in themselves are timid, inept, insensitive, without dash or daring conviction—and thus undo all the verbal lesson. In our time nobody has drawn a harsher indictment of the teacher of the humanities than the classicist William Arrowsmith, who has proclaimed that we lack educators—

> by which I mean *teachers* in the Socratic sense, visible embodiments of the *realized* humanity of our aspirations, intelligence, concern, skill, scholarship; men ripened or ripening into realization, as Socrates at the close of the *Symposium* embodies his own definition of love. Our universities and our society need this compelling embodiment, this exemplification of what we are all presumably at, as they have never needed it before. It is *men* we need now, not programs. It is possible for a student to go from kindergarten to graduate school without ever encountering a *man*—a man who might for the first time give him the only profound motivation for learning, the hope of becoming a better man. Since the humanities aim at humanization, their meaning and end are always, I believe, an exemplary man. Hence the humanities stand or fall according to the human size of the man who professes them. The teacher is both sanction and goal of the education he gives. This is why it is completely reasonable that a student should expect a classicist to live classically. The man who teaches Shakespeare or Homer runs the supreme risk. This is surely as it should be. Charisma in a teacher is not a mystery or nimbus of personality, but radiant *exemplification* to which the student contributes a correspondingly radiant hunger for becoming. . . . The teacher, like his text, is thus the mediator

between past and present, present and future, and he matters because there is no *human* mediator but him. He is the student's only evidence outside the text that a great humanity exists; upon his impersonation both his text and his student's human fate depend. For student and teacher alike, ripeness is all.[13]

If all this is true, or even a reasonable approximation to the truth —allowing for rhetorical exaggeration—the preparation for teaching is even more difficult than anyone has yet supposed, for it is no longer enough to *know* a great deal, including a great deal about effective teaching procedures. One must also—perhaps above all—*be* a great deal. What our students need is, then, better, deeper, wiser human beings— who will thus communicate the fullness of their humanness to their classes. But starting with our own limitations as human beings, we who are teachers can at least face up to the fact that we are teaching ourselves. And go on from there.

11

Humanities Curricula

We have seen that, strictly speaking, any subject *can* be taught humanistically: mathematics, geology, physical education, home economics, music, art, and literature. Dewey has wisely said, "Knowledge is humanistic in quality not because it is *about* human products in the past, but because of what it *does* in liberating human intelligence and human sympathy."[1] Good humanistic teaching is teaching that has such results. Furthermore, humanistic teaching and humanistic learning do not entirely depend upon there being a formal organization of topics and activities—which is to say, a curriculum: one can imagine a teacher who proceeded almost entirely *ad hoc,* taking whatever was at hand for the object of a lesson, and inducing, thereby, savoring, evaluative, appreciative attitudes. (This might be taken as descriptive of the way a wise parent teaches.) But most professional teachers and nearly all schools want and believe in an ordered sequence of learning activities. Indeed, there are no commoner questions in educational circles than these: How shall we organize the material of the course? Where shall we start and what shall we include? What relationships should we stress? What books and other materials will prove most useful? In fact, for some reason, teachers and other educators find it easier and more comfortable to talk about curriculum than about the instructional process itself. Yet, nearly everyone is willing to admit that any ultimate separation of the two is mischievous. Surely no curriculum is so ingenious or comprehensive that it is "teacher-proof." And yet there are curricula which will tend to stimulate both teachers and pupils to more effective teaching and learning.

HUMANITIES CURRICULA

The Elementary Grades

At least since the time of Pestalozzi and Froebel it has been impossible to think of the schooling of young children apart from singing and dancing and drawing and story telling—activities that are about as humanistic as it is possible to be. Still, it is possible (and accurate) for a recent book on the humanities in the schools to say, categorically: "At the present time, few humanities programs for the elementary schools exist."[2]

In recent years very detailed sequences of learning activities have been devised for music and literature, and to some extent for the visual arts and crafts, but remarkably little exists, either in the way of books or of curriculum guides, that would help the teacher in relating the arts to one another, much less in developing the conception of man's achievements as objects of appreciation.

Of course in many ways the primary grades are the *least* appropriate times for insisting upon sharp distinctions between subjects and fields. How particularly pedantic it would be to try to decide whether to categorize a kindergarten unit on wild flowers as "science" or "humanities"; or to insist that a second-grade project on American Indians must belong to the social studies and therefore *not* to the humanities. No, the point is not to parcel out all the manifold activities of the early grades into neatly demarcated groups, but rather to ask the question whether more effective ways can be devised of encouraging the appreciative attitudes in young children, helping them genuinely to like an ever more complex type of song or story and to see the importance as well as the fascination of raising questions about man as a creator. Thus, one experimental humanities course designed for fourth, fifth, and sixth graders in Tampa, Florida, "concentrates on famous people who have contributed to literature, music, art, architecture, and philosophy" throughout Western history.[3]

Few activities could be more valuable—and are less in evidence—than sensory training for children. We think of small children, when they are healthy of mind and body, as intensely alive, aware of the manifold wonders of the world they inhabit, constantly surprised and frequently delighted by rocks and worms, scurrying clouds and droning bees, the teacher's new dress and a funny, knobby carrot. But all this is to say that they are greatly motivated to learn to see and listen and smell and taste and to feel textures and the tone of their own muscles. For we do learn, or fail to learn, to perceive beyond the rough outlines of objects and beyond classifications and expectations. How many children ever discover that winds do far more than howl, that only in the funny papers does a dog say "Arf"? How many are taught, at some appropriate point, to *look* at houses and trees when they want to draw them, and not be content with another conventionalized sketch that serves its purpose in being recognized *as* a house or tree? Even quite a young person can learn to catch on the face of a friend a characteristic expression and record it in pencil or words: a perceptive teacher can improve on the chances of his learning this skill unaided. How crude is that child's seeing that is willing to settle for "flower" to name what he sees, as if the difference between marigold and peony were miniscule. If, as we are told by all language experts, it is far easier to teach a young child, as against one well advanced in his teens, or an adult, to speak authentic French or Spanish (perhaps it gives us a bit of start to add, unabashedly, Chinese?); does this not signify something about the child's ability to learn to listen, with uncanny accuracy, to a great variety of nonlanguage sounds too?

The imaginative teacher will think of dozens of games and excursions to develop sensory discrimination, ranging from blindfold sniffing-identification and Essalen-type concentrations on the particular feel of one's left shoulder or tongue, to something as ancient as the nature-walk, but now prepared for and sharpened by achievements to be aspired to. But are there not whole curricula waiting to be developed which would provide a more systematic development of sensory powers than can be accomplished by the occasional and cursory lesson of the unusual teacher?

From a heightened and more discriminating awareness of the richly sensuous, qualitative world in which we live, it is no great leap to a world extended by a fertile imagination. Again no teacher starts from scratch in this respect either, for young children are famously (and in some circles, notoriously) fertile in their imaginations—or is this a romanticized stereotype? Well, better say what's true, that children differ in this respect at least as much as in "intelligence" or physical prowess. Some youngsters are exceptionally literal-minded, having no more than the most rudimentary inclination to weave worlds of fantasy and make-believe, and little power of inventiveness in peopling and furnishing such worlds. Are there teachers who make no effort to develop imaginative capacities in the odd belief that imagination is something each person either has or has not, or, again, in the supposition that it is ubiquitous among children, perhaps even needing more curbing than encouragement? It is barely possible. Or is the block, rather, that no one knows anything about stimulating and improving imaginative abilities? But this is patently false, for there have always been teachers themselves imaginative enough to tease out, cultivate, and refine the imaginations of their pupils. There are the great exemplars of imaginative power, the coiners of fairy tales, fables, myths, and other sorts of stories, but it is one thing to learn to delight in the imaginative excursions conducted by others, and something else again—however natural it seems to move from one to the other—to be one's own tour guide, for are there not illimitable fables, myths, and stories still to be invented and transcribed in words, oral or written, in tableaux, in line and color, in pantomime, in dance?

Some will say that now we have gotten over into *creativity;* but, alas, the word has, from overuse, become almost as distasteful as "appreciation." Yet there is such a thing—or better, say, such a characteristic; and from the researches of such psychologists as Richard Crutchfield and such art educators as Herbert Read and Schaeffer-Zimmern, no one can beg off by pleading the total mysteriousness of the subject. Something is known about its nature, and about its cultivation, even in children who have seemed to be inevitable plodders. The humanities have no monopoly on creation, of course, but where else are the possibilities so manifold?

Aristotle would have agreed, we think, to the importance of stimulating such powers as imagination and creativity in children, but he would have drawn the line if anyone had had the audacity to suggest in his presence that children have philosophic interests and capabilities that also deserve tapping. And whether from Aristotle's influence or some other reason, philosophic study in American schools has been exceptionally uncommon below the college level. Only recently, however, this has begun to change, so that today a course in logic or ethics is no longer unusual in high schools. But once we transcend the identification of philosophy with philosophy books, there is no reason why such a study is not appropriate and interesting in the lower grades. Take a topic of such ancient lineage as "What is man?": nine-year-olds can be as fascinated with this challenge as their seniors. True, if we are to credit Piaget's and other studies of the development of children's capacities for moral judgment, it is possible to be premature in raising questions of principle with respect to human conduct, but children's almost universal interest in science fiction testifies to the possibility of helping them open up large cosmological questions for speculation and wonder. And this in turn quickly shades over into various problems of a religious nature: divinity, existence before and after mundane life, prayer, ritual, holiness and unholiness, mana, taboo, and many others. Although, admittedly, this is ground that a teacher must trend upon with delicate and sensitive feet, children have been often ill-served by the kind of timidity that says, since somebody may conceivably be offended, better avoid such subjects altogether. Most teachers feel safer with the far away and the long ago, and without question, comparative religion is a lively field for young and old alike, but there are ways too of dealing sensitively with religious matters much closer to home.

Another approach to elementary level humanities that appears to be growing in popularity is one that is psychological/philosophical, often aimed at helping the child toward a better sense of his own uniqueness or of some of the distinctive values and characteristics of various regional or ethnic groups. For instance, in Fairfield, Connecticut, sixth-grade students take a course, intended as a bridge to junior high school, called "Discovering Who I Am," which involves role-playing, exploration of several media of art creation (not now art for art's sake, but art expression as a means toward self-identity), and a study of symbol systems. Such themes as Honesty, Fairmindedness, Self-acceptance, Rejection, Friendship, and Responsibility are searched out in poetry, short stories, and other materials.

Then there is the whole problem of beginning the development of an historical sense in the young child, a sense of continuity, of change through influence, of the diachronic understanding of cultures and civilizations. And much else. In many ways, the problem of teaching the humanities is much easier at the elementary level than subsequently. The young child does not have to be helped to put the humanities back together again, because he has not yet taken them apart, has not yet learned that a gulf separates the several disciplines from each other, and that it is not respectable to mix categories and classifications. What is important, above all, is that the humanities not be allowed to fall by the wayside, in the supposition that they are less important than certain other subjects, or in the mistaken belief that some very particular talents and rare abilities are required of the teacher before she dare teach art, music, dance, or philosophy, either individually or in concert.

Finally—lest this, in spite of its commonness, not go without saying —the elementary grades are a time for acquiring basic "literacies" in the arts. The feasibility of deferring the teaching of reading until high school years is scarcely ever mentioned, so obvious is it that most students want to read at a much younger age, and that so much other learning is dependent upon the possession of this skill. But the rudiments of drawing, painting, modeling, reading music, singing, playing a musical instrument, dancing, and much else can obviously be taught early along, and need not be thought of as deterrents to spontaneous expressiveness. Possession by virtually all children of such skills, even in very modest degree, could make much later teaching/learning the more effective and the more enjoyable.

Modes of Integration in Secondary Schools

Generally in the past students' exposure to the humanities has been through taking literature, history, music, art, each taught without more than casual reference to any of the others. Today the very concept "humanities" is fast coming to mean an interrelation of subjects: literature and history; the allied arts; film, drama, and fiction; philosophy, religion, and literature—and almost every other combination imaginable of these and many other fields.[4] If we concentrate here on some five "modes of integration," it is in full recognition that these modes themselves can be variously combined, and that other modes—for example, "Regional and Ethnic Studies," an exploration of the humanistic products and interests of Blacks, Chicanos, Native Americans, India, West Africa, etc., can be exceptionally interesting.[5]

Cultural history.   Perhaps the richest of the synoptic disciplines is history. Anything can be and most things are, some place or other, studied historically.

Most people when they hear "history" probably still think of kings and presidents, wars and treaties, discovery of new lands and migrations of peoples. Time was when a typical history book, dealing, say, with England in the time of Queen Elizabeth I might find occasion barely to mention the place of the theater in London, and even the activities of William Shakespeare. Today any comprehensive history, unless it specifically confines itself to politics or economics, is likely to devote a considerable space to intellectual and artistic happenings. For notable instance, Will Durant's ten-volume *The Story of Civilization,* extending from the ancient Hebrews and Greeks through the eighteenth century concerns itself as much with philosophers, scientists, writers, artists, religious leaders, and popular morality as with kings and warriors. Thus, in the final volume one chapter is devoted to the Seven Years War and one to Mozart, one to the Industrial Revolution and one to Kant, one to Catherine the Great and one to Samuel Johnson; and the volume is entitled *Rousseau and Revolution.*

But increasingly scholars are writing books that are wholly or mainly devoted to arts and ideas, perhaps with only brief mention—reversing the more usual emphasis—of political happenings. Typically these books are organized around the concept of epochs. Thus, the Age of Greece will trace literature from Homer and Hesiod down through the great tragic dramatists of the fifth century; discuss the Parthenon and other Greek temples (with pictures, of course); briefly describe—since so little is known on the subject—the state of Greek music and dance; spend a chapter on vase painting; sketch the rise of philosophy and its blossoming in Socrates, Plato, and Aristotle; and pay at least some attention to Herodotus and Thucydides as the progenitors of historiography. Then it will pass on to the Roman civilization, thence to the Middle Ages, and so on. The attempt will be made, characteristically, to show how a religious or philosophical idea influenced the arts, the extent to which such a concept as "classical" or "romantic" has similar meanings in painting, sculpture, architecture, music, literature, and philosophy; the ways in which the arts have overlapped or been deliberately combined —or separated—at various times; and also, of course, the ways in which artists and critics within each of the arts influenced succeeding ages.

So common is the historical approach by epochs that Joseph Satin in his *The Humanities Handbook* speaks of *the* "Humanities Approach" taking for its first step the placement of "contemporaneous examples of works from different areas side by side to find their common elements."[6] Thus he finds, during the Age of Reason, Montesquieu's *The Spirit of the Laws* and the form of the classical symphony equally characterized by "symmetry and balance." Then he would have this common element "traced across all areas of culture during a given period."[7] For instance, eighteenth century painting, the astronomy of Newton, and the heroic couplet turn out to be as balanced as Montesquieu and the symphony of Haydn. Although these very examples may embarrassingly illustrate the dangers of simplistic epoch-characterization, there *are* interesting and even illuminating parallels, analogies, and similarities to be discovered among certain of the achievements of any age. Perhaps the inductive exercise wherein the student is himself encouraged to hypothesize such connections, and then to seek by a wide-ranging exploration to verify his hypotheses is an even more valuable experience than the much commoner procedure whereby the student tends to accept on faith the textbook's or lecturer's assertions about the defining characteristics of this or that age. Surely there is an important place here too for the production, by both student and teacher, of apparent counterexamples. Thus, in the above case of the "Age of Reason," what is to be said of Hume's skeptical attack on reason, of Rousseau's sentimentalism, of Blake's paintings? Yet, perhaps on close examination these examples will turn out to be only apparent exceptions to the proposed rule. And that of course is fine too, pedagogically.

Because it is not easy in our time to interest large numbers of students in historical studies, especially when, as often happens, recent and contemporary times are neglected either from the impulse to stay back in the relatively remote past when (at least so it seems to us) things were simpler, or just from not having time to get beyond, say, Impressionism or The Gay Nineties, some teachers today are making an effort specifically to relate past and present. One way this may be done, of course, is to start with the present and then to do flashbacks to show influences, positive or negative, upon the newer modes and styles. For instance, it is commonly said today that we are witnessing (or participating in) a reaction to "Puritanism." Well, then, how is this evident in music, fiction, morals, religion, and the vernacular of post-World War II in America and Western Europe? Now, how *does* this contrast with Victorian times? with the late seventeenth century? with the Middle Ages? And, by the way, how "Puritanical" were the Puritans?

Or, again, one may leap to, rather than start from, the present, as when, having examined the "Return to Nature," the repudiation of conventional manners and morals, the attack on established authority, the surge toward individualism discernible in France and America in the late eighteenth century, the challenge may be laid down to find similar (as well as conflicting) phenomena in the present.

Still again, without at all stressing epochs, the cultural historian may interest himself (and hopefully his students) more in tracing influences, ideological or stylistic, or even in terms of certain feelings. Thus Edmund Burke Feldman in his exceptionally handsome book, *Varieties of Visual Experience,* speaks of "The Style of Objective Accuracy," "The Style of Formal Order," "The Style of Emotion," and "The Style of

Fantasy," and shows examples from painting and plastic arts of each of these in different periods.[8] It would not be impossibly difficult to add other arts to such a scheme.

A novel, multi-media approach to cultural history called "Educational Programming of our Cultural Heritage" has been tried out in the Berkeley, California, area for several years.[9] EPOCH is in large measure a resources center, featuring a large table with concentric circles that represent periods of time since man's beginning, and wedges through these circles that represent areas of the earth's surface. But prominent among the resources is a large collection of slides which can be projected —six or seven at once—on the many-faceted walls of the basic room. These, then, with taped music and various sound effects, are arranged in programs around various themes. This is one of the humanities projects that draws rather heavily upon archaeology and other branches of anthropology.

Themes and variations.   Cultural history is usually written in a chronological manner, and, as we have noted, with emphasis upon cross-sectional displays of epochs. Another way of doing history that has recently found an increasing number of adherents is that which centers upon certain themes or key ideas, and shows how various arts and other disciplines may illuminate these. Take for instance the Pennsylvania Humanities Commission's Humanities courses, which are organized around some six large themes: Man's Search for Truth, Man's Search for Freedom, Man's Search for Beauty, Man's Relationship with the Natural World, Man and Society, and Man's Relation to God.[10]

Particularly popular in such thematic courses is the idea of "Freedom," which can be traced through many theories and practices, starting with the Greeks, the Renaissance, the eighteenth century—or wherever —showing some of the variations in interpretation that philosophers, religious prophets or reformers, political rebels and revolutionaries, pamphleteers and journalists, among others, have made with respect to this richly ambiguous concept. Another idea that is popular in such a treatment is "Nature," which admits of a display of the spectrum among artists from naive realism to abstract expressionism and even more puristic theories.

A currently developing project in England concentrates upon such themes as "War and Society," "Education," and "Love." Instead of developing a consecutive historical account for all pupils to follow, packets of suggestive material, pictures, films, leaflets, book lists, and records, are gathered to serve as a starting place for the development of individual or small group student projects, as they explore some of the ramifications of one or another of these big ideas.[11]

Focus and fringe.   Broadly educated teachers have typically always taught their own field broadly. The good physics teacher often manages to give his students a feel for mathematics and aspects of chemistry and biology that may bring new illumination to these other subjects. The teacher of physical education is often in a favorable position for teaching physiology, nutrition, and various ethical concepts that get summarized under "fair play" and "group spirit." But no teacher is better situated to use his specialization as a take-off point for excursions into other subjects than the teacher of a humanistic subject.[12]

The teacher of literature can hardly help but be involved in the subjects which literature itself touches upon—which is every subject. Yet, this is not to say that some teachers do not adroitly manage to be narrowly formalistic in their literary teaching, avoiding wherever possible the human, dramatic content of the writing to concentrate on structures, styles, techniques and purely literary background. But the opportunity is there continually to show the relationships between poetry and music, verbal description and portrait or landscape painting, and history seen fictionally and discursively. Such writers as Cicero, Montaigne, Hume, Nietzsche, and Unamuno test the distinctions between philosopher, historian, and man of letters. The problems which the protagonists of drama face, not less in the comic than in the tragic genre, are inescapably philosophical and, more particularly, ethical in nature. Much of the world's great poetry is devotional and in other ways religious in character. Indeed, probably no teacher in the school has more frequent opportunity to relate his discipline to others than does the teacher of literature.

The music teacher works in a medium which from the time of Pythagoras has been recognized as mathematically ordered, and it has also obvious relationships to physics and engineering acoustics. The joining of music and verse for song affords an obvious linkage of the arts that is yet altogether too seldom explored from both the literary and musical viewpoints in close conjunction. The complex art form of opera, as well as other kinds of theater involving music, show the fusion of dance and scene painting and stage architecture with verbal and musical components. The rich relationships music bears to social forms and practices and to every aspect of human nature indicate that there is no end to the paths one may take starting from a musical center. Once again the teacher of the visual arts has the opportunity—and increasingly many would say the obligation—to show painting and sculpture as not by any means isolated from the other arts, from history, philosophy, and religion, or indeed from the sciences—one thinks of the mathematics of perspective, of optics, of the psychology of perception, etc. Rather art should be presented as having exceedingly numerous connections with ideas and feelings and events beyond its immediate borders.

Fortunately, many of the new textbooks in literature, music, and the visual arts reflect the growing recognition of the humanistic setting of each of the arts. It is the rare book in the history of music, for instance, that does not now contain reproductions of paintings and statues and buildings that relate to musical achievements.

Increasingly popular are courses at the high school level with theater at the focus; since theater itself often involves music, dance, and stage and costume design, in addition to drama, it rather easily becomes integrative.

And, after a long struggle to become respectable, film is at last coming into its own as a humanistic subject. Although many of the film courses that are springing up on every hand do not yet go beyond showing and discussing the films themselves—now, often, with some attempt at *making* films too—this art form is particularly rich in the opportunities it affords to explore virtually every aspect of human lives and values. It has been pointed out that the typical college freshman has seen twenty movies for every novel he has read and has spent more time watching television than he has going to school.[13] The motivation is unsurpassable!

Administratively, there is one obvious advantage to achieving a measure of integration by keeping one or more of the arts at the focus. The regular teacher, though he might feel insecure faced with the task of giving equal attention to several arts, can normally equip himself, to the extent that he is not already well prepared, to relate his specialization to other humanistic subjects, perhaps calling in colleagues for an occasional presentation, something very much more easily managed than a team-teaching arrangement.

The aesthetic mode of integration.   One way of integrating philosophy, literature, music, art, film, dance, architecture and other arts is by a concentration on certain principles or issues taken from the study of aesthetics.

For instance, this can be done historically. That is, one can, starting (inevitably) with Plato and Aristotle, march down through the centuries, discovering the different ways in which beauty and the arts have been viewed. It is interesting, for example, that the Greeks had no word or phrase quite corresponding to our "fine arts"; that there have been long stretches in which many people shared the belief that high mountains are ugly, a kind of blight on the landscape; that Thomas Jefferson listed landscape gardening as being on a par with painting, music, poetry, sculpture, and architecture; and so on. It is interesting too—though this may be *more* historical than philosophical—to speculate about why some peoples have been much more productive in certain arts and much less so in others, or productive only at certain stages. Where were the German painters to match Beethoven, Schubert, and Brahms, say? Why has English music been so relatively inferior to the standards set in poetry by Chaucer, Shakespeare, and Milton? Where is the Russian visual art to set alongside the productions of its great novelists and composers? In the Renaissance many of the very finest of the world's painters were Italian, but which nineteenth century Italian painters are to be compared with Cezanne or Van Gogh? Perhaps these discrepancies have something to do with the way the arts, in general or separately, are regarded in different times and places. Still again, consider the differing status of the artist in different times and places, including the area of freedom or constraint within which he has worked.

Or, proceeding more analytically (as distinct from historically), a teacher could interestingly engage high school students in questions about taste, and its reputed indisputability; or about the moral dimensions, if any, of art; or about such artistic "roles" as creator, performer, critic/interpreter, audience; or about problems like that raised in Chapter 5 above, as to similarities and differences among the arts and humanities, on the one hand, and the sciences and technologies, on the other.

But, for purely illustrative purposes, let us briefly follow another sort of approach from the point of view of philosophical aesthetics. Suppose the question be raised as to wherein the several arts are similar and wherein dissimilar. We *call* both music and painting arts, but what do they have in common? Are there elements that all of the arts share? Are there respects in which the arts tend to group, say, architecture with music, and dance with film?

All the arts have a physical basis. Unheard music, Keats said, is even sweeter than heard; perhaps, but is it music? His own poem exists as marks and sounds, which constitute its possibility for continuing existence.

Suppose the question be put, What in the case of each of the arts does the artist *start* with. If such answers as "with an idea," or, "with an image," or "an intent," or "an inspiration"—then the initial question has to be sharpened. No, consider the artist as—whatever else he be—a craftsman, one who with greater or lesser skill modifies some aspect of the environment. Now, put the question: What, in the case of each *kind* of art, does the artist start with as material, as matter, as stuff. Or, if he is thought of as imposing order or form, *on* what does he set to work?

The easiest case, perhaps, is that of sculpture, which has the most obviously palpable reality. Think of the smocked teacher handing a seven-year-old a piece of clay. The challenge, voiced or tacit, is: make something. Do something with it. The clay, in his or far more skilled hands, is, to start with, unformed. Not really, some literalist reminds us. What, after all, would it be like to have a piece of clay, or anything else, that had *no* form? Well, then, no particular form. Its form is accidental, and almost totally uninteresting. It represents—and this was Aristotle's definition of matter—potentiality, not achievement. It is something to be done with. Yet, here again, an objection occurs: it has been prepared, dampened, for instance, to be made more malleable, or dried if it was too wet to mold. Perhaps some impurities were removed. Potentiality is never unlimited. The blob of clay represents certain possibilities—more to the skilled craftsman than to the novice—but not an infinite number. You cannot make a poem of it, or a sun, or a limeade.

If the clay (or a block of marble or wood, etc.) is the sculptor's material, what is the painter's? Here we have to think of both a surface and some sort of pigments. But the problem thickens somewhat when it is asked what is the poet's or story teller's material, or the composer's. Still again, what of the choreographer? Joyce Cary, who was normally exceedingly sensitive to the problems of all sorts of artists, once said that whereas the painter dealt in colors and lines and the musician in tones, the literary artist dealt in emotions. It is an odd kind of error. Did he mean that other artists do not traffic in emotions? Or, equally absurdly, that the poet has no material starting place, nothing on which to operate, no relatively unformed stuff to mold and shape?

Yet is is hard to say exactly what the material basis of the poem or story is. In one way of thinking, it is sounds. But this answer is at a high level of abstraction. It links the composer and the poet, for instance; just as an analogous assertion that the painter deals in sights, in visible matter, fits the case of the sculptor and architect (et al.) too. One way of becoming a little more concrete is to specify that the sounds in which the poet deals are those that are made by human voices. Yet, such an answer is incomplete, for at least two reasons: for one thing, a string of nonsense syllables is an odd kind of poem, or perhaps we will not want to call it a poem at all, however rhythmic, funny, or ominous-sounding ("Jabberwocky"); besides, a poem may exist in print, as well as in sound. (One may not think it proper that poems be read silently, but they are, all the same, and do not stop being poems thereby.) Shall we say that *words* are the material of the literary artist, realizing that words are sometimes marks, sometimes sounds? But words are an abstraction from language, which includes syntax and not merely a vocabulary. If one thinks of there being several kinds of language, mathematical, musical, etc. (some people speak of "body-language"), then it will be necessary to say something like, "verbal language."

Now, to what extent is music an analogous case with literature? One may be tempted to narrow down sounds to tones; but that would be too narrow, for this would then exclude certain sounds that do not have pitch, such as taps made by a snare drum or the clash of cymbals. Also, should one not specify silences, as well as sounds?

What does the choreographer start with? Human bodies, their stances and movements? Notice, that in the case of dance and music, the basis for permanence, the notation, has a very different relationship with the ultimate aesthetic experience than does the painting, statue, or building. For most of us, anyway, the musical notes are directions for performance, and it is the performance that affords us whatever pleasure we take in music.

"Form" is a concept no less tricky than "material." In its broadest sense, it stands for all the characteristics a given bit of matter has or is given. That is, if materiality is equivalent to potentiality, form is equivalent to realization or achievement. Middle A, as a note, is formed when it is played by a harpsichord, but formed differently when sung by a male voice. But normally, we look at more complicated forms such as "A" having taken its part in a tonic chord, or better still, being included in a tune, or a section of symphony.

Given a very commodious meaning, "form" may refer to everything an art work represents, says, means; but more commonly a distinction is made between form and content, where form refers to structure, shape, arrangement. In this meaning, form usually admits of some sort of schematization. For instance, a teacher may wish to concentrate attention on the "composition" within a painting, by sketching on the board the distribution of the main masses, now independent of color or representation. Or the arrangement of musical "ideas" may be indicated by some such scheme as: A-B-A-C-A-D-A. The successes and failures of a character in a novel, may be plotted on a graph, or a plot shown to have the form of an hour glass. The distribution of figures on a stage may be indicated by "blocking" diagrams, and letters may show the rhyme scheme of a poem.

The word "content" suggests a rather curious metaphor, with the form being the container, and something else the contained. But what? Meaning, perhaps. But such a metaphor may be—indeed, often is— seriously misleading. It strongly suggests that what the artist does is to *have* an idea (truth, insight, theory, explanation, etc.) and *then* he casts about for a form in which to enclose it. As if to say, I have this stew, but what will I serve it in? Or, now that I've bought the present, what shall I wrap it in for safe delivery? Perhaps not just safe, either, but attractive. The container, the form, ought not to disgrace, ought if possible even to enhance, what it carries. Or take a practical problem like providing shelter from wind and rain: if the house is good-looking to boot, that's a bonus.

Such a way of thinking more or less fits everyday conversational needs, in which what one has to say can be said in half a dozen different ways, indifferently; and in which occasionally, one may be stopped by this problem: I know what I want to say, but I can't think how to put it. In the latter instance, container and contained are still pretty distinct. But jump to the case of music. One can easily imagine a composer who has been given a "program" or an opera libretto and been agitated by the necessity of writing music to "fit." One can even imagine an untrained person thinking of a tune and not knowing how to notate it. But what kind of sense would it make for someone to say, "I have this wonderful tune running through my head, but I can't think how to express it musically." He doesn't mean *orchestrate,* or *harmonize* or anything like that: he means to find a form for his content. Or rather he does not mean that because he can't.

This alleged inseparability of form and content in music is precisely what has appealed to so many aestheticians as the paradigm case. Perhaps it is unfair to try to get other arts into this same state of integration, but it is at least an instructive exercise.

So, let us *not* say form and content, but form and—some other sorts of things, not utterly opposed, but for some purposes separable, or anyway distinguishable. For instance, take a "formalist" position in painting, which we have already alluded to in another context.

The representative element in a work of (visual) art may or may not be harmful; always it is irrelevant.[14]

Or again:

To appreciate a work of art we need bring with us nothing but a sense of form and colour and a knowledge of three-dimensional space.[25]

This is a wonderfully controversial statement, one that infuriates some people, delights others, but just bewilders the many who think that paintings exist in order to portray, to represent "outside" reality. It is not at all hard to take an analogous position with respect to sculpture; even less hard with music. But what about literature? Well, it will be said (properly), the case is different. In literature, it is not so *much* a matter of representation, though there is plenty of descriptive poetry and prose. It is rather a matter of other sorts of meaning. Would a formalist in literature have to attend exclusively to the sounds of the words? Or the shape of the words and lines on a page, even? (There have been poems printed as diamonds and hour glasses, etc.) Or perhaps a formalist in literature would be one who would take the less outrageous position that it doesn't matter *what* a poem or a novel is about, or what the author's ideas are. It can be about woodchucks or God, trash heaps or Beatrice —and the worth of the work is not affected by *which.* Or, again, it can be said that the poet's ideas, as ideas, as propositions, are likely to be trivial, or anyway dubious, but still sublime in the way they are put.

What oft was thought
But ne'er so well expressed.

Or what if one raised the question as to what "formalism" might mean in the case of architecture. It is not that anyone wants a building to represent anything besides itself. (Or is that quite so? What about the banks that look like small Roman temples?) Yet consider an architect who proudly announced that he had created a structure that had no function whatsoever. This is not hard to imagine: think of Washington's monument. Or is that to be cited as sculpture, instead? Certainly there have been architects who insisted that leaky roofs have *nothing* to do with the merit of their achievement.

Another whole cluster of questions is suggested by the much-invoked norm, "uniqueness of the medium." Is "medium" the same as "material"? Is it the same as "message"? By what curious circumstance has "media" (a singular noun) come to refer to television, and to a minor degree to radio and film? Anyway, as relatively new media, television and film raise many questions about derivativeness and uniqueness. Take two extreme cases: (1) a straight filming of, say, a production of the Metropolitan Opera or the Royal Ballet at Covent Garden; (2) an entirely abstract animation. In the first case, the camera is being used simply as a means of conveying what would of course be better seen in person. In the second case, there is a creation of something that could exist in no other form. Does that make the latter somehow more "genuine," "authentic"—in short, a unique use of the medium? And anyway, how important is that? Or, for much less extreme cases, take the films of Fellini, Kadar, and Bergmann. In being from beginning to end created as films, are they preferable to the film version of a play like "Henry V" or a novel like *Women in Love?*

Film, dance, music, painting, sculpture, architecture, literature: these, we say, are arts. Why do we thus lump them together under such a heading? Wherein are they alike? It is always interesting to see whether or to what extent something said about one art applies to another. (Tragedy is a means of purging the spectator of certain emotions, for instance. The architectural motto: form follows function. "You should not create stainless steel flatware according to designs made for sterling." etc.) There will be likenesses and similarities. What about the alleged similarity of "the aesthetic experience"? Suppose an experience of watching a play, listening to music, or looking at a large painting: suppose them all to be equally rapt, intent, appreciative. Are they quite a lot alike?

The issues raised here, and many others as well, have of course been debated orally and in print for a very long time. They are not, needless to say, the kind of questions that admit of definitive, right-or-wrong answers. But they are to many persons both interesting in and of themselves and illuminating of aesthetic experiences. It is curious that it has long been assumed that whereas high school students are capable of thinking about the causes of World War I, or the expansion of gas when heated, or the death of Lady Macbeth, or the inequalities of educational opportunity, they absolutely must wait until college to ponder problems of aesthetics.

The popular arts.   The increasing emphasis upon the Youth Culture and upon the evils of ethnocentrism have led many teachers of humanistic subjects to call into question the sacrosanct status of Shakespeare, Mozart, Rembrandt, Michelangelo, Dickens, and the other giants in the history of Western Civilization. Perhaps it is futile or even vicious to insist that every child experience masterpieces that are in form and content distant from his own everyday experience. The ghetto child who simply tunes out when the class discusses (or anyway the teacher discusses) "Julius Caesar" may be rejecting such literature not only as irrelevant to his own life, but even as just another instance of the imposition upon him of the traditional culture of White Supremacy. The Mexican-American child may love to sing—but *not* German lieder. Indeed, "Hark, hark, the Lark" will probably seem just plain silly to a great many children who collect Beatle records, never miss an episode of "Mission Impossible" or an issue of *Mad* and are wrestling with what, if anything, to smoke, and with whom, if anyone, to begin sexual experimentation.

Aesthetic values are, after all, we are reminded, not exhausted by the "canon" of master works. If the child is really excited by a new protest singer and really bored by Purcell, why not start with where he is? If a young person is profoundly thrilled by "Easy Rider" and left cold by Ibsen's "Ghosts," why struggle to establish the "real" superiority of the accepted drama to the popular favorite?

Sophisticated professors of literature are now to be heard asking whether a child of the inner city might not learn more about humanistic values by being given a camera and some film, than from an anthology of poetry.

In short, we are witnessing today a massive attack upon the traditional denigration of popular arts, and a new attempt to take them seriously. Perhaps most teachers who are thinking along these lines hope for a gradual weaning away of their students from their present tastes, but some are as disillusioned as anybody else with traditional arts, traditional philosophy, traditional religion, and with history of any kind, and call for a massive reorganization of the humanities to concentrate upon the present, the near at hand, the "real," the popular. Here, they say, is a new opportunity for integration that may at last reach students where they live.

Here, as so often, dogmatism is hard to avoid. It is *not* essential to cater to students' present tastes to teach them effectively. There have been instances of young black men and women, out of the rural South, being plunged without special preparation into an undiluted Great Books program and set to reading Platonic Dialogues, Virgil's *Aeneid*, Harvey's *Circulation of the Blood*, Dostoevsky's "Notes from Underground," and William James' *Psychology;* becoming fascinated and entering avidly and perceptively in the discussions. Sometimes high school students to whom Mozart is no more than a distant and slightly unpleasant rumor can, through the offices of a skillful teacher, quickly delight in "The Marriage of Figaro." Yet, once a teacher has disabused himself of the notion that a student has to have become acquainted with a certain list of works and to have formed certified opinions (if not feelings) about them in order to be educated, he is at least ready to entertain the possibility of concentrating attention upon the present and even upon the presently popular.

"Popular" is, of course, another tricky concept. It has been said that " 'popular art' suggests easy availability and possibly a substantial permeation of everyday life."[16] Perhaps the single best beginning along these lines is, not to guess or assume, but to *find out* what sorts of art one's students *do* presently find easily available—including the sense of that term that means "intelligible"—and permeative of their everyday life. Notoriously, these sorts of interests tend to change rapidly. The examples that might be put down here could be obsolescent before the book should be printed, but it is certain that *some* music and *some* performers will at any given time be popular among many young people

—never, of course, *all*. It is certain, too, that there will always be very popular movies and television programs and ways of dancing. It is not at all certain that any poetry or prose fiction, any painting or sculpture, any philosophy or history will enjoy popularity, although the recent vogue of Rod McKuen, Zen and Yoga, and Peter Max-style painting must be taken into account. The sudden emergence of psychedelic posters, light shows, and supergraphics remind us, too, that it is risky to discount the exceptionally novel.

But whatever it is that *is* popular among the students of a certain class, it is a fairly safe bet that even the most enthusiastic devotees will not have gone far in analysis and understanding of their favorites. Of course the teacher may well feel somewhat beyond his depth in this area too, but often the combination of his conceptual tools and the intuitive grasp of his students will be equal to the challenge.

Some of the most interesting questions about the whole phenomenon of popularity should themselves prove fruitful for class discussion. For instance, in our time and part of the world, what *are* people's main interests? In 1966 a cross section of adult Americans were asked by Roper interviewers to name subjects in which they had "a good deal of interest." Perhaps the most interesting result was that there was *no* subject that was named by half of the respondents! Religion had 49%, sports 47%, and music 46%. A little over a third were interested in cooking. History, science, and literature were bunched at right around 1/5th, and 13% claimed to be interested in art. Of these same respondents more had fewer than 25 books in their homes than had more than 100. The college-educated had more interests and a slightly different order of list, but the pollsters said that even of this elite group only 10% could be called "culturally active."[17] What now if the question is put about teenagers, or some other age group? Some classes might like to make a survey, or in other ways play sociologists.

Again, suppose the question were raised about what if anything strobe lights have in common with rock music, or more generally why there are groupings in popularity of kinds of art and other activities? Many classes would gleefully respond to this recent definition of "pop": "popular, transient, expendable, low cost, mass-produced, young, witty, sexy, gimmicky, glamorous, and last, but not least, Big Business."[18] Is this another adult "put down"? But that very question and the suspicion that lingers behind it suggest a particular reason why it is often especially hard just now to get students even to entertain the possibility that they might like the philosophy, art, and letters of other times and other places, and therefore created by persons who are, at least now, *very* old.

At the secondary level, anyway, there is by now no shortage of models for both small and large integrations of the humanities,[19] though in the providing of "packages" of material (books, slides, films, tapes, records, etc.), in detailed syllabi, in teachers' manuals, we lag far behind the natural science curriculum projects. But since humanists are notoriously (and sometimes perversely) individualistic, there will long remain a certain fondness for making a fresh start. And indeed, why not, if only one has the time and energy—and the right colleagues? "Curriculum making" has to the outsider, doubtless, a certain dull sort of sound, but provided that one sees the curriculum as a proper way of promoting more effective teaching and learning, the challenge is unsurpassed and the promise of educational reward very great indeed.

12

Humanistic Learning

The bafflingly broad and vague word "humanities" and its cognates and derivatives were dealt with in Chapter 6 by trying to show certain family resemblances among humanistic approaches to characteristically "humanistic" objects. Besides approaches and objects, we spoke also of *effects,* intended and actual, of "humanistic" experiences.

If education means change—and it makes no sense to say that one has at the same time been educated and stayed the same—then the educator is required to ask what changes he and his fellow learners seek in behavior or (if that word is too closely bound up with "behaviorism") in human functions, ranging from the gross and overt to the subtle, secret, and evanescent, and for all the manifold reasons and causes that poets and painters not less than psychologists and sociologists show. Or, in order to focus attention now upon traits and characteristics of human beings, and not just their accidental acts, let us say, *dispositions.* Our concern as educators, then, is with effecting certain changes in (yes, our own but also our) students' dispositions to behave, respond, function, act —indeed, to *be.* Whether we are, at any given time, thinking of curriculum, materials, teaching, school organization, or any of the other more-or-less controllable variables, we need to ask what we are after, what are the ends to which these are paths. If then the delineation of the ends, the effects, does not start modifying the means, something has gone drastically wrong, and the process has to be started anew.[1]

But it is always hard to organize educational goals. Are there seven that are *cardinal?* Or forty-seven? Or one—as in the Educational Policies Commission's latest pronouncement on the subject.[2] The goals of humanistic education, similarly, can be made few or numerous. Here we will begin with two very large ones, and then list several others of somewhat smaller scope, without worrying much over the possible subsumptions and the actual overlaps.

PERSONAL KNOWLEDGE

There is no assumption more common than that education is about, and teaching and learning aim at, knowledge. Thus, in the successful case the pupil passes from a state of ignorance to a state of knowing. We will suggest presently that this way of thinking can tyrannize educational processes; for the present, we join in the universal praise of knowledge —but with the insistence that there are *kinds* of knowledge, all of them valuable. If the natural and (to a lesser extent) the social and behavioral sciences are devoted to impersonal knowledge, we hereby counter with the proposal that the knowledge most relevant to the humanities is personal, though this is not at all to suggest that there is not also, as we have continually noted, thinking and inquiry—and ultimately knowl- edge—of a scientific sort included in the humanistic disciplines. No, there is *objective* knowing in the humanities but there are also, to use Carl Rogers' trichotomy, *subjective* knowing and *interpersonal* know- ing.[3]

> We ask a person who attends a cocktail party how he feels, and he answers, "I feel fine; I feel very happy." Yet when we see him leave the cocktail party, he may suddenly look sad. . . . He may *feel* sad, bored, indifferent, but he *thinks* the feelings which are put into him by the situation. . . .[4]

In this passage Erich Fromm recognizes a truth often neglected and even explicitly denied: that one can be wrong, even profoundly wrong about his own feelings. The orthodox position goes like this: feelings are pri- vate, inside one, inaccessible to others except indirectly and by report. I may falsify my account of how I feel, but whatever it is I feel, I feel just that way. They are my feelings. So I am the court of last appeal on at least this one aspect of the entire world: my own feelings.

But, in opposition to this widespread opinion, Fromm's account rings true. One knows it best of all at first hand: "I thought I was having a good time, but now I recognize that I wasn't—not even then." "Little did I realize then how really happy I was." "I must have been furious, for I found out later that while he was talking I ripped my napkin into shreds."

It seems that we can be wrong about our own feelings, even (or perhaps especially?) about what we *want*. C. I. Lewis, one of the most perceptive philosophers of the twentieth century, went so far as to say, once:

> At least half of the world's avoidable troubles are created by those who do not know what they want and pursue what would not satisfy them if they had it.

Hence, knowing one's own feelings and wants, as well as knowing the feelings and wants of others, is an empirical enterprise, fraught, like all empirical inquiry, with hazards and uncertainties.

We will return to intra-subjective knowing, but let us look for a time at knowing others, not now as objects, but as other subjects. Carl Rogers thinks that we carry on all kinds of cognizing by means of hypotheses, even interpersonal or phenomenological knowledge:

> Here I 'know' that you feel hurt by my remark or that you despise yourself or that you have a strong desire to get 'to the top of the heap' or that you believe the Republican Party to be an excellent organization or that you are concerned about thermonuclear war. These knowings, like those described before, are all hypotheses. But in these instances, the way of checking these hypotheses is to use whatever skill and empathic understanding is at my command to get at the relevant aspect of your phenomenological field, to get inside your private world of meanings, and see whether my understanding is correct. I may simply ask you bluntly if my hypothesis is correct, but this is often a very inadequate method of inferring your private world. I may observe your gestures, words, and inflections and base my inferences on these. Or I may—and here is the essence of my experience in psychotherapy—create a climate which makes it psychologically safe and rewarding for you to reveal your internal frame of reference.[6]

Rogers says further about subjective knowing:

> I may 'know' that I love or hate, sense, perceive, comprehend. I may believe or disbelieve, enjoy or dislike, be interested in or bored by. These are all hypotheses, which we often check ... by using the ongoing flow of our preconceptual experiencing as a referent. So I may check my hypothesis by asking, 'Do I really hate him?' As I refer to my experiencing I realize that it is envy rather than hate which I feel. ...[7]

There are ways in which a person can develop his capacity to bring parts of himself out into the open through humanistic creation, and ways too in which we can learn more about others by more intimately relating their achievements with the self responsible for those achievements. The present point is nearly related, yet different; now it is a matter of clarifying, understanding, even coming to admit, ownership of our own feelings, so that some provisional hypothetical formulations of those feelings do not rest as self-evident, inscrutable truths, but are testable, checkable, validatable. (Possibly the word "verifiable" should be reserved for more scientific hypotheses, "objective" knowing.) What Rogers is mainly talking about, of course, is the therapeutic, and perhaps to some extent the teaching, situation. But it strikes us that much of what he says has especially close bearing on humanistic products and experiences, for here too we have a kind of psychological protection that many of us seem to require for the exploration of these exceedingly intimate aspects of ourselves. That is, about very much humanistic experience, there exists the "as if" flavor, the sense that to dwell inside this work is, in some important way, to dwell inside the imagination. Even in the most realistically representative painting, novel, or statue, "reality" is *re*presented not presented. The spectator of even the most pitiable scene on stage or screen knows that he is not present in somebody's living room or on the street corner. He can therefore invest his feelings with a certain impunity denied him in his confrontations with real persons directly. For some persons, weak in their imaginative powers, this very fact makes of the fictional world of art something too insipid to bother about. For others, too insecure about their own emotional adjustment to risk even an imaginative flight into certain threatening territory, only certain kinds of light-hearted or highly-distanced art can afford pleasure. But most persons, especially if their education has helped them in this respect (and this respect has remarkably little to do with the usual indices of educational *achievement*) are able to embark upon the seas of art to explore hitherto obscure sides of human nature—including themselves. From looking at an Hellenic statue of Apollo they can know something about what confident and powerful serenity is like[8]; from a rollicking German student song, they can participate in a side of life they may know little about at first hand; from Plato's "Symposium," they may experience a conjoining of intellectuality and revelry that is novel; from Solzhenitsyn, they may participate in a dogged persistence to survive under conditions that make life very nearly insupportable. All this is not simply the addition of a quantum of raw experience: it is, rather, an extension of one's sympathetic and empathic grasp of "what it is like. . . ." Everybody knows something of the ego-gratifications that come from identification with a hero; but we have it in us to be Iago and Fagin and Babbitt and Willy Loman as well, so that from *these* somewhat reluctant identifications, we can know something about the shadow sides of our own and of others' beings.

Unamuno put it well:

> The fact is, every human being has within him the seven cardinal virtues and their corresponding mortal sins: he is humble and he is proud; he is sober and he is gluttonous; and he is chaste and licentious, charitable and envious, generous and stingy, diligent and lazy, long-suffering and quick to wrath.[9]

He also said: ". . . One enjoys a work of art because one creates it in oneself, recreates it, and recreates oneself in so doing."[10]

But in saying "work of art" the philosopher (and writer of fiction) Unamuno is surely speaking for much of philosophy too: indeed it is likely that he would not want to draw too fine a line between these fields; and this, if we remember that some but not all philosophy has many of our humanistic qualities, suits us very well too.

We have spoken, then, of knowledge—particularly personal, subjective knowledge. But at this point it is well to remember that the effect we are mainly after is not a *body* of knowledge, but a *disposition to know,* which involves a disposition to intuit, to think, to carry on thought-experiments, to ponder, to wonder, to imagine, to inquire, and much else. Above all, the aim is to develop a wide-ranging, a *versatile* knower, and would-be knower.

FEELING

Deliberately contrary to the common assumption that knowing and feeling constitute a natural, even cosmic, dichotomy, we have continually emphasized their interpenetration, indeed their final inseparability. Furthermore in the section immediately above, we have seen that when knowing becomes personal, it necessarily has to do with those feelings that make persons persons.

Of course for some purposes one can legitimately speak now of knowing, now of feeling, and it is time now to say something, however brief, about that intended effect of humanistic learning which is the enrichment of our affective life.

However much fuzzy thinking is in evidence about "education of the emotions," it must be put down to the credit of educational thought —and to some extent educational practice, also—in recent years that people are beginning to assume that the schools are legitimately and even importantly charged with a responsibility for the sensitizing and development of pupils' feelings. Intellection and reasoning are not and should not be the whole of life.

One recent commentator has spoken of humanists as "People delegated to articulate and service an ecology of survival values." He goes on to show how a work of art or other humanistic product can point the way toward the limitations of reason as a guide to life:

> For years I thought the stress in Lear's great, "Oh reason not the need," fell on "need." It falls rather on the outrage of "reason" presuming to measure human needs. The humanist's function is to *imagine* needs when these have been lost to self-bedazzling reason.[11]

Unfortunately, though, students often acquire early and abandon late, if ever, a strong prejudice against either betraying—the word is pejoratively significant—or expressing their feelings. The distinction between thinking and feeling is invidious, for many of the educative forces with which they are surrounded urge them to replace emotional by rational responses. The person, for instance, who becomes angry or highly incensed, who perhaps waves his arms around, rises out of his seat and paces the floor, lets his voice rise in pitch and get louder, all in the course of a discussion, may be told that his behavior is unseemly, and cautioned toward greater decorum. He is given to think that becoming educated consists largely in controlling the emotions, in not letting his feelings "run away with him," or get in the way of his thoughtfulness. Less so today than in former times, no doubt, but it appears still widely the case that the quiet child, the undemonstrative child, the child who has gained close control of his feelings except upon carefully regulated occasions (as spectators, though not players, at a basketball game, etc.) is the one who gains the approbation of his elders. It may well be that this kind of education—or should one say "conditioning"?—is responsible for putting many persons out of touch with their own emotions through some sort of process of repression. In this process, they become negatively responsive to the emotional expression of others, and (therefore?) are inclined to be relatively undiscriminating with respect to emotions, and even upon occasion "sloppy," and "sentimental," or "cold" and "unfeeling."

It has often been remarked that we learn to look at nature differently from having experienced landscapes through the eyes of painters. But artists are the educators of our emotional feelings as well as of our sensory feelings. D. H. Lawrence once said, "My field is to know the feelings inside a man, and to make new feelings conscious. What really torments civilized people is that they are full of feelings they know nothing about: they can't realize them, they can't fulfill them, they can't live them. And so they are tortured."[12] Such a statement may suggest to some people—what their own education has prepared them to believe as being desirable—that feelings should somehow be gotten rid of by being made conscious, much as Freud advocated bringing the contents of the consciousness up into the light of day. But this is quite contrary to Lawrence's (or our) point. He sees the novel (which he was particularly discussing, but art generally too) as opening up the life of feelings, making for a richer emotional life, than we normally attain without such help. And this enlightenment continues not only while we are reading, but thereafter *because* we have read.

Yet the point is not just to *have* feelings, or to have *more* feelings (as if they came in bushels or gallons), but to have feelings that are consonant with, harmonious with, of a piece with, the larger occasion. In this context, "occasion" now is intended to have both external components, such as the objects or events we respond to, and internal components, the other parts of our psychic life, such as thoughts and ideas and moods and attitudes. Take, for instance, "genuineness" as a characteristic of feelings. Lawrence (again to follow his lead) believed that it is possible, indeed common, to "fake feelings," to palm off on oneself feelings heard about, easily recognized, and named externally, but never really *had*. In fact, this is his definition of "sentimentality": to pretend to feel what one doesn't really feel. The great advantage of faked feelings is that they do not really upset one, and can be turned off upon demand.

Properly understood, feelings are not the opposites of or antithetical to thoughtfulness, except insofar as, from the influence of the rigorous sciences, thoughtfulness has come to be *defined* as cognitive activity stripped (by a cool kind of violence) of its feeling quality. Every perception, for instance, has its own feeling quality.[13] We tend to know something about the objects and occurrences of our on-going life by noticing how we feel about them. Particularly is this true of the persons with whom we relate: what would it be like to be able to say, "I know him very well, but I have absolutely no feeling about him one way or the other"? Oh, if we are being cautious, we say, regarding some characterization of another, "Anyway, that's how I feel about him" or we confess that we are "prejudiced" or we identify our response as "subjective," and of course we do know that our feelings change, and so must not be regarded as infallible indicators of an objective state of affairs. Still, to try to know someone by inhibiting our feeling response to him would be much like coming to know a painting by keeping our eyes shut.

G. H. Bantock has said:

> We are always being told that the function of our education is to make children think. . . . It is equally necessary to teach children how to feel; for some such feelings are as important a way of taking the world, as apprehensive of aspects of reality, as are our cognitions. In this sense at least they can become ethically desirable.[14]

But from a humanist's point of view, philosophers and historians have altogether too often themselves inhibited their feeling responses in accordance with a lofty rational ideal that takes mathematics and the natural sciences as models; so we return to the artist-as-educator, who may help us know in ourselves that "fear" or "joy" is as crude a classification as "red" or "loud." The fear response to a voice when one thought himself alone is apt to be very different from the fear response to the doctor's scalpel or to the yet unopened but dreaded letter. The artist helps us in very much finer discriminations than these rough-and-ready examples indicate.

But he helps us extend our emotional life, too, beyond what may be the relatively narrow confines of our direct workaday experience. Today the word "exciting" is hugely overused as an adjective of praise, but its very prevalence suggests our need for excitement. Almost anyone can be excited by a flourish of trumpets and a roll of drums, or by a realistic battle scene filmed, but one of the immense gains from a cultivation of our aesthetic responses comes from being excitable by a subtle modulation, by a seemingly small but significant change of behavior in a character on the stage, by the placement of a gargoyle on a cathedral ledge. The exact transfer of such sensitivity to nonaesthetic, or anyway nonartistic, situations is a matter still somewhat mysterious, but we hope and believe it is not slight.

Nobody has made this point as well as the philosopher, C. J. Ducasse, who argued that it is an essential "part of the education of a complete man" to develop the capacity to distinguish exceedingly subtle and delicate nuances of feeling.

> ... However greatly we admire a man's moral character and his intellectual attainments we perceive an unmistakable lack in him if he does not also possess taste and delicacy of sentiment. A man is not fully human if he is undeveloped in the feeling-dimension of his being.[15]

Having dealt, even though sketchily—considering the immensity of the topics—with personal knowledge and feeling, we may pause before going on to somewhat less commodious categories of the desired effects of humanistic teaching/learning to relate these ends to the "approaches" previous listed. These we called the appreciative, the empathic, the *person*al, the imaginative, and the inclusively relating. We will make direct links between the imaginative and corresponding effects. The "inclusively relating" we will link up in the next chapter with the effect of integration. But the *person*al, empathic, and appreciating apply to two or more of our effects, so that we will not essay to make a point-for-point relation between the two lists.

Our next aim, goal, or intended effect is:

SENSIBILITY

This characteristic (as we noted before) has been defined as "capacity to feel . . . ; exceptional openness to emotional impressions . . . ; delicacy of feeling. . . ."[16]

One way of understanding the meaning of this heavily-charged word is through thinking of what an excess of this characteristic would consist in. Physiologically, one's skin may at times become overly sensitive, so that even the smallest touch will be intolerable. More generally, one may be "thin-skinned," excessively open to the slings and arrows of even everyday fortune, too readily put upon, so responsive to pleas for sympathy that emotional exhaustion is quick and inevitable. The word "hyperaesthesia" for such a state affords an illuminating link back to normal and desirable aesthetic sensitivity.

Surely excess in this direction is very uncommon; but altogether too usual, at least in Anglo-American culture, is "hypoaesthesia," deficiency in emotional responsiveness, dullness toward affect. Even commoner is a selective deficiency in sensibility. A great many persons have developed to the point where they respond sensitively to auditory but not visual stimuli, or the other way around; to the expressions of children but not of old people; to near-to-home but not distant tragedy; to up-to-date events, but not the long ago—or in some other ways develop calluses or blind-spots; or perhaps better say *fail* to develop certain capacities that do not just (somehow) "naturally" emerge.

Yet this account too may be misleading for seeming to suggest that one either has or lacks a certain sort of sensibility; or that sensibility is a kind of responsiveness that can be measured in ergs or watts. The sensibility that can be considered humanistic is one that is discriminating, that represents a subtly precise response to the uniqueness of an occasion or an object. In this respect the gross classifications represented by the names of "the emotions" mislead us. *Joy, jealousy, anger, pity.* Perhaps Rose is a rose is a rose, but pity is not pity is not pity. Something of the same point is made negatively by such a word as "schmaltz," (literally "rendered fat") to signify sentimentality, gushy emotionality— which of course in turn suggests turning a spigot, or getting an *automatic* response to a manipulative stimulus.

But the painter is precisely the person who knows that one stroke, one additional dot of color can change the entire emotional quality of a canvas. The highly-trained musical ear is very disturbed by a transposition from one key to another. The poet knows that there are no real synonyms: every word has a different feel and therefore a different meaning. The philosopher worth his salt knows that there are subtle but important differences between two ethical theories that the unwary would call identical: in being different, they signify different ways of life. The historian of sensibility responds to and reflects the *quality* of life led by a black slave in the Mississippi delta, rejecting crudely stereotyped accounts. And the person knowledgeable about religion understands differences in ritual or in creed that the less expert would dismiss as unimportant.

But more important still, that person who has penetrated beyond the kind of sensitivity directly associated with his own discipline or art to an "integrated, humanistic outlook" will have, by definition, achieved a wider-ranging sensibility.

EXPRESSIVENESS

In this section, we consider the effects of increasing self-expressiveness and of developing an awareness of expressiveness in others.[17] Historians have sometimes insisted that their job is simply to "tell what happened," to rise above the biases of nation, religion, region, race, even of temperament and personal values, and to look at the past with an unclouded, beady eye. "All right, so this is, strictly speaking, an ideal impossible to realize," they might admit; "nevertheless, it *is* the ideal, and the closer one approximates to it, the better." Other historians have likened themselves more to the artist, who usually has less hesitation in admitting that there is something of himself in all his creations.

Perhaps there really are historians and philosophers so objective, so self-effacing, that in reading their works our attention is riveted entirely on what they are talking about. But there are other philosophers, like William James, and other historians, like Gibbon, who are always visible in their own pages. It is not that they are literally talking about themselves, of course, but that they are personal, rather than impersonal in their creations. In reading them, as in reading Goethe or Ibsen, or in seeing an El Greco or hearing something of Haydn, it is impossible not to be aware of him who is speaking. No, this is an exaggeration. Better say: it is impossible, once one has learned this way of responding. There are many forces in the school environment militating against this sort of sense of the personal, this responsiveness to expression. Pupils are constantly being trained—one almost wants to say programed—to be objective, to get rid of the personal factors; it is interesting that "ad hominem" is the name of a logical fallacy. Consequently, many students have to learn (or relearn) to acknowledge and take pleasure in this humanistic sense of person-to-person communication, often over the gap of centuries.

It may even be taken as a defining characteristic of humanistic works, that they are inescapably personal, that they are not just recordings of facts. They are the gestures made by human beings who have something in them, something *of* them, that requires manifestation, annunciation. And it is precisely this about them that accounts for a significant amount of their value. This is not to say that we have to know, from independent sources, something about the lives of the creators; but rather that we do know something about their lives *from* their creations. Some students need help in learning to enjoy this expressiveness, very much as they may have to get over their inhibition about moving their lips when they read poetry.

They may require even more help, and it is more likely that a given student will need help, in developing his own capacity for self-expressiveness. Contrary to some belief, this skill is not developed simply by engaging in artistic exercise—although some are helped—by such activity. One can scribble poetry or drawings until kingdom come without advancing a jot toward expressiveness. Indeed, there seem to be ways of protecting oneself, of keeping oneself back, by such "outlets." Genuine creativity always entails a certain threat because it means an opening of oneself, without quite being able to predict the outcome. In this way it is like love. Once again this brings to mind Keats' conception of "negative capability," of "being capable of being in uncertainties, mysteries, doubts, without any irritable reaching after fact and reason."

A FULLER RESPONSIVENESS TO SYMBOLS

Of course, anything that serves as an expression of a feeling, a mood, an insight, a state of being, for someone, may in turn serve as a symbol to someone else, through which he gets back to the person whose need for expression was the inception of the creative act. Yet, in another way, the created object as symbol refers outwardly, to the world, to mankind. To fail to see so is to be caught in a kind of psychologizing trap. The point can be illustrated from the use that is often made by therapists of children's drawings: they are taken as symptoms of the child's self-image, his fears and hopes, his attitudes toward his parents and siblings, and the like. Similarly, "Hamlet," the "Mona Lisa," and *Huckleberry Finn* have been used for the purpose of diagnosing the psychiatric problems of their creators. Such interpretation has a place, and a use, but it is very limited, and in many contexts it is patronizing, simply because it refuses to accept the artifact in the way it was intended. Furthermore, it reduces the criteria by which such creations are to be judged to this alone: how well does the work enable us to understand its creator? Some works inferior by every other standard may be exceptionally transparent in this way; and some of the greatest of humanistic products may yield us only a teasingly evanescent glimpse of its creator. Jung understood this point much better than did Freud, once saying, "What is essential in a work of art is that it should rise far above the realm of personal life and speak from the spirit and heart of the poet as man to the spirit and heart of mankind." Jung was especially insistent, too, as against some psychoanalytic critics that, "art is not a morbidity"—not, that is, best understood as a symptom of a disease. On the contrary, there tends to be about it that which transcends its own specificity and concreteness, so that in a sense it is about the great *recurrences* in the life of the race: birth, initiation, severance from parents, marriage, location, death.[18]

Some people become annoyed at the suggestion that works of art "mean more than they say," symbolize aspects of the world that somehow elude more straightforward signification. Perhaps they are reacting to a vague mystification cultus sometimes perpetrated by sophisticates; but sometimes, perhaps more often, they are misled by two common assumptions: that art is appropriately and properly simple, there to be enjoyed by anyone who inclines that way; and that, in the words of the early Wittgenstein, "Anything that can be said at all can be said clearly"[19]—that is, can be said in the mode cultivated by purely rational disciplines. But Jung warns against such reductiveness as itself betraying an unreasonable fear of superstition and metaphysics. "The poet," he says, "now and then catches sight of the figures that people the night-world—the spirits, demons and gods. He knows that a purposiveness out-reaching human ends is the life-giving secret for man; he has a presentiment of incomprehensible happenings in the pleroma. In short, he sees something of that psychic world that strikes terror into the savage and the barbarian."[20] But even if the artist's vision is less occult, he may manage by the richly-fused multiplicity of meanings in his symbol to convey that which could yield to no other vehicle. Once again we need to remember T. S. Eliot's formulation, which, though intended to describe John Donne and others of the Metaphysical school, perfectly describes his own work at its best; he speaks of how a poet amalgamates disparate experience. When an ordinary man

> falls in love, or reads Spinoza, and these two experiences have nothing to do with each other, or with the noise of the typewriter or the smell of cooking; in the mind of the poet these experiences are always forming new wholes.[21]

If such is the poet's (and, more generally, the humanistic creator's) talent with symbolic expression, of packing into a single symbol such a multiplicity of allusions, with their implied relations, then what is required of us who are confronted with such achievements is the capacity for unpacking them, for realizing their meaning. And once again there arises the necessity of learning to be aware of, to respond to, this sort of symbolism. A failure in this regard dooms one to settle for a much diminished universe.

IMPROVEMENT OF THE IMAGINATION

No human characteristic is harder for the humanist to deal with than literal-mindedness. Some persons find it hard, nearly impossible, to say, As if. . . . The historian for all his dedication to telling the truth about what happened cannot see the importance of actuality unless he is able to contrast it with contrary-to-fact possibilities. What if Caesar had not crossed the Rubicon? What if Cleopatra's nose had been a quarter of an inch longer? If Charlemagne had not lived, would the dark ages have stayed unlighted? What if, to take James Thurber's jocular example, Grant had been drunk at Appomattox (and surrendered his sword to Lee)?

The philosopher too must sometimes seriously entertain departures from actuality. Plato defended his Republic as a glimpse of an ideal, though unrealizable, state. Leibniz admitted that this is not necessarily the best imaginable, but only the best of all *possible,* worlds. Are there imaginable languages in which some conceptions would be ineffable? What if a demon interposed himself between us and our thoughts, making them come out all wrong—then would there be anything indubitable: Descartes' great question. "Philosophy, beginning in wonder, . . . is able to fancy everything different from what it is. It sees the familiar as if it were strange and the strange as if it were familiar."[22]

The religious thinker too, unless he be the most rigid dogmatist, will depend for the sensitivity of his interpretations on being able to imagine gods and devils, heavens and hells, damnations and salvations conceivably different from the arrangements of the actual universe; and he will have some empathy with those whose rites and beliefs differ from his own.

Marianne Moore in a fine poem speaks of poets as "literalists of the imagination," able to present for inspection, "imaginary gardens with real toads in them. . . ."[23] Surely she is right in suggesting how serious is the imagination of the creative artist, so that his creations may seem more, not less, real than the space-time continuum we literally inhabit.

Any creator, of course, is required to be imaginative, the chemist as much as the sculptor, the astronomer as much as the choreographer, for creation *is* a departure from the tried and true, an adventure, an imagining of novelty; and correspondingly, the understanding of a novel creation is reserved for the imaginative. For a long time Einstein *boggled* the imaginations of so many people that he was widely regarded as unintelligible, as before him the non-Euclidian geometers had seemed too. Freud with his talk about the unconscious went beyond the imaginations of many men, and was therefore thought to be talking balderdash. But in the humanities, imagination, whether for purposes of creation or for appreciation, tends to have great scope, to involve (as we have said repeatedly in other contexts) a relatively large portion of the self, exceeding the sheerly cognitive and involving affect, feeling, mood, vision.

But what is imagination? At its simplest, it is nothing more than the power to call up an image, to remember the look or taste of something and to hold that sensation in the mind, in the absence of the thing itself. But more important for our purposes is that about "imagination" which connotes a formative power, which cuts away from horses and men to the creation of centaurs and endows the gods with power over lightning, space, and mortality; that invents the sounds that Don Giovanni would utter when threatened by supernatural revenge and condemnation; that designs a habitation at Chartres able to inspire reverence in the irreverent. In the creative artist's imagination it is that which enables him to make an expression for his psychic state. Wallace Stevens called the imagination "the power of the mind over the possibilities of things. . . ."[24] but wrote even more tellingly about it when he had to imagine imagination poetically:

After the leaves have fallen, we return
To a plain sense of things. It is as if
We had come to an end of the imagination,
Inanimate in an inert savoir

It is difficult even to choose the adjective
For this blank cold, this sadness without cause.
The great structure has become a minor house.
No turban walks across the lessened floors.

The greenhouse never so badly needed paint.
The chimney is fifty years old and slants to one side.
A fantastic effort has failed, a repetition
Is a repetitiousness of men and flies.

Yet the absence of the imagination had
Itself to be imagined. The great pond,
The plain sense of it, without reflections, leaves,
Mud, water like dirty glass, expressing silence

Of a sort, silence of a rat come out to see,
The great pond and its waste of lilies, all this
Had to be imagined as an inevitable knowledge,
Required, as a necessity requires.[25]

That is, one way of imagining imagination is to imagine its temporary suspension, presumably the blank space which a creative artist will experience after a major effort or a period of inspiration. We note all the words for dullness and inaction: inanimate, inert, blank, cold, lessened, plain, silence; and inevitably we consider their opposites, the condition of flourishing movement, exotic costumes and struts, warmth, richness, novelty, lushness, animation, newness, color, tone, and greatness. The poignancy of the poem comes in the realization of how many whole lives may be characterized as inertly unimaginative, and how much of the lives of most of us.

Coleridge assigned the name "fancy" to the limited kind of imagination noted above, the mere combining of elements already given in memory, and reserved "imagination" for a larger meaning. The "primary imagination" he regarded as the unifying agency of the human being, that which enables us to perceive, to create, to exist. The secondary imagination is, he said, a kind of echo of the primary, but existing consciously. "It dissolves, diffuses, dissipates, in order to recreate; or where this process is rendered impossible, yet still at all events it struggles to idealize and to unify. It is essentially *vital,* even as all objects (as objects) are essentially fixed and dead."[26]

The emphasis upon the imagination as vital and as subjective, as identified with process in contradistinction to product, object, inertness, death, fixity, runs through many of those who have addressed themselves to the problem. There is an important lesson, here, for the teaching of the humanities. Too often, the study has focused upon products, art objects, and achievements as ends in themselves—there in all their *finished* state, to be analyzed, understood, admired, perhaps even revered, but with altogether little emphasis upon their power to stimulate and to vitalize the being of the students. Something has gone wrong with that education in the humanities that does not make students livelier, more free-wheeling, better capable of inventing, of—as someone described the act of creation—"thinking aside."

THE CULTIVATION OF PLAYFULNESS
AND SENSUOUSNESS

Here the sober reader may come to the end of his patience, especially if he happens to think how often humanists, especially in the universities, are portentous and pontifical—pretentious in every way but that which suggests a capacity to imagine things other than they are. Yet, the childlike quality of the artist has often enough been noticed and wondered about: not only his naïveté and credulousness, but his delight in play. Schiller said that man is completely human only when he is playing —that is, having put aside the compulsiveness that attends work and the performance of duty, he is a free spirit.

An important part of today's youth culture consists in the revolt against puritanical repressiveness, particularly the prevailing notion that there is something intrinsically good about doing that which is serious, competitive, high-pressured, and unpleasant—at least in the sense that one would not at all want to do it except for certain derivative values; and something necessarily bad about doing that which is humorous or light-hearted, sociable, easy-going, playful, nonstriving, and pleasant.[27] Norman O. Brown has won many followers among youth for his celebration of life, spontaneity, and joy, turning, as he does, Freudian psychoanalytic theory away from its traditional concentration on neurosis toward a cultivation of healthiness. He admits that Freud did not succeed in articulating a satisfactory theory of art, but that in his book on Wit, he comes close to one:

> Art as pleasure, art as play, art as the recovery of childhood, art as making conscious the unconscious, art as a mode of instinctual liberation, art as the fellowship of men struggling for instinctual

liberation—these ideas plainly fit into the system of psychoanaly-sis.[28]

He who thought that the only justification of aesthetic experience lay along these paths would be profoundly wrong, but so would he who neglected this fact. Perhaps every civilization through its inevitable mores, conventions, laws, and customary patterns of behavior has been seen as an enemy of the anarchic forces of men. At least in retrospect the Victorian Age has come to symbolize this kind of inhibition to a singular degree, but in our own time there is a far higher degree of awareness of this phenomenon, not alone as it existed in past ages, but of course very much in our own. That about art work which is anarchic, at least in the sense of encouraging fresh ways of perceiving and being while rebelling against stereotype, dogma, and rigid categories, is respon-sible for the deep suspicion with which puritans in all ages have looked upon both the producers and consumers of art objects.

The empirical evidence is not at this point clear about the effects of pornography upon behavior: some say that it encourages, others that it sublimates prurient conduct; but that it often gives some sort of outlet to lust, as well as to many other basal impulses is affirmed by art lovers and haters alike. But some have looked forward to a time when these aspects of art could be thought to show the way to a freer, less hemmed-in, and repressive society. The connection here with dreams and with play is clear, for in these three forms of activity, above all others, persons of all ages have a kind of license to indulge instinctual drives that in most contexts must be kept discreetly under wraps.

THE GAIN OF A MYTHOPOEIC SENSE

Of all the objectives this is the subtlest, most tenuous, most difficult, and perhaps most arguable. Still, it should not be avoided.

What is myth? The answers given to this question are numerous and conflicting. One meaning now popular is so utterly foreign to our present purposes that we will mention it in order to discard it: myth is a wide-spread misconception, a prevalent lie or mistake, as in "the myth of racial superiority" or "the myth of American invincibility." Another popular conception is one equally foreign to our purposes: that myths are prescientific explanations of the universe that are wholly and properly replaced by scientific accounts. Of course there is *something* in this, but he who believes it is the whole truth is precisely the one whose humanistic education is, in this respect, deficient.

Yet even among the closest students of myth and mythology there is no substantial agreement. Richard Chase says, "The word 'myth' means story: a myth is a tale, a narrative, or a poem; myth is literature and must be considered as an aesthetic creation of the human imagination."[29]

Gayley in large measure agrees, saying that myths are "stories of anonymous origin, prevalent among primitive peoples and by them accepted as true, concerning supernatural beings and events, or natural beings and events influenced by supernatural agencies. . . ."[30]

The anthropologist Malinowski, on the other hand, says:

> The myth in . . . its original living form, is not a mere tale told but a reality lived. It is not in the nature of an invention such as we read in our novels today, but living reality, believed to have occurred in primordial times, and to be influencing ever afterwards the world and the destinies of men.[31]

But whatever myth was for eighth century B.C. Ionians, fifteenth century Aztecs, eighteenth century Navajos, or twentieth century Australian bushmen, our question is: What can myth reasonably be—if anything—for us who live in a post-industrial, hypercivilized, mainly urban, highly literate society? The first question is, Why bother? The starting place for answering this question is simply that to a lot of us certain myths have an uncanny fascination. The adjective is chosen with care. Almost all children enjoy at some stage hearing the tales of Zeus and Prometheus and Orpheus. But for them the stories are precisely like Grimm's tales or the Fables of Aesop or even Peanuts and Popeye. (Not that there *aren't* some likenesses.) Yet, some of these same children—not all—will as adults return to those myths and ponder upon them, feeling anew their power. Meantime, of course, they will have deliteralized them. Now they will not believe, if they ever did, that Prometheus brought fire to man in a hollow reed or that thunder and lightning emanate from Zeus, and will of course know something about the psychological origins and functions of myths among those who gave them birth. But they will also, and this is the big point, detect that in some deep sense, the myths have not been superseded by creedal religions, science, philosophy, or even literature. It is very hard to say what this sense is.

One of the commonest occurrences in the Platonic dialogues is for Socrates, at the end of a long, arduous argumentation which has still not been quite conclusive or convincing about the nature of the universe or man's fate, to say, "But let me tell you a myth. . . ." Afterwards, he was wont to say, "Perhaps this is something like the truth." *Not* the truth, but having to do with it, glancingly suggestive of it. That is, a myth is a narrative account of supernatural (or proto-natural) events. It tends to have a certain timelessness about it, and to cut athwart many of our rational distinctions and categories.[32]

Particularly it confounds the distinction between fact and fiction, between a pragmatic, utilitarian conception of force or power and the primitive conception of *mana*. Richard Chase has written:

> Whatever has impersonal magic force or potency and is therefore extraordinarily beautiful, terrible, dangerous, awful, wonderful, uncanny or marvelous has *mana*. . . . In this sense myths do not show us what is *less* than ordinarily natural; they show us what is *more* than ordinarily natural.[33]

We agree with Philip Wheelwright about the importance of keeping alive *"the permanent possibility of genuinely mythic experience,"* which he says is possible only to those who can become as little children.

> Mana is a borderland idea, whose mode of existence lies between the personal and impersonal, between the natural and supernatural, and between the subjective and objective. . . . Primitive man . . . does *not* make the distinctions which appear logically and experientially axiomatic to us moderns.[34]

At least part of what myth conveys is a sense of a universe larger than man and his immediate experiences, of powers exercised from afar. Whatever be his cries of bravado, that he is master of his fate and captain of his soul, men have always come back to the realization of their own limitations and ultimate helplessness. Now, this realization may be simply overwhelming, and may suggest that we are pawns of absolutely ineffable, transcendent forces. But myth seems always to suggest through its narrative that supernature too can be somehow comprehended, taken in. Not explained, exactly, or wholly understood, so as to make everything predictable. But given a sort of setting.[35] This transcendent reality, or, alternatively, this substratum of myth, is, as Ernst Cassirer has said, not "entirely incoherent ... not bereft of sense or reason. But their coherence depends much more upon unity of feeling than upon logical rules."[36] The primitive mind, he says, ignores and rejects our boundaries between plants and animals, and animals and men. "Its view of life is a synthetic, not an analytical one. . . . Nothing has a definite, invariable, static shape. By a sudden metamorphosis everything may be turned into everything. If there is any characteristic and outstanding feature of the mythical world, any law by which it is governed—it is this law of metamorphoses."[37]

Myth for the adult cannot be what it is for the child. Myth for us today cannot be what it was, or even is, for the primitive mind. But it need not be nothing. And it shades over into a sort of religious quality, too, especially if one can, with Whitehead, generalize this quality into the attitudes of *awe* and *reverence,* or with Rudolph Otto speak of the "sense of the Holy."[38] That person who has been trained out of his sense of awe toward the universe and a reverence for that about it which is holy, has been miseducated. The humanities ought to make a difference in this regard.[39]

SENSE OF FORM

We have had occasion to oppose "formalism," the aesthetic theory that *only* form counts in the work of art; that content, representation, any reference to the realm of feeling, idea, object, or event outside the charmed circle of the aesthetic spell is all a distracting irrelevancy. Such a theory is too precious, too dichotomous of the human self—as if we could, by throwing a switch, sever our relations with the rest of reality. As if we should want to, even if we could!

And yet formalism, like so many "isms," exaggerates and carries to an untenable extreme, a sound and important idea. History can be read as an account of an endless string of events, "one damned thing after another," as someone remarked. Philosophy can be reduced to a set of outcomes, a list of assertions or beliefs. Music can be and often is heard as only a succession of more or less agreeable sounds. A story can be thought of as a report of happenings that go on for a while and then stop. But these are precisely the kinds of attitudes characteristic of those to whom history is bunk, philosophy is futile, music is, though perhaps delectable, no more than amusement; and stories are as vain and silly as the gossip of fishwives.

Form, said Santayana

> does not appeal to the unattentive; they get from objects only a vague sensation which may in them awaken extrinsic associations; they do not stop to survey the parts or to appreciate their relation, and consequently are insensible to the various charms of various unifications; they can find in objects only the value of material or of function, not that of form.[40]

The logician and mathematician go farther than anyone else in abstracting form, whereas the humanist tends to see form as embodied, sees things *as* formed, sees them to be what, in large measure they are, because of that form. Aristotle described form as the realization of what had, previously, been only the potentiality of matter. The best example of all is the human being. A child passes through one or more stages in which he seems to be neither this nor that; in body and personality alike he is in between, transitional; then, with luck and good management, he becomes—what he is. His body develops its true stature, his mind and spirit take on their distinctive shape. He comes to have his own unique way of being; and then those who come to know him will know that about him which is his formed self.

But ultimately there is a consonance between the form of a person and the forms he apprehends. As we learn better to penetrate to the form that upon apprehension seems resident in (and not just projected upon) objects and events, *we* are formed thereby—which in turn facilitates formed perception.

Perhaps the Gestaltists are right in insisting upon an isomorphism between certain perceptions including perceptions of value, and external reality, so that it may be as true to say of a certain landscape that it is sad, as that it is bare or gray. In any case, it can scarcely be doubted that form applies as much to experiences themselves as to objects. What Carroll C. Pratt tantalizingly says of music has, perhaps, a large generalizability:

> The ears of those who love music are filled with the form but not with the material of emotion. In this sense music is the language of emotion. . . . *Music sounds the way emotions feel.*[41]

When a human being or a human expression has sufficiently achieved its form to be genuinely distinctive, we may speak of the emergence of style. Style, said Whitehead, is marked by the two qualities, attainment and restraint; the sense for style is "the most austere of all mental qualities. . . ."

The love of a subject in itself and for itself, where it is not the sleepy pleasure of pacing a mental quarter-deck, is the love of style as manifested in that study. . . .

Style is the ultimate morality of mind.[42]

If humanistic education has done its work for an individual, he will resist the forces of "socialization"—which some people today seem to think are sufficient to explain everything important about a man—at least sufficiently to allow a place for a quest of life style.[43] It is an unending but unpostponable task.

THE CONSUMMATORY

An appropriate ending of our list—though it could be lengthened without falling upon trivialities—is that effect which consists in a developed capacity for relatively intense and culminative consummations. In one way, as John Dewey never tired of showing—Heraclitus too, twenty five hundred years earlier—there are no endings: life is a stream; experiences melt and dissolve into each other; time has no stop. Yet, there is not just experience but, sometimes, "an experience." "That," we say, "was an *experience!*"—and thereby set it off from its immediate context, tending to assign it the form of a beginning, a middle, and an end.[44] It was Aristotle in the *Poetics* who first showed how this apparently banal formula is potent. The beginning is that from which something further proceeds but does not itself have (necessary) antecedents; the middle is that which flows out of something and on into something else; and the end is that which is the issue of everything that has gone before, but from which it is not necessary or desirable to go on.

The objects that we seek out with an appreciative approach tend to be those that will reward us with a sense of closure, a sense of synthesis, a drawing together, sometimes of a complex that up until then seemed hopelessly and frustratingly diverse and confused. But we differ from each other in possession of "a sense of an ending," a capacity for realization.

Perhaps everyone's life is full of incompletions, fallings short, breakings-off, non-realizations, but as Maslow has so often and tellingly said, we all know something about reaching peaks. Some people seem to be almost wholly dependent upon fortune for their peak-experiences, the windfall, the manna from heaven; others seem to be—what would be the opposite of "accident-prone"?—fortune-prone.

A very great deal of education seems and is preparatory—that is, has its ends more or less distant from immediate experience. Humanistic education at its best holds forth promises both in its means and in its very fulfillments; it says, "See how good this is? There's more where that came from." The tendency, the disposition toward experiences that pull together, synthesize, bring to a fulfilling ending: what better objective could education espouse?[45] Perhaps only that wholeness of self, that integration of personality that will be our concern in the final chapter.

This list of intended and actual effects of humanistic learning is of course not complete—nor could it be, for who is to say where the consequences of any learning stop? In any case, it would be easy to think of other items, such as the decrease in parochialism in time and place and in ethnocentrism, or to emphasize once again in this context points dwelt upon previously, such as the help humanistic learning can have on becoming ethically humane. However, the list is already so long as to threaten to topple, to seem, perhaps, grandiose or pompous in its ideality. Yet, we are not talking about paragons and utopias, angels and heavens. We are not trying to imagine the perfect humanist. Rather, our concern is with growth, progress, development toward what are, in a generous sense, "behavioral goals," though they are very hard to reduce to operational measurements. Yet how much more important it is to know, to the extent that we *can* know, whether a person has made a gain in the quality and liveliness of his imagination or in his sensibilities, whether he has brought his feelings and cognitive impulses into closer accord, than whether he recalls this or that collection of facts. To the shame of educators, we are still, to a considerable measure, teaching and examining for the trivial out of a certain laziness and embarrassment about the profound and sublime.

13

The Humanities and the Whole Man

One dissatisfied with the present condition of the humanities could make out a case that its apologists have sometimes been its worst enemies. Take the following bit of rhetoric, the like of which has been heard on innumerable occasions:

> Ours is an age of incredible scientific progress. Consider the amazing advances which have allowed us to put men on the moon, instantaneously broadcast pictures all over the globe, unleash the power latent in the nucleus of the atom, (etc.). But man does not live by means alone. However advanced we are scientifically, many of us still live lives of "quiet desperation." The richest nation in the world has not learned to feed, clothe, and educate many more than half of its citizens. We are still plagued by wars and the threats of wars.

> Therefore, the place for the humanities is not less but greater than ever, for it is to the humanities that we must go for answers to the real human problems. (Etc.)

Such a claim constitutes a vast embarrassment for the humanist. He realizes that if a student should take those words seriously and come to him for the promised answers, he would have to send him away empty-handed and disillusioned, for answers of that degree of definiteness are rare in the humanities. Where ends and values are involved, the humanist may suggest and explain other men's answers, including some very great men indeed; he may helpfully clarify the questions; he may stimulate and direct the inquirer's imagination; he may help him acquire better ways of evaluating hypothetical solutions—and much more. But he cannot give him answers—not, anyway, in good faith.

Another claim made in behalf of the humanities, or some of them, is that they, unlike other subjects, are directed at the whole man. Science and technology, it is said, deal with man the knower, man the controller, man the manipulator, perhaps man the worker; but the humanities suffer no such partiality: they alone address man as a whole.[1]

But again this is to claim too much. If any subject or cluster of subjects really addressed man as a whole, what need would there be for any others? Academic men will always debate about what *the* most important parts of the curriculum are (from which it does *not* follow that they are all equally valuable, or even that some should not be discarded), but we hope to have passed beyond the stage of either scientists' or humanists' thinking that they alone represent the truth and the light. One of the distinctively human activities is thinking in terms of numbers and configurations of space. Another is inquiring into the disposition and changes of heavenly bodies. Another is the building of electrical generators. None of these parts of man is done justice to by the humanities. Therefore, the humanities are also partial rather than all-inclusive. Indeed, humanists can be not only partial but partisan, not only exclusive but narrow. Some humanists act as if they thought the genus *man* was effectively exhausted by the painters of the Italian High Renaissance, others that slavery was forgivable to the Periclean age, still others as if humanity were totally revealed by British historiography.

All the same, the humanities taken at a relatively high degree in integration, *do* often address more of man than the sciences, technologies, and other areas of human endeavor. The sciences achieve their rigor, their elegance, their dependability, at a considerable cost: that is, by expurgating human functions with great severity; ruling as out-of-bounds huge areas of human concerns, attitudes, and behaviors, in the interest of rigor, precision of generalization, and dependability of prediction. In being very much concerned with man as a sensory and emotional being, a being somewhat given to worship and idealization as well as to derogation and destruction, the humanities go beyond man-as-knower, though for humanists too, knowledge has plenty to do with the case.

One way of seeing the relative breadth of the humanities' concern with humanity is to think of some such classification of human functions as Carl Jung's. He speaks of four great kinds of psychic functioning: sensing, intuiting, feeling, and thinking.[2] Now a science, most particularly psychology, can be and is concerned with all these functions, as Jung himself demonstrates; but no science, even psychology, *uses* the full range of functions in its own investigations and inquiries. Mainly, of course, we think of scientists as *thinking* types (as it is to be noted that

Jung is especially concerned with *types* of men, as indicated by their primary proclivity for functioning). However, it would not be right to exclude intuition, especially in the process of hypothesis-formation from the scientist's procedures. And despite how closely he schools himself in the control of his feelings, he will, of course, experience elation, disappointment, uneasiness, fear, hope, and other emotions in the course of his work, like other men. Also he will use his eyes, and perhaps other senses, in the observational aspects of his work. But note the strict limitation on all these nonthinking acts. To the extent that he uses his senses, it is for the purpose of getting signals—consider Bertrand Russell's famous and just claim that a blind man can know the whole of physics—or of making factual observations. As scientist, he never *feasts* his eyes, or listens for the sake of the sounds alone, or images a variety of sensations purely for the satisfaction taken in the fancy. He is not concerned in his work to elicit feelings on the part of others—except possibly those of approval of his achievement. And for him intuition has a very cautious, tentative role, with everything depending upon empirical or formal validation of the hypotheses formed.

Of course the several humanities differ among themselves with respect to the relative importance of these psychic activities. In history and philosophy, the sensory elements are not of great importance; nor in religion either, except in certain rituals. But in the arts, there is an undeniable primacy of the sensory and perceptual. In everyday life, we tend to use our eyes and ears, for instance, mainly to afford us signals for action. The bell rings, the light turns green, a mud puddle appears in our path, the clothing looks wrinkled, our hands dirty—and we act accordingly. The perception's whole importance is bound up with warning against or promoting another act. Once we get our signal, our attention is diverted from the sight or sound. Most photographs are for the purpose of remembering, or occasionally of recognizing[3]; but a painted picture is to *look* at, to dwell upon. Some stainless steel forks and knives are purely functional: others one takes up, eating apart, to touch and notice. A house, an office building, a church ought to serve certain practical ends, but each ought to transcend practicality too and invite our lingering and searching gaze from various vantage points. The poem we read is not for giving us information; if it is good, we return to it over and over, even after we "know what it says" and savor its images and sounds.

Just as the several humanistic disciplines differ among themselves with respect to their sensuousness, so too do the arts, even though the arts taken generally, are properly thought of as taking a good part of their value from the pleasure they give us in the use of our senses. A person congenitally deaf could master the principles of harmony and compose "faultless" fugues, but there are obvious ways in which he could not enjoy music. Yet, some prose fiction and even some drama, depends relatively little upon sensuousness. For instance, take a novel in which the writing is not, except occasionally and incidentally, imagistic, in which setting plays little part, and in which the rhythm and euphony of language are slight, but with plot, idea, and characterization bulking very large. Still, this kind of art work must be considered an extreme—or let us say rather that along a continuum stretching from the most purely and richly sensuous art to the most drily abstract philosophy and the most factual and theoretical kind of history, the sort of fiction mentioned would be well over toward the latter pole.

All the same, it remains generally true that the arts are, among other things, celebrations of our senses, with certain affinities with physical games, sexual play, eating, lying in the sun, and leaping into a cool pool after a sauna bath. As we noted before, Norman O. Brown has found in Freud's writings, but particularly in his fascinating work called *Jokes and their Relation to the Unconscious,* a virtual aesthetics emphasizing "Art as pleasure, art as play, art as the recovery of childhood, ... art as a mode of instinctual liberation. ..."[4]

When Jung talks about sensation, it is not mainly the delight in sensousness that he has in mind, but the perception of *objects,* the sense of the world being composed principally of things. This too bulks large in the arts, particularly *some* arts. Most obviously there are the relatively static arts of sculpture, painting, architecture, and virtually all of the crafts, wherein artifacts, space-occupying objects, are the products of the artist's creative acts and the source of the spectators' aesthetic satisfaction. (Pushed too severely, the distinction becomes misleading, but there is *some* important difference between the arts of *process*—music, literature, dance, film, etc.—and the arts of stasis.) But sensation is important too in the representational aspects of art works. A painting may occupy a space four feet by seven, but represent a space of as many yards or miles, in which the sensed objectness of that tree or rock or hill or barn is an intimate part of the experience of the painting. The point is perhaps even clearer from literature, in which the created work has little importance as an object in itself. (Though the very size of a copy of *War and Peace* may have its own effect.) We are seldom very conscious of the poem existing as an object in the same way that a statue or a building is an object. But the poem or story is usually about objects or persons with their distinctive characteristics: ox-eyed Hera, Joseph in his coat of many colors, muscular Samson with his flowing locks, Beatrice with her pure beauty, Grendel, the hunchback of Notre Dame, swarthy Othello; wind-swept heaths and rivers running blood, haunted houses and stately mansions, triremes and donkeycarts and *wagonlits* on the Orient Express; Louis Quatorze interiors and a share cropper's cabin, the holy Ganges and a stagnant lagoon. These as objects existing in our imagination are indispensable to the quality of the story or the poem. The historian too may give us a strong sense of place, may enliven our conception of the thirteenth century University of Paris by taking us inside a lecture hall, may make the American Civil War real by an account of the terrain at Appomattox, or help us to see as well as to understand the short Napoleon. Even the philosopher, normally some degrees of abstraction above physical objects, may employ our visual or tactile imagination as in Plato's cave, Lucretius' hooked atoms, and Descartes' ball of wax.

Intuition is a much more subtle function than either sensation or sensory feeling, but whatever be the limitations on our understanding of it, it is not here intended as an occult phenomenon. It may be glanced at first as part of the creative process of the artist himself, whatever his medium.

Art is by its very nature a craft, which is only to say that with respect to every kind of art, there is a group of skills, mastery of which is necessary to the artist who would achieve and not merely yearn for expression. Nevertheless, there are wonderfully dextrous workers in every medium who are smiled at by their fellows for "having nothing to say." Manipulative skills are of little worth (beyond impressing the gullible with one's virtuosity) unless they are in the service of insight into the larger vision. The artist who amounts to anything creatively must be a person who engenders ideas, though these may be musical or visual ideas instead of the kind that are necessarily associated with verbal language.

Now, in the case of the arts—perhaps more than in philosophy and history—these ideas, these insights, these proposed solutions to problems, whether of a strictly aesthetic or a larger sort, are very apt to come as flashes, sudden hunches. And in the process material previously unordered, or ordered only in conventional ways, falls into a new and interesting configuration. But this is just what is meant by intuition, an immediate way of "knowing" or perceiving that makes up in "startle" what it wants in the way of external evidence.

Creative persons in all fields employ intuition, but in the highly rational and rigorously empirical fields of investigation, intuitions are discarded if they are not borne out by careful processes of verification.[5] In the arts, they are often retained if they have about them the ring of plausibility: it is more important, aesthetically, that an idea be interesting than that it be *true*—if a choice has to be made. And this is precisely what it is about the arts that scandalizes rationalists from Plato to modern positivism.

The much discussed mysteriousness of intuition is mainly a matter of the suddenness and even in retrospect, the inexplicability, of the idea's emergence. Sometimes this is expressed as the "givenness" of a work's starting point. Someone—was it Valéry?—said that a poet's first line comes from the gods: the rest he must write himself.

Now, just as the artistic creator employs intuition, so must he who would appreciate the resultant expression rehearse this intuition for himself. There are persons too severely rational, too closely wedded to the explicit citation of empirical evidence, to enjoy the more glancing, fleeting ways of art. Strictly speaking, a spectator cannot tell with certainty about another's character from looking into his eyes. Yet to appreciate the work of the portrait artist one must see, immediately and, as it were, indubitably, the character *in* the face. To look appropriately at Michelangelo's "Pieta" one must realize directly Mary's state with the dead Jesus on her lap. Unless in hearing the Agnus Dei of Bach's B-minor Mass one knows by acquaintance the dominant mood therein—even to try to name it may be a mistake—justice is not done either to Bach or oneself. In dramatic art, the spectator's or reader's intuition may be directed variously: to what the creative artist is saying in his own person; to the nature of a character inside the work; or, *through* such a character, to something or someone else.

In some of what was just now said about intuition, we had already shaded over into emotional feeling; indeed, to keep them rigidly apart is itself an important mistake. But intuition is a way of knowing or trying to know, whereas feeling is—feeling. Typically, in full-fledged aesthetic experience, we both feel and know our feeling. But if pursued too relentlessly, the cognitive can inhibit feeling itself. Part of coming to experience aesthetic value consists of a surrender of oneself to the feelings that the artist is providing, or perhaps better yet, conducting.

———————

Finally, there is the psychic function that is thinking. Man, said Aristotle, is the rational animal. He meant of course not that man is exclusively rational, for that is reserved to divinity, but that man alone among animals is, even part of the time, rational. This search for the distinctive trait may well have led not Aristotle alone, but thinkers ever since, to exaggerate the importance of rationality. Why, after all, should we be demeaned by sharing certain characteristics with other animals?

Nevertheless, man can and does think, reason, analyze, advance and test hypotheses, deduce, and—to pick a very general verb—intellectualize; and it is not necessary to stop to defend or justify such acts. Nor is there needed any explanation that the philosopher, the historian, the religious scholar thinks: everybody knows they do; it is their job, in very large part. It is equally clear that the musicologist, the art and literary historian, and the critic are intellectuals. But it has sometimes seemed to the naive that composers and poets and painters and sculptors *feel,* not think. Yet, once one thinks about what these creative sorts do *when* they're creating, it is apparent that typically, as John Crowe Ransom once put it, their actions are more cool than hot. There is about artistic creation a strong element of problem-solving. The poet searches for the right word, the painter for a way of filling up a "hole" in his work, the composer for an interesting variation on his announced theme, the choreographer for a way posturally to convey (say) raptness. Such problems are solved—if they are solved at all—by thinking.

Some thinking is typically required of the appreciator too. For instance, unless a listener remembers a certain theme or motif, he may miss a considerable part of the value of the music; unless one puts two and two together, he is likely to come out nowhere in a mystery novel; if one does not understand the kind of problem flying buttresses were intended to solve, one is, in an important sense, not fully seeing the cathedral.

Furthermore, part of what one gets from works of art, or some works of art, is intellectual grasp, and sometimes even facts, as when one may learn from a novel something about the emperor Claudius or the flora of the Yorkshire heaths.

This quick survey of Jung's four primary psychic functions has had the purpose of showing how relatively full is the humanist's use of his psyche, especially on the aesthetic side of the humanities, both in creation and appreciation. Again, we make no claim that it is complete, or that in comparison with certain nonhumanistic disciplines, it is not somewhat deficient in this or that respect. Yet, it is no idle claim that there is a particular affinity between the humanistic side of the curriculum and the conception of "the whole child,"—indeed, the whole person, whatever his age. This is the more true when one considers that these presently delineated functions are not typically kept by the humanist distinct and apart from each other. To the contrary, there is that about the humanities which strongly tends toward *integration*—and this in several ways, but for present purposes we are thinking particularly of psychological integration. That is, the person behaving humanistically tends to involve an exceptionally large portion of his own being in his acts, not acting just as a thinker *or* with appropriate emotional response *or* intuitively *or* with full use of his senses, but in all of these ways, and at least sometimes, in all of them simultaneously.

To integrate is to form into a whole, to unify, to pull together, to synthesize. Although there is a legitimate place for analytic, highly specialized scholarship in the humanities, the whole subject is infused with a nisus toward wholeness.

All disciplines can be integrative. The sciences are ever trying for larger syntheses, more comprehensive explanations: consider Einstein's spending the last decades of his life in search of the greater outreach of a field theory. There have been attempts to bring together the several contributions of economics, sociology, political science, geography, anthropology, and psychology in the interests of a synoptic description of human institutions and behavior.

But humanists try for something still larger—at least some do. Very often they fail, coming out with fuzzy generalizations, sloppy categorizations, shoddy and makeshift syntheses, and empty rhetoric. Most philosophy is trival, most religion is embarrassing, most art is deservedly ignored or forgotten. But there are stupendous successes too: massive consolidations of qualities so diverse as, for most of us, to forbid linkage: the book of *Job,* the *Phaedrus,* Jesus' "Beatitudes," *The Divine Comedy, The Canterbury Tales,* Chartres Cathedral, the *Ninth Symphony, The Brothers Karamazov, The Decline and Fall of the Roman Empire, The View of Toledo,* Michelangelo's *David,* Spinoza's *Ethic.* Of course, there are many others, some the equal of any of the previous works in magnitude and focus; others of smaller scope, or of lesser degree of unification, but still remarkable achievements of synthesis.

Humanistic creators and teachers have often set out quite self-consciously to attack or at least to unsettle the conventional wisdom that resides in such polarities as: Present/Past, Ridiculous/Sublime, Process/Product, Dream/Waking, Mine/Thine, Object/Subject, Self/Other, Sad/Funny, True/False, God/Devil, Pious/Erotic, and even Part/Whole.[6]

Humanistic integration has kinship with, but no monopoly on, love, compassion, care, concern, accepting, and kindness, for all these attitudes and qualities are gathering-in, pulling-together movements, as distinct from hate, suspicion, cynicism, mistrust, jealousy, ridicule, and hierarchical discrimination, which pull apart, reject, spew out. Perhaps this explains why satire is a less satisfying type of art than humor, and why pathos is less fulfilling than tragedy, which, as many commentators have shown, is ultimately affirmative in outlook. This would suggest too a subordination of analytic philosophy to visionary philosophy,[7] muckraking history to history-as-pageant, religion as denunciation to religion as worship. The humanities have their shadow side too, and it is indispensable, for it is part of human life to take apart, denounce, and push away, but the return movement is the truly fulfilling one: the gathering of the sheaves, the consummation of the marriage, the shout of triumph, the adoration of the divine.

Greater than the developing ability to comprehend the integrations achieved by others, greater even than the ability to effect such integrations oneself, is the integration, the individuation of the self. Here is the greatest challenge, the greatest aspiration of humanistic education.

We have used the word "individuated" as well as "integrated" to suggest that through the humanities progress can and should be made not only to wholeness but to distinctiveness. It is, after all, the neurotic, the person who identifies with one role, and the thoroughly conventional person, who are absurdly predictable. Molière's doctors and misers are laughable because they have completely one-track minds.[8] The person mainly eager not to depart from the decrees of custom wants not to be noticed, but to blend into the human landscape. And the neurotic too is one who has lost his resilience, lost his ability to cope by novel means, and falls back upon some symptomatic behavior that is only just better than not coping at all. But the person best able to be creative, most adventuresome, most delighted with the immense range of human experience is precisely the person who is most distinctively and uniquely himself.

"To be that self which one truly is." Kierkegaard's great words, echoed and elaborated in our day by Carl Rogers, who has written repeatedly of what it is like to be "living in the good life . . ." "To be part of this process means that one is involved in the frequently frightening and frequently satisfying experience of a more sensitive living, with greater range, greater variety, greater richness."[9] Such a person can be trusted, can trust himself, to make decisions about life simply because he is whole, autonomous, integrated.

So to say is not, however, to separate off the single individual, no matter how glorious, from mankind. For, as Buber has taught us, hate is a relationship that can exist only between partial beings, but mutual love is necessarily between whole beings. Even short of love, the recognition of another person as a subject, a "Thou," proceeds from the whole being:

> The primary word *I-Thou* can only be spoken with the whole being.
> The primary word *I-It* can never be spoken with the whole being.[10]

The helping of a student to achieve such wholeness, and thus to be put into human relationship with human beings is the ultimate mission of the teacher. It is a great lot to ask of a teacher, that he become equal to this task. William Arrowsmith has said what the student wants now

> is models of committed integrity, as whole as they can be in a time of fragmented men, and pertinent to the anguish of existence in a hard time.[11]

And more and more teachers are asking how they can become this, which is to say, themselves. This is our hope and our justification: that we can so ask.

Notes

INTRODUCTION

1. Jean-Jacques Rousseau, *The Emile,* William Boyd, trans. (New York: Teachers College Press, 1962), Book I.
2. J. T. Plumb, *The Crisis in the Humanities* (Baltimore: Penguin Books, 1964).
3. Howard Mumford Jones, *One Great Society* (New York: Harcourt, Brace & Company, 1959), p. 8.
4. In Scheila Schwartz, *Teaching Humanities* (New York: The Macmillan Company, 1970), p. 27.
5. Jerry L. Walker, "Humanities: A Question of Values," in Schwartz, *op. cit.,* p. 33.
6. Charles Keller, "Humanities in the High School," in Schwartz, *op. cit.,* p. 70.
7. J. H. Billington, "The Humanistic Heartbeat Has Failed," *Life* (May 24, 1968), p. 32, cited in Edmund Burke Feldman, *Becoming Human Through Art,* (Englewood Cliffs, N.J.: Prentice-Hall, Inc., 1970), p. 174.
8. Jon Roush, "What Will Become of the Past?" *Daedalus* (Summer, 1969), p. 641.
9. Harold Taylor, ed., *The Humanities in the Schools* (New York: Citation Press, 1968), pp. 24-25.
10. For these and other classifications of the fine arts, see James L. Jarrett, *The Quest for Beauty,* (Englewood Cliffs, N.J.: Prentice-Hall, Inc., 1957), Chapter 2.
11. James L. Jarrett, *The Educational Theories of the Sophists,* (New York: Teachers College Press, 1969), p. 68.
12. Two irreverent critics of education have recently expressed their amusement over the superstitious belief "that the study of literature and other 'humanistic' subjects will result in one's becoming a more decent, liberal, tolerant and civilized human being. ..." They go on to wonder if the professor of literature or other self-styled "humanist" would "dare to offer his own life as an illustration of the benefits that will accrue from humanis-

tic studies." N. Postman and C. Weingartner, *The Soft Revolution: A Student Handbook for Turning Schools Around* (New York: Dell Publishing Company, 1971), pp. 38-39.

CHAPTER 1

1. See Werner Jaeger *Paideia: The Ideals of Greek Culture,* Gilbert Highet, trans. (New York: Oxford University Press, 1939), Vol. I, Book II, Chapter 3.

2. Sophocles, "Antigone," C. M. Bowra, trans.

   Indeed, the person who is unrefined, uncultivated, ungracious was called by Plato ἄμουσος, "unmusical." See F. M. Cornford, "The Doctrine of Eros in Plato's *Symposium*" in *Plato,* Gregory Vlastos, ed., (Garden City, New York: Anchor Books, Doubleday and Company, Inc., 1971), Vol. II, p. 119.

3. Plato, *The Republic,* Paul Shorey, J. L. Davies and D. J. Vaughan, trans., in *The Republic of Plato* (London: Macmillan and Co., 1895), 398 a-b.

4. *Ibid.,* 401e-402.

5. Plato, *The Protagoras,* W. K. C. Guthrie, trans., in Hamilton and Cairns, *op cit.,* p. 339.

6. Isocrates, "Antidosis," 238c, in James L. Jarrett, *The Educational Theories of the Sophists,* (New York: Teachers College Press, 1969), p. 230.

7. *Loc. cit.*

8. *Ibid.,* p. 231.

9. Aristophanes, "The Clouds," Arthur S. Way, trans., in Jarrett, *The Educational Theories of the Sophists,* p. 113.

10. W. J. Ong considers man's first 500,000 years to be wholly in the oral tradition. The first script appeared around 3500 B.C., alphabets around 1500 B.C. See *Knowledge and the Future of Man,* (New York: Holt, Rinehart & Winston, 1968).

    Antisthenes the Cynic said, "If you intend a boy to live with Gods, teach him philosophy; if with men, rhetoric." But he also said, according to Diogenes Laertius, that the great advantage he had gained from philosophy was the "ability to hold converse with myself." *Lives of Eminent Philosophers,* R. D. Hicks, trans., (Cambridge, Mass: Harvard University Press, 1958), Vol II. p. 9.

11. Aristotle, *Politics,* in John Burnet, trans. and ed., *Aristotle on Education* (Cambridge, Cambridge University Press, 1903), Book VIII, Chapter 3.

12. *Loc. cit.* and *Odyssey,* IC, 7ff.

13. *Loc. cit.*

14. H. I. Marrou, *A History of Education in Antiquity,* George Lamb, trans., (New York: The New American Library of World Literature, 1956), p. 220.

15. See Bruno Snell's *The Discovery of the Mind*, T. G. Rosenmeyer, trans. (Cambridge, Massachusetts: Harvard University Press, 1933). Especially Chapter 11, "The Discovery of *Humanitas*, and Our Attitude Toward the Greeks."

CHAPTER 2

1. *Apology*, Hugh Tredennick, trans., in Hamilton and Cairns, *op. cit.*, 19b-c.
2. *Ibid.*, 33a.
3. *Ibid.*, 3 a-b.
4. "In the field of philosophy, humanism must be regarded, quite frankly, as a Philistine movement, even an obscurantist movement." C. S. Lewis, *English Literature in the 16th Century*, (Oxford: Clarendon Press, 1954), pp. 30-32.
5. Jacob Burckhardt, *The Civilization of the Renaissance in Italy*, (New York: Mentor Books, 1960), p. 191.
6. Pico della Mirandola, "Oration on the Dignity of Man," A. R. Capognigri, trans., (Chicago: Gateway Editions, Inc., 1956), pp. 3-4.
7. *Ibid.*, p. 6.
8. *Ibid.*, p. 14.
9. *Ibid.*, p. 38.
10. P. O. Kristeller, *Renaissance Thought: The Classic, Scholastic, and Humanist Strains* (New York: Harper Torchbooks, 1961), p. 133.
11. *Loc. cit.*
12. Crane Brinton, *Ideas and Men*, (Englewood Cliffs, New Jersey: Prentice-Hall, Inc., 2nd edition, 1963), p. 218.
13. Montaigne, "Of the Education of Children," L. E. Rector, trans.
14. *Loc. cit.*
15. *Loc. cit.*
16. *Loc. cit.*
17. *Loc. cit.*
18. Chaucer, *Canterbury Tales*, General Prologue, lines 293-300.
19. Strictly speaking, Gutenberg's invention was anticipated by the Chinese in the 11th century, but for some reason the earlier achievement was abandoned.
20. Rabelais, *Gargantua and Pantagruel*, Thomas Urquhart and Peter Le Motteux, trans., Vol. II, Chapter 8.
21. Baldassore Castiglione, *Book of the Courtier*, Leonard Eckstein Opdycke, trans., (New York: Charles Scribner's Sons, 1903; original edition, 1528), Section 43.
22. *The Great Didactic of John Amos Comenius*, M. W. Keatinge, trans. (London: A. and C. Black, 1921), Vol. I, Part II, p. 3.

23. From a letter of Martin Luther dated March 1, 1517, as cited in Bruno Snell, *op. cit.,* p. 255.
24. Crane Brinton, *op. cit.,* p. 201.
25. John Edwin Sandys, *Harvard Lectures on the Revival of Learning* (Cambridge: at the University Press, 1905), p. 30.
26. Cited in *Ibid.,* p. 31.
27. J. A. Symonds, "The Renaissance," *Encyclopaedia Britannica,* 9th edition, pp. 127-128.
28. Reprinted by permission from Richard McKeon "Culture and the Humanities," in Ben Rothblatt, ed., *Changing Perspectives on Man,* p. 288. Copyright © 1968 by the University of Chicago Press.
29. W. J. Ong, *The Presence of the Word* (New Haven: Yale University Press, 1967); Eric Havelock, *Preface to Plato* (Cambridge, Mass: Harvard University Press, 1963); Marshall McLuhan, *The Gutenberg Galaxy,* (Toronto: Toronto University Press, 1962).
30. Ong, *op. cit.,* p. 35.
31. That is, read *silently,* a skill more astonishing and more recent than most people realize.

CHAPTER 3

1. See Ficino, in Kristeller, *op. cit.,* p. 133.
2. Leon Battista Alberti, "On Painting," John R. Spencer, trans. (New Haven: Yale University Press, 1966) p. 161.
3. Leonardo da Vinci, *Leonardo da Vinci on Painting,* Carlo Pedretti, compiler, (Berkeley, University of California Press, 1964.)
4. Aristotle, "Poetics," Butcher trans., V. 4.
5. But consider Blake:
God us keep
From Single Vision and Newton's sleep.
6. Earlier Sir Thomas Browne affords an interesting (partly because unusual) example of an eminent man of letters whose interests were divided among science, magic, and religion.
7. Quoted in Katharine Gilbert and G. Kuhn, *A History of Aesthetics* (Bloomington: Indiana University Press, rev. ed., 1953), pp. 203-204.
8. See Ernest Lee Tuveson, *The Imagination as a Means of Grace:Locke and the Aesthetics of Romanticism.* (Berkeley: University of California Press, 1960).
9. John Locke, *An Essay concerning Human Understanding,* Book III, Chapter 10.
10. Cited in R. S. Crane, *The Idea of the Humanities* (Chicago: The University of Chicago Press, 1967) Vol. I, p. 68.

11. Canto I., lines 27-39.
12. *Traité du Poème Épique,* Book I, Chapter 1. Cited in Monroe C. Beardsley, *Aesthetics from Classical Greece to the Present* (New York: The Macmillan Company, 1966), p. 142.
13. Alexander Pope, "Essay on Criticism," Part i, lines 88-89.
14. Sir Joshua Reynolds, *Discourses on Art,* III.
15. Samuel Johnson, *Rasselas,* Chapter 10.
16. John Herman Randall, Jr., *The Career of Philosophy* (New York: Columbia University Press, 1962), p. 746.
17. David Hume, "On the Standard of Taste," *Essays and Treatises on Several Subjects.*
18. David Hume, *Treatise on Human Nature,* Introduction.
19. *Loc. cit.*
20. Cited in Crane, *op. cit.,* p. 92.
21. Reprinted by permission from Ronald S. Crane, *The Idea of the Humanities,* p. 111. Copyright © 1967 by the University of Chicago Press.
22. Barnaby Keeney, first director of the National Endowment for the Arts and Humanities, recently said, "Education in the Humanities . . . has very much the same purposes as in the eighteenth century, with the addition of objectivity." "The Humanities: Episode or Continuing?" *Educational Record,* Summer, 1969.
23. As Randall has shown, *op. cit.,* Vol. II, pp. 99-171.
24. Jean-Jacques Rousseau, *Emile,* William Boyd, trans., (London: William Heinemann, Ltd., 1956), Book III.
25. Immanuel Kant, *Critique of Judgement,* Bernard translation, cited in Randall, *op. cit.,* Vol. II, p. 175.
26. Randall, *op. cit.,* Vol. II, p. 198.
27. Friedrich Schiller, *On the Aesthetic Education of Man,* Reginald Snell, trans., (New York: Frederick Ungar Publishing Co., 1954; originally published 1795), Second Letter, p. 26. Romantics generally (though not unanimously) were antipathetic to science. Keats, for instance, complained that science robbed the rainbow of its mystery.
28. *Op. cit.,* Fifteenth Letter, p. 80.
29. *Ibid.,* Twenty-first Letter, p. 99n.
30. *Ibid.,* Twenty-sixth Letter, p. 125.
31. *Ibid.,* Twenty-seventh Letter, p. 139.
32. S. T. Coleridge as cited in Randall, *op. cit.,* p. 505.
33. Ralph Waldo Emerson, "Education."
34. *Loc. cit.*
35. Herbert Spencer, "What Knowledge Is of Most Worth?" in *Education* (New York: D. Appleton and Co., 1883).
36. John Henry Newman, *The Idea of a University,* Discourse 7, Section 10.

37. Matthew Arnold, "Literature and Science," *Discourses in America* (London: Macmillan and Co., 1885), p. 127.

38. T. H. Huxley, unpublished address to the Senate of London University, cited in Cyril Bibbey, "The Scientific Humanist: Huxley," *The Educated Man: Studies in the History of Educational Thought,* Paul Nash, Andreas M. Kazamias, and Henry J. Parkinson, eds., (New York: John Wiley and Sons, Inc., 1965) p. 273.

39. See Maurice Merleau-Ponty, *The Primacy of Perception,* James M. Edie, ed., (Evanston: Northwestern University Press, 1964).

40. Henri Bergson, *Laughter,* C. Brereton and Fred Rothwell, trans., (London: Macmillan and Co., Limited, 1911), p. 161.

41. "For a traditionally sports-oriented nation, 'culture' is now ascendant: '. . . there are more piano players than licensed fishermen, and as many painters as hunters. There are twice as many people listening to concerts and recitals as at Major League ball games. Boaters, skiers, golfers, and skin divers are fewer than theatergoers.' The Metropolitan Museum of Art . . . draws over three million visitors a year." Bernard Rosenberg and Norris Fliegel, *The Vanguard Artist* (Chicago: Quadrangle Books, 1965)pp. 181-182; citing *New York Times Magazine,* September 20, 1965, p. 30. On this general topic see also J. L. Jarrett, "Countering Alienation," *The Journal of Aesthetic Education* (January-April, 1972).

CHAPTER 4

1. W. J. Ong, "The Knowledge Explosion in the Humanities," in *In the Human Grain* (New York: The Macmillan Company, 1967), p. 49. He goes on to say that within the anthropological knowledges there exists the problem of "communication between the integrator and the specialist." Whether he is right in saying that "integration is not so much the business of the physical sciences . . . " or not, he is certainly right in seeing this as a serious problem for those who deal with humanity. It is hard enough now, but if the integrator had to take account of the findings of sociology, political science, economics, etc., his job would become overwhelming.

   Erwin Panofsky makes a somewhat similar distinction between "the sphere of *nature* and the sphere of *culture*" where culture has to do with the "records left by man." "The History of Art as a Humanistic Discipline" in Theodore Meyer Greene, ed., *The Meaning of the Humanities* (Princeton: Princeton University Press, 1938), p. 95.

2. Albert Einstein, *Origin of the General Theory of Relativity,* (Glasgow: Jackson, Wylie and Co., 1933.), pp, 20-21.

3. From Ralph Barton Perry, "A Definition of the Humanities," in *The Meaning of the Humanities,* ed. with an introduction by Theodore Meyer Greene, with a Preface by Robert Kilburn Root (copyright © 1966 by Princeton University Press) p. 3. This and subsequent selections are reprinted by permission of Princeton University Press.

4. *Ibid.,* p. 36. See Note 3 above.

5. *Ibid.,* p. 34. See Note 3 above.

6. *Ibid.,* p. 37. See Note 3 above.

7. E. M. Forster distinguishes between "story"—a series of *and-thens*—and "plot," in which causality is shown. His famous example: the-king-died-and-then-the queen-died is a story; the-king-died-and-then-the-queen-died-of-grief is a plot. *Aspects of the Novel* (New York: Harcourt Brace Jovanovich, Inc., 1927) Chapter V. History is or should be concerned with plots—but of course with plots having to do with real, not fictional, persons and events.

8. Perry, *op.cit.,* p. 39. See Note 3 above.

9. *Ibid.,* p. 40. See Note 3 above.

10. Ernst Cassirer, *An Essay on Man* (Garden City, New York: Doubleday & Company, Doubleday Anchor Books, 1944), p. 43.

11. From *Realms of Meaning* by Philip Phenix, p. 5. Copyright © 1964 by McGraw-Hill Book Company. This and subsequent selections are used with permission of McGraw-Hill Book Company and the author.

12. *Ibid.,* p. 6. See Note 11 above.

13. *Ibid.,* pp. 141-142. See Note 11 above.

14. *Ibid.,* p. 143. See Note 11 above.

15. *Ibid.,* p. 187. See Note 11 above.

16. *Ibid.,* p. 193. See Note 11 above.

17. *Ibid.,* p. 208. See Note 11 above.

18. *Ibid.,* p. 215. See Note 11 above.

19. *Ibid.,* p. 188. See Note 11 above.

20. *Ibid.,* p. 239. See Note 11 above.

21. *Ibid.,* p. 253. See Note 11 above.

22. Note, for instance, that within the National Endowment for the Arts and the Humanities, the Humanities Endowment and the Arts Endowment are quasi-independent.

23. Phenix, *op.cit.,* p. 325. See Note 11 above.

24. If space permitted, other accounts that would be interesting to examine are those of Moody E. Prior in *Science and the Humanities* (Evanston: Northwestern University Press, 1962), W. T. Jones' *The Sciences and the Human-*

ities (Berkeley and Los Angeles: The University of California Press, 1965), and Harold Gomes Cassidy's *Science and the Arts* (New York: Harper & Brothers, 1962).

25. Reprinted by permission from Ronald S. Crane, *The Idea of the Humanities,* p. 158. Copyright © 1967 by the University of Chicago Press.

26. *Ibid.,* pp. 168-169. See Note 25 above. William James was another to look at the humanities primarily as the study of great human achievements: " . . . In a broad sense the humanities mean literature primarily, and in a still broader sense the study of masterpieces in almost any field of human endeavor. . . . You can give humanistic value to almost anything by teaching it historically. Geology, economics, mechanics, are humanities when taught with reference to the successive achievements of the geniuses to which these sciences owe their being. Not taught thus, literature remains grammar, art a catalogue, history a list of dates, and natural science a sheet of formulas and weights and measures.

"The sifting of human creations!—nothing less than this is what we ought to mean by the humanities." "The Social Value of the College-Bred," *Memories and Studies,* (New York: Longmans, Green, and Co, 1911), p. 312.

27. Aristotle, *Poetics,* 26-27, S. H. Butcher, trans.

28. Crane, *op. cit.,* p. 170, emphasis added. See Note 25 above. An interesting recent interpretation of the humanities which resembles somewhat that of Crane is Frederick Olafson's "Philosophy and the Humanities" in *The Monist* for January 1968. Olafson characterizes the humanities "as having a special affinity with the study of that subclass of human cultural achievements that are thought of as the achievements of assignable individuals or groups of individuals." (p. 30) He excluded most scientific achievements from this subclass by the following device: " . . . When the production of an individual human mind is of such nature that it calls for appraisal in terms of a reasonably well-worked-out and available canon of truth, it is *to that extent* withdrawn from the peculiar sphere of the humanities." (p. 31) Also Olafson, perhaps somewhat reluctantly, acquiesces in a fundamental distinction between the humanities considered as historical studies and the productive arts. His article is very much worth pondering at length.

CHAPTER 5

1. C. P. Snow, *The Two Cultures: And a Second Look* (Mentor Books, 1964).

2. Herbert Read, *Education through Art,* (London: Faber and Faber, 1943), p. 11.

Oliver Rieser has expressed a common anti-dualistic sentiment: "It is my impression that this dualism of the 'scientific' and the 'humanistic' is at the root of many of our troubles, social as well as intellectual. If we could devise courses in integrated education which would cultivate a rapport between both fields . . . , the rivalry of 'art versus science,' for example, would vanish." *The Integration of Human Learning,* (Boston: Porter Sargent Publisher, 1950), pp. 54-55. Our response to that is that such high-level integration is fairly easily and appropriately available in the primary school grades but is exceptionally difficult to manage further along. This should not count it out as an ideal, of course, but neither should it be supposed that there is something inherently vicious about effecting integration of either the sciences or the humanities which specifically excludes the other, any more than that there is anything wrong about teaching music as music, instead of *always* trying to integrate it with literature, or painting.

3. Michael Polanyi, *The Study of Man* (Chicago: The University of Chicago Press, 1959), p. 37.

    Peter Hilton has pointed out that "facts decline in importance as a science advances. Indeed it has often seemed to me that the historian or the student of literature has a far heavier load of facts to carry around (or store in notebook or library) than the physicist." "Arts and Sciences: Differences and Similarities," *Science v. Arts,* Alan S. C. Ross, ed., (London: Methuen & Co., Ltd., 1967) p. 29.

4. Michael Polanyi, *Ibid.,* pp. 38-39.

5. J. Bronowski, *Science and Human Values,* (New York: Harper Torchbook, 1959), pp. 30-31.

6. *Ibid.,* p. 31.

7. *Ibid.,* p. 67.

8. Alan S. C. Ross, *op. cit.*

9. Herbert J. Muller has taken the "residue" approach to the humanities. Unfortunately, his expression of the present fuzziness about the humanities is more convincing than his own attempt to clarify the issue: " . . . We have no clear definition of the humanities. . . . In effect, the humanities are what is left in the curriculum when the sciences and technical and vocational studies have been separated out." Herbert J. Muller, "The 'Relevance' of the Humanities," *The American Scholar,* Winter 70-71, pp. 104-105.

10. Harold L. Burstyn, "Tradition and Understanding: The Science and the Humanities," *School and Society,* November, 1969, p. 420. Burstyn goes on to argue, interestingly, that a failure to understand this basic difference between the sciences and the humanities accounts for the present overemphasis upon method in education. Crane Brinton has made popular the distinction between cumulative (scientific) and noncumulative (humanistic) study. But the words do not seem quite right, since we do possess and cherish an accumulation of poetry, philosophy, etc. Joseph Schwab uses the

happier term, "revisionary" for scientific knowledge. See Brinton, *op. cit.*, Introduction, and Joseph Schwab, "Structure of the Disciplines: Meanings and Significances" in G. W. Ford and Lawrence Pugno, *The Structure of Knowledge and the Curriculum* (Chicago: Rand McNally & Company, 1964), p. 18.

A physicist, M. Delbrück, has recently written: "The books of the great scientists are gathering dust on the shelves of learned libraries. And rightly so. . . . While the artist's communication is linked forever with its original form, that of the scientist is modified, amplified, fused with the ideas and results of others and melts into the stream of knowledge and ideas which forms our culture." "A Physicist's Renewed Look at Biology: Twenty Years Later," *Science* (12 June 1970), p. 134.

11. James Conant has said, in *Modern Science and Modern Man*, "Science is a dynamic undertaking directed toward lowering the degree of empiricism involved in solving problems; or, if you prefer, science is a process of fabricating a web of interconnected concepts and conceptual schemes arising from experiments and fruitful of further experiments and observations."

Ernest Nagel: "It has been the perennial aim of theoretical science to make the world intelligible by disclosing fixed patterns of regularity and orders of dependence in events," in "The Place of Science in a Liberal Education," Both Conant and Nagel are quoted in Moody E. Prior, *Science and the Humanities,* (Evanston: Northwestern University Press, 1962), pp. 12-13.

Also, Lewis Mumford has recently written: "Unfortunately, the ultimate effect of the methodical seventeenth century advance in clarity of description and in fidelity to observed fact was to devalue every aspect of human experience that could not be so treated—to devalue, and eventually exile, the human personality." "Reflections: The Megamachine," *The New Yorker* (Oct. 10, 1970), p. 110.

12. The point is much in debate among social scientists now, and certain modifications need to be made in their case, but it remains true that the economist, sociologist, and psychologist are thought to have an obligation to describe things in an impersonal way. Thus, a psychologist who happens to *feel* that there are qualitative differences among races is obliged by his professional commitment to let his "data speak for themselves," and if they show nothing to support his feelings, he must go along with the facts. At this writing, a considerable controversy has been created by a psychologist's contention that the prejudice today typically works otherwise so that in the interests of egalitarianism, investigators are consciously or unconsciously suppressing facts.

13. Sometimes one hears "generalizations" spoken of as if, *per se,* they were always loose and illegitimate. But a science without generalizations would not be a science at all, obviously.

14. William Rohwer, Jr., "Prime Time for Education: Early Childhood or Adolescence?" *Harvard Educational Review,* (August, 1971), pp. 316-341.
15. Bronowski, *op. cit.,* p. 31.
16. John Crowe Ransom, *The World's Body* (New York: Charles Scribner's Sons, 1939) *passim.* See also William James, *The Principles of Psychology* (New York: Henry Holt and Company, 1890), II, p. 361.
17. Bronowski, *op. cit.,* p. 27.
18. Mao Tse-tung, "Talks at the Henan Forum on Literature and Art," cited in Conor Cruise O'Brien, "Politics and the Morality of Scholarship" in Max Black, ed., *The Morality of Scholarship,* (Ithaca: Cornell University Press, 1967), p. 59.
19. See James L. Jarrett, *The Quest for Beauty* and Philip Wheelwright, *The Burning Fountain* (Bloomington: Indiana University Press, 1954).
20. Louis Arnaud Reid, *Ways of Knowledge and Experience* (London: George Allen & Unwin Ltd., 1961).
21. Suzanne Langer in *Philosophy in a New Key* (New York: The New American Library of World Literature, Inc., 1948), Chapter 8; in subsequent works she has made out an important case for music having "presentational" instead of the more usual "representational" significance. Hans Keller has argued for music as a "mode of thought," a rival to philosophy. ("Toward a Theory of Music," *The Listener,* June, 1970, *passim.)*

CHAPTER 6

1. William James, *The Varieties of Religious Experience,* (New York: The Modern Library, 1939, first published, 1902). ". . . The very fact that (would-be definitions of religion) are so many and so different from one another is enough to prove that the word 'religion' cannot stand for any single principle or essence, but is rather a collective name. The theorizing mind tends always to the oversimplification of its materials . . . Let us rather admit freely at the outset that we may very likely find no one essence, but many characters which may alternately be equally important to religion." p. 27.
2. Ludwig Wittgenstein, *Philosophical Investigations* (Oxford: Basil Blackwell, 1953), esp. pp. 31-32.
3. One of the best accounts of appreciation is John Dewey's: "In one of its meanings, appreciation is opposed to depreciation. It denotes an enlarged, an *intensified* prizing, not merely a prizing, much less—like depreciation—a lowered and degraded prizing. This enhancement of the qualities which make any ordinary experience appealing, appropriable—capable of full assimilation—and enjoyable, constitutes the prime function of literature, music, drawing, painting, etc., in education. They are not the exclusive

agencies of appreciation in the most general sense of that word; but they are the chief agencies of an intensified, enhanced appreciation. As such, they are not only intrinsically and directly enjoyable, but they serve a purpose beyond themselves. They have the office, in increased degree, of all appreciation in fixing taste, in forming standards for the worth of later experiences. They arouse discontent with conditions which fall below their measure; they create a demand for surroundings coming up to their own level. They reveal a depth and range of meaning in experiences which otherwise might be mediocre and trivial. They supply, that is, organs of vision. Moreover, in their fullness they represent the concentration and consummation of elements of good which are otherwise scattered and incomplete. They select and focus the elements of enjoyable worth which make any experience directly enjoyable. They are not luxuries of education, but emphatic expressions of that which makes any education worthwhile." From *Democracy and Education,* by John Dewey, pp. 278-279. Copyright © 1916 by The Macmillan Company. Reprinted by permission.

4. Whitehead has said, "... Traditional educational methods ... are far too much occupied with intellectual analysis, and with the acquirement of formularized information. What I mean is that we neglect to strengthen habits of concrete appreciation of the individual facts in their full interplay of emergent values ..." *Science and the Modern World* (New York: The Macmillan Company, 1925), p. 284.

5. William James, *The Principles of Psychology* (New York: Henry Holt and Company, 1890), Vol. II, p. 308.

6. Carl Jung, *Aion: Researches into the Phenomenology of the Self,* R. F. C. Hull, trans., (New York: Pantheon Books, Inc., 1959), p. 32.

7. Carl Jung, *op. cit.,* p. 33.

CHAPTER 7

1. Michel de Montaigne, "Education," L. E. Rector, trans.

2. John Locke, *Some Thoughts Concerning Education,* #47.

3. Mircea Eliade, "A Cosmic Territorial Imperative?" *The Center Magazine* (July-August 1971), pp. 22-23.

4. John Holt, discussion, *Daedalus* (Summer 1969), p. 733.

5. G. John Roush, "What Will Become of the Past?," *Daedalus* (Summer, 1969), p. 643.

6. For more on the "It's good because it's awful" way of thinking, see Susan Sontag, "Notes on Camp," *Against Interpretation,* (New York: Farrar, Straus, and Giroux, Inc., 1964).

7. For the classic statement against high culture as inherently divisive, see Leo Tolstoy, *What Is Art?*

8. Clive Bell, *Art* (London: Chatto & Windus, 1914).
9. Eduard Hanslick, *The Beautiful in Music,* Gustav Cohen, trans. (New York: The H. W. Gray Co., 1891).
10. Jose Ortega y Gasset, *The Dehumanization of Art and Notes on the Novel,* Helene Weyl, trans. (Princeton: Princeton University Press, 1948).
11. In an unusually interesting article, "The Function of History," *Encounter* (June, 1971), J. H. Plumb has traced the move, after the Russian revolution, away from "literary history" to historical analysis, a process greatly aided by the development of the social sciences. He says that it is now hard to imagine a scholar's contemplating a large-scale narrative history. Writing of a recent collection of papers on the study and teaching of history, he says, "The fascinating aspect of this book is that no one adopts the view that history has any direct lessons to teach. It can expand the mind, stimulate the imagination . . ." etc., but no one apparently "believes that there is a coherent vision of the past which ought to be taught to the young." (p. 75.) Fragmentation is rampant, along with the hunger "to be like natural scientists. . . ."
12. George Steiner, *Language and Silence* (New York: Atheneum, 1967).

   Martin S. Dworkin has warned that "We must not sharpen the senses without educating the spirit, lest we raise generations of moral cripples who can see, to be sure, but without thinking or caring." "Toward an Image Curriculum: Some Questions and Cautions," *The Journal of Aesthetic Education,* April 1970, p. 132.
13. George Steiner, "To Civilize Our Gentlemen," *op. cit.,* p. 61. Speaking as a scientist, Sir John Crockcroft has said, "For all too obvious reasons, we are no longer at all confident that a literary, humanistic education does very much to make men better or incapable of political stupidity, social confusion, or personal vileness." "A Transatlantic View of What Knowledge is Worth Having," in Wayne C. Booth, ed. *The Knowledge Most Worth Having,* (Chicago: University of Chicago Press, 1967), p. 97.

   In a Louis Harris poll conducted in 1969, high school students listed history as the "most irrelevant" subject in their course of studies. See Herbert I. London, "The Relevance of 'Irrelevance': History as a Functional Discipline," *New York University Education Quarterly,* (Spring, 1971), p. 9.

   Another "vice" that might have here been adumbrated—it has been alluded to in various contexts above—is that of a certain condescension regarding the sciences. In our time, as we have noted, C. P. Snow has exposed this attitude most effectively. But for a classical statement, the following by Bishop Berkeley can hardly be improved upon: "As in reading other books a wise man will choose to fix his thoughts on the sense and apply it to use, rather than lay them out in grammatical remarks on the language: so in perusing the volume of nature methinks it is beneath the dignity of the mind to affect an exactness in reducing each particular phenomenon to general rules, or showing how it follows from them. We should propose to ourselves nobler views, namely, to recreate and exalt the mind with a prospect of the beauty, order, extent, and variety of natural things: hence, by proper inferences, to enlarge our notions of the grandeur, wisdom, and beneficence of the Creator. . . ." George Berkeley, *Principles of Human Knowledge,* #109.

CHAPTER 8

1. Duane Manning, *Toward a Humanistic Curriculum,* (New York: Harper & Row, 1971), p. 3.
2. Ryland W. Crary, *Humanizing the School* (New York: Alfred A. Knopf, 1969) pp. 259-260.
3. Robert Blume, "Humanizing Teacher Education," *Phi Delta Kappan,* March, 1971, p. 411.
4. Carl Weinberg, *Education and Social Problems,* (New York: The Free Press, 1971) p. 15.
5. See, for example, Edgar Z. Friedenberg, *The Vanishing Adolescent,* (New York: Dell Publishing Co., Inc., 1959); Jonathan Kozol, *Death at an Early Age* (New York: Bantam Books, 1967); Herbert Kohl, 36 *Children* (New York: The New American Library, 1967), Paul Goodman, *Growing up Absurd* (New York: Vintage Books, 1952).
6. Ivan Illich, *Deschooling Society* (New York: Harper & Row, 1971).
7. Yet once again it is necessary—partly because of the huge tendency of apologists for the humanities to be led into exaggeration by their enthusiasm—to be explicitly cautionary: there is nothing to forbid the hater and despiser of the humanities being humane; and, yes, it is possible for the sensitive humanist to be ethically ugly. Furthermore, there is no more *automatic* transfer of fictional sympathy to real life sympathy than there is of reasoning in mathematics to reasoning in politics; but as all studies of transfer say, abilities can be broadened beyond their initial context by enlightened effort.
8. Walter Pater, *The Renaissance,* Conclusion.
9. We need reminding, too, that an environment can be too bland and innocuous. For instance, in a recent symposium, Wolf Kahn, a painter, commented: "In our crowded environment, the individual who derives satisfaction from the density of visual stimuli is a happier person than the aesthete, the nostalgic, who is revolted by the vulgarity of it all." "Uses of Painting Today," *Daedalus* (Summer, 1969), p. 750.

10. Reprinted by permission from Herbert Marcuse, *An Essay on Liberation* (Boston: Beacon Press, 1969), pp. 25-26. Copyright © 1969 by the Beacon Press.
11. *Loc. cit.* See note 10.
12. *Op. cit.,* p. 38. See note 10.
13. *Op. cit.,* p. 43. See note 10.
14. Robert Coles, "The Words and Music of Social Change," *Daedalus,* Volume 98, Number 3 (Summer, 1969) p. 692. Reprinted by permission from *Daedalus,* Journal of the American Academy of Arts and Sciences, Boston, Massachusetts.
15. *Ibid.,* p. 693.
16. James S. Ackerman, "Two Styles: A Challenge to Higher Education," *Daedalus,* Volume 98, Number 3 (Summer, 1969) p. 857. Reprinted by permission from *Daedalus,* Journal of the American Academy of Arts and Sciences, Boston, Massachusetts.
17. Stuart Hampshire, "Commitment and Imagination," *The Morality of Scholarship,* Max Black, ed., (Ithaca: Cornell University Press, 1967), pp. 50-51.

CHAPTER 9

1. "Rationale and Definition of the Humanities," New York State Education Department, in Scheila Schwartz, *op. cit.,* p. 28.
2. On the subject of the general theory of values, see C. I. Lewis, *An Analysis of Knowledge and Valuation,* (La Salle, Illinois: The Open Court Publishing Company, 1946); DeWitt H. Parker, *Human Values* (New York: Harper & Brothers, 1931); Ralph Barton Perry, *The General Theory of Value,* (New York: Longmans, Green and Company, 1926); and Stephen Pepper, *The Sources of Value* (Berkeley and Los Angeles: The University of California Press, 1958).
3. We think there is good reason for not identifying value with pleasure, as many have done—the main reason being that certain very exalted gratifications, such as those associated with love, deep friendship, religious experience, and tragic catharsis are not appropriately or rightly instances of pleasure—yet pleasure is a fairly reliable index of the value present on most occasions.
4. See C. I. Lewis, *op. cit.,* Book III.
5. De Witt Parker, *op. cit.,* Part II.
6. In a very valuable article, Harry S. Broudy has argued that "What ought not to be assumed is that the Humanities taught for specialized purposes will automatically have humanistic results." He lays down the ingredients

necessary for a subject of study to provide value orientation, with indications of the different ways in which philosophy, history, and literature operate. "Science 'Versus' Humanities in the School Curriculum: A Philosophical Analysis for the Present Crisis," *Journal of Philosophy,* Nov. 6, 1958. See especially pp. 998-990. See also James E. McClellan's "Why Should the Humanities Be Taught" in the same issue of the *Journal of Philosophy.*

7. Leonard Meyer has shown in detail how the satisfaction of music consists in large part in the syntactical and subsequent satisfaction of expectations. See *Emotion and Meaning in Music* (Chicago: University of Chicago Press, 1956), *passim.*

8. Abraham Maslow, *The Psychology of Being* (Princeton: D. Van Nostrand Company, Inc., 1962), p. 89.

9. *Ibid.,* pp. 83-84. Italics in original are here omitted.

10. *Ibid.,* p. 104.

11. *Ibid.,* pp. 104-105.

12. See J. L. Jarrett, "Coming to Know Persons, Including Oneself," *The Monist,* January, 1968.

13. Ralph Barton Perry, "A Definition of the Humanities," in T. Greene, *op. cit.,* p. 39.

14. Cited by Antony Flew, "What is Indoctrination?" *Studies in Philosophy and Education,* Spring, 1966, p. 302.

15. See John M. Rosenfeld, "The Arts in the Realm of Values," *Daedalus,* Summer, 1969. Also: J. M. Rich's *Education and Human Values* (Reading, Massachusetts: Addison-Wesley Publishing Company, 1969).

16. For an elaboration of this point, see J. L. Jarrett, *The Quest for Beauty* (Englewood Cliffs, N.J.: Prentice-Hall Inc., 1957), Chapter 13.

Paul Goodman, who is so often cranky, speaks perceptively on the question of openness of the teacher about his own values: "When A. S. Neill says that his pupils don't know his religion, drug attitudes, or politics, I am simply baffled. He can't be taking his pupils very seriously.... If the young don't hear opinions about such things from a knowledgeable and trusted adult, from whom should they hear them?" *New York Review of Books,* (September 23, 1971), p. 22.

CHAPTER 10

1. Paul Goodman, *op. cit.,* p. 22. "I don't know any academic means of passing on the humanities; the schools do more harm than good, for they turn the young off. If the humanities do seem to survive, poorly, it is by contagion; some of us take them with surprising eagerness, some young people catch on."

2. An eminent humanist, Roger Shattuck, has gone so far as to say, "*Any* significant truth is unteachable; only the husk can be conveyed. . . . I know intimately the work of only a few great minds. All of them without exception state or imply in a significant context that each person must learn for himself, from his own experience. There is no substitute." ("Thoughts on the Humanities," *Daedalus,* Summer, 1969, p. 678). Doubtless this is true, but what exactly does this imply? That there is no significant teaching? Not unless teaching is thought, indefensibly, to be some kind of implanting, or direct transmittal of truth. "Husk" is surely an exaggeration. An excellent coach can teach a young child to swim in a few hours, though nobody ever supposed that in some way the child can acquire this skill and not "learn for himself." Only a very peculiar (though probably widespread) conception of teaching would suppose some contradiction to exist between teaching and learning for (not *by*) oneself.

3. Letter to George and Thomas Keats, Dec. 21, 1817 in Lionel Trilling, ed., *The Selected Letters of John Keats* (New York: Farrar, Straus, and Young, Inc., 1957), p. 92.

4. As a matter of fact, there has been just recently a flurry of interest in Bach on the part of some Rock devoteés.

5. Or, in Harry Broudy's perceptive phrase, *enlightened cherishing:* neither enlightenment nor cherishing is enough by itself. See, among other places, Broudy, "The Role of the Humanities in the Curriculum," *The Journal of Aesthetic Education,* Autumn, 1966, pp. 17-27. Reprinted in Scheila Schwartz, *op. cit.,* pp. 276-284.

   R. G. Collingwood, *The Idea of History* (Oxford: Oxford University Press, 1946) pp. 245-246. Philip Phenix has said, "Historical understanding is personal insight expressed in ordinary language, informed by scientific knowledge, transformed by esthetic imagination, and infused by moral consciousness." *Op. cit.,* p. 240.

6. Thucydides, *History of the Peloponnesian War,* Book II, Chapter 47, 53, A. Crawley, trans., in *Greek Historical Thought: From Homer to the Age of Heraclitus,* (New York: The New American Library, 1952), p. 168.

7. Thomas Hobbes, *Leviathan,* Chapter XIII.

8. Donald Michael has written: ". . . What has to be done increasingly, I believe, is to teach *styles* of life, to teach what it means to be, to grow, to become actualized, to avoid alienation, to enlarge one's self. The only way a teacher can teach these things is to *be* these things." "Tomorrow's Sources of Actualization and Alienation," in Robert R. Leeper, ed., *Humanizing Education: The Person in the Process* (Washington, D.C.: Association for School Curriculum Development, 1967), pp. 40-41.

9. An interesting problem, not here treated, is that of the respects in which the teaching act itself may have aesthetic qualities. See Donald Arnstine,

"Aesthetic Qualities in Experience and Learning," C. M. Smith, "Style and Education," and Monroe C. Beardsley, "Aesthetic Theory and Educational Theory." All in Ralph A. Smith, ed., *Aesthetic Concepts and Education* (Urbana: University of Illinois Press, 1970).

10. Martin Buber, "Dialogue," *Between Man and Man,* Ronald Gregor Smith, trans. (Boston: Beacon Press, 1955) Section II, p. 19.
11. "Education," *op. cit.,* pp. 99-100.
12. *Ibid.,* p. 101.
13. William Arrowsmith, "The Future of Teaching" in Calvin B. Lee, ed., *Improving College Teaching: Aids and Impediments* (Washington, D.C.: American Council on Education, 1967), p. 60. Reprinted by permission.

CHAPTER 11

1. John Dewey, *Democracy and Education, op. cit.,* p. 269.
2. Scheila Schwartz, *op. cit.,* p. 285.
3. Frances Hufford in Richard R. Adler, ed., *Humanities Programs Today* (New York: Citation Press, 1970), pp. 42-45. Some thirty-five recently developed humanities courses, mainly interdisciplinary, team-taught, and at high school level are described in this book. Jack Strauss and Richard Dufour, "Discovering Who I Am: A Humanities Course for Sixth Grade Students," *Elementary English,* January, 1970, pp. 85-120. In the same district, high school students may elect a humanities course called "The Humanities in Three Cities: Ancient Athens, Renaissance Florence, and Modern New York."
4. Having looked at many dozens of examples, Scheila Schwartz has said, ". . . The only definite pattern found in humanities courses is that they are interdisciplinary. . . ." *Op. cit.,* p. 325.
5. Another form of synoptic integration is afforded by courses centering upon religious experience, interpreted historically, cross-culturally and comparatively, philosophically, or in other ways. To those who see religion as in some sense anti-Humanistic, Clyde Holbrook's words are an important corrective. Conceived in comprehensive terms, "religion finds its principal aims of instruction and scholarship consonant with those of liberal education. Emphasis falls upon informative, appreciative, and critical purposes rather than upon the stimulation of devotional attitudes or the inducement to doctrinal conformity." *Religion, A Humanistic Field* (Englewood Cliffs, N.J.: Prentice-Hall, Inc., 1963), pp. 36-37.

   Thayer S. Warshaw has had success in a public high school teaching the Bible "as a source book for the humanities." (Scheila Schwartz, *op. cit.* pp. 186-192.) There are other signs today that teachers and administrators are beginning to move beyond the timidity which for years made them observe the separation of church and state by pretending that religion did not exist.

6. Joseph Satin, *The Humanities Handbook* (New York: Holt, Rinehart, and Winston, Inc., 1969), p. 4.

7. *Ibid.,* p. 5.

8. E. B. Feldman, *Varieties of Visual Experience* (Englewood Cliffs, N.J.: Prentice-Hall, Inc., rev. ed., 1972.

9. Mark Luca, of the School of Education, University of California, Berkeley, was the inventor of this scheme. Miss Dorothy Bennett has been in charge of the ESEA Title III project, run in cooperation with the Berkeley Unified School District.

10. *A Pennsylvania Humanities Report,* prepared by the Bureau of Curriculum Planning, Pennsylvania Department of Public Instruction, Harrisburg, 1967.

11. Lawrence A. Stenhouse's "Humanities Curriculum Project," now associated with the University of East Anglia. In England, "humanities" often embraces, and is even considerably slanted toward, the social sciences. In part this reflects the fact that there the social sciences have not gained as clear a recognition and identification as in the United States.

12. E. B. Feldman's *Becoming Human through Art* (Englewood Cliffs, N.J.: Prentice-Hall, Inc., 1970) is a notable example of a book about the visual arts, with many references to other fields.

13. See W. R. Robinson, *Man and the Movies* (Baton Rouge: Louisiana State University Press, 1967), pp. 34ff. Quoted in Franck Machel's "Movies and Man's Humanity," Scheila Schwartz, *op. cit.,* pp. 193-194.

14. Clive Bell, *Art* (New York: Stokes, n.d.), p. 25.

15. *Ibid.,* p. 27.

16. Francis T. Villemain, "Aesthetic Education in Social Perspective," *Journal of Aesthetic Education,* April 1970, p. 11.

17. Elmo Roper, "How Culturally Active are Americans?" *Saturday Review,* May 14, 1966.

18. Richard Hamilton quoted from George Melly, *Revolt into Style,* reviewed in the *Times Literary Supplement,* January 22, 1971, p. 98. For a brilliant analysis of popular art as "not the degradation of taste but its immaturity," see Abraham Kaplan's "The Aesthetics of the Popular Arts," in James B. Hall and Barry Ulanov, eds., *Modern Culture and the Arts* (New York: McGraw-Hill Book Company, 1967), pp. 62-78.

19. Furthermore, there are, currently, highly promising activities in elementary-grade humanities. A notable instance is the series of texts that Paul Brandwein and associates are preparing under the Harcourt Brace Jovanovich imprint; another is the work of the CEMREL Aesthetic Education team, especially in the development of games to facilitate the understanding

of dramatic structure and components. For background see Manuel Barkan, Laura H. Chapman, and Evan J. Kern, *Guidelines: Curriculum Development for Aesthetic Education* (St. Louis: Central Midwestern Regional
Educational Laboratory, Inc., 1970).

CHAPTER 12

1. "The 'humanities' have insisted that they are the road to wisdom, to goodness, to truth. But they have been strikingly unsuccessful in demonstrating
   precisely *how* they lead to these goals. Too often wisdom is equated with
   information, goodness with a genteel life-style cultivated in certain academic circles, truth with skillfulness of argument." Bennett Reimer, *A
   Philosophy of Music Education,* (Englewood Cliffs, N.J.: Prentice-Hall,
   Inc., 1970) p. 147.
2. Educational Policies Commission, *The Central Purpose of American Education* (Washington, D.C.: National Education Association of the United
   States, 1961).
3. Carl Rogers, "Toward a Science of the Person," in T. W. Wann, ed.,
   Behaviorism and Phenomenology, (Chicago: Published for William Marshall Rice University by the University of Chicago Press, 1964), p. 115. See
   also L. A. Reid, *Ways of Knowledge and Experience* (London: George
   Allen & Unwin Ltd., 1961) and W. P. Montague, *The Ways of Knowing*
   (London: George Allen & Unwin Ltd., 1925).
4. Erich Fromm, "The Creative Attitude," in Harold H. Anderson, ed., *Creating and its Cultivation,* (New York: Harper & Brothers, Publishers, 1959)
   p. 50.
5. C. I. Lewis, *An Analysis of Knowledge and Valuation,* pp. 372-373.
6. Carl Rogers, "Toward A Science of the Person," in T. W. Wann, ed.,
   Behaviorism and Phenomenology (Chicago: Published for William Marshall Rice University by the University of Chicago Press, 1964), p. 115.
   Reprinted by permission of the author.
7. *Ibid.,* p. 111.
8. See Rainer Maria Rilke's great poem, "Archaischer Torso Apollos" in *Der
   Neuen Gedichteanderer Teil.*
9. Miguel de Unamuno, *Three Exemplary Novels and a Prologue,* (New
   York: Albert & Charles Boni, Inc., 1930) p. 28.
10. *Ibid.,* p. 22.
11. R. J. Kaufmann, "On Knowing One's Place: A Humanistic Meditation,"
    Daedalus, (Summer, 1969) p. 709.
12. D. H. Lawrence, "State of Funk," *Assorted Articles* (London: M. Secker,
    1930), p. 98.

13. Suzanne K. Langer has, building on a metaphysical conviction of White-head, gone farther than anyone else to show the human centrality of feeling. See *Mind: An Essay on Human Feeling,* Vol. I (Baltimore: The Johns Hopkins Press, 1967). For a psychologist's treatment of the structure of emotional meaning, see Joel Davitz, *The Language of Emotion* (New York: Academic Press, 1969).

    See also Wayne Shumaker, *Literature and the Irrational* (Englewood Cliffs, N.J.: Prentice-Hall, Inc., 1960) for a detailed investigation of the resemblances between much literary expression and primitive tendencies.

14. G. H. Bantock, "The Education of the Emotions," *Education, Culture, and the Emotions,* (London: Faber and Faber, 1967) p. 79. Reprinted by permission of the author.

15. C. J. Ducasse, "Are The Humanities Worth Their Keep?" in Adrian Dupius, ed., *Nature, Aims, and Policy,* (Urbana: University of Illinois Press, 1970) pp. 273-274.

16. *The Concise Oxford Dictionary,* third edition, 1934.

17. I suggest that aesthetic perception requires an ability to perceive affect in portrayed figures, to recognize affect in oneself, and to experience the unpleasant as well as the pleasant. ... I am implying ... an *ability to empathize,* that is, to project one's own feelings outward and to perceive those one can recognize outside." Pavel Machotka, "Visual Aesthetics and Learning," *Journal of Aesthetic Education,* (July, 1970) p. 125.

18. Carl Jung, *Modern Man in Search of a Soul* (New York: Harcourt, Brace & World, Inc., 1933) p. 168.

19. Ludwig Wittgenstein, *Tractatus Logico-Philosophicus,* (London: Kegan Paul, Trench, Trubner & Co., Ltd., 1922) p. 27.

20. Jung, *loc. cit.*

21. T. S. Eliot, "The Metaphysical Poets," *Selected Essays,* 1917–32. (Harcourt, Brace and Company, 1932), p. 247.

22. William James, *Some Problems of Philosophy* (New York: Longmans, Green & Co., 1911). He said in another place "that philosophic study means the habit of always seeing an alternative, of not taking the usual for granted, of making conventionalities fluid again, of imagining foreign states of mind. In a word, it means the possession of mental perspective." From a letter, reprinted in Horace Kallen, *The Philosophy of William James,* (New York: The Modern Library, n.d.) p. 58. It is an almost perfect statement of the humanistic attitude toward life.

    For a particularly searching account of the place of imagination in humanistic thinking, see, A. W. Levi, *Literature, Philosophy and the Imagination* (Bloomington: Indiana University Press, 1962.)

23. Marianne Moore, "Poetry," *The Collected Poems of Marianne Moore* (New York: The Macmillan Company, 1941).

24. Wallace Stevens, *The Necessary Angel* (New York: Vintage Books, 1951), p. 51.

25. Wallace Stevens, "The Plain Sense of Things," *The Collected Poems of Wallace Stevens* (New York: Alfred A. Knopf, Inc.). Reprinted by permission of the publisher.

   We were reminded of this poem by Maxine Greene's "Imagination" in Ralph Smith, ed., *Aesthetic Concepts and Education,* pp. 303-304. The entire essay deserves careful reading and so do many of the other pieces in this excellent collection.

26. S. T. Coleridge, *Biographia Literaria,* Chapter XIII.

27. However, it must be said that very often the "youth culture" too is humorless, and lacking in either playfulness or spontaneity. A rejection of gray Puritanism is only a first step. I owe this point and many others in this chapter to a personal communication from Professor James Stone of the San Francisco State College Humanities Department.

28. Norman O. Brown, *Life Against Death* (Middletown, Connecticut: Wesleyan University Press, 1959) pp. 65-66. William Glasser in *Schools without Failure* (New York: Harper and Row., 1969) has emphasized the necessity for encouraging laughter, anger, and other feelings in all classrooms.

29. Richard Chase, *Quest for Myth* (Baton Rouge: Louisiana State University Press, 1949,) p. 73.

30. Charles Mills Gayley, *The Classic Myths* (Boston: Ginn and Company, 1911) p. 1.

31. Malinowski, "Myth in Primitive Psychology," in C. G. Jung and C. Kerenyi, *Essays on a Science of Mythology* (New York: Pantheon Books, Bollingen Series XXII, 1949, R. F. C. Hull, trans.) p. 7.

32. Kerenyi has said, "Mythology, like the severed head of Orpheus, goes on singing even in death and from afar." *Ibid.,* p. 5.

33. Richard Chase, "Notes on the Study of Myth" in John B. Vieckery, ed., *Myth and Literature* (Lincoln: University of Nebraska Press, 1966) p. 70.

34. Philip Wheelwright, "Notes on Mythopoeia," *Ibid.,* pp. 62-63.

35. Cf. Harold H. Watts' "Myth and Drama," *Ibid.,* esp. p. 79.

36. Ernst Cassirer, *An Essay on Man* (New Haven: Yale University Press, 1944) p. 81.

37. *Loc. cit.*

38. Rudolph Otto, *The Idea of the Holy,* John W. Harvey, trans. (New York: Oxford University Press, 2nd ed., 1952.)

39. I. A. Richards has said: "The saner and greater mythologies are not fancies; they are the utterance of the whole soul of man and as such, inexhaustible to meditation. They are not amusement or diversion to be sought as a relaxation and an escape from the hard realities of life." *Coleridge on*

Imagination (London: K. Paul, Trench, Trubner & Co. Ltd., 1934) p. 173. Mircea Eliade has said that one of the functions of teaching the arts, especially those that are difficult and precious is that this gives the student a sense of initiation into a select company—a common event in all mythology. But he goes on to say that "it is especially the 'escape from Time' brought about by reading—most effectively by novel reading—that connects the function of literature with that of mythologies. . . . The reader is confronted with a strange, imaginary time, whose rhythms vary indefinitely, for each narrative has its own time that is peculiar to it and to it alone. . . ." One wonders whether the day will come when this desire to transcend one's own time—personal, historical time—and be submerged in a "strange" time, whether ecstatic or imaginary, will be completely rooted out. As long as it persists, we can say that modern man preserves at least some residues of "mythological behavior." Traces of such a mythological behavior can also be deciphered in the desire to rediscover the intensity with which one experienced or knew something *for the first time;* and also in the desire to recover the distant past, the blissful period of the "beginnings." Mircea Eliade, *Myth and Reality* (New York: Harper & Row, 1963, Willard R. Trask, trans.), pp. 192-193.

40. George Santayana, *The Sense of Beauty,* (New York: Dover Publications Inc., 1955) p. 96.

41. Carroll C. Pratt, *Music as the Language of Emotion* (Washington: Library of Congress, 1952) p. 26.

42. Alfred North Whitehead, *Aims of Education and Other Essays,* (London: Williams & Norgate Ltd., 1932), p. 19.

43. See Gordon Allport, *Becoming* (New Haven: Yale University Press, 1955) p. 39. Alfred Adler has said, "What is frequently labeled 'the ego' is nothing more than the style of the individual." "The Fundamental Views of Individual Psychology," *International Journal of Individual Psychology I,* 1955, p. 5.

44. John Dewey, *Art as Experience* (New York: Minton, Balch, 1934) *passim.* And we have not only a rage for order but also its opposite, which is a strong impulse behind both the creation and the seeking out of humanistic products, as Morse Peckham has demonstrated in *Man's Rage for Chaos* (New York: Schocken Books, 1967).

45. Clearly many persons have something about them that strongly militates against bringing matters to a happy close. Like the protagonist in Alan Sillitoe's "The Loneliness of the Long-Distance Runner," they will, from a perverse impulse, slow down in sight of the goal in order to ensure their defeat.

CHAPTER 13

1. Cf. A. D. Graeffe, *Creative Education in the Humanities* (New York: Harper & Brothers, 1951), p. 6. Also, Herbert Read, *Icon and Idea,* (New York: Schocken Books, 1962) p. 18.

2. Carl Jung, *Psychological Types,* H. Godwin Baynes, trans., (New York: Harcourt, Brace & Company, Inc., 1923). Jung's classification relates each of the functions to both introverted and extraverted subjects, for a much more complex schematism than that employed here. Incidentally, Herbert Read has said that schools have universally taught art according to the "standard of the extraverted thinking type." (*Education through Art,* p. 104.) In the same work he has shown how the skillful teacher can move children from play to art in each of the four Jungian aspects. See p. 223.

3. We are not, however, forgetting that photographs can be works of art, and increasingly often are.

4. Norman O. Brown., *op. cit.,* pp. 65-66.

5. Frank Barron has reported that in a study of creativity "only 25% of the general population is classified as 'intuition' types. . . . , yet 100% of the creative architects . . . and 92% of creative writers . . . were so classified." *Creative Person and Creative Process* (New York: Holt, Rinehart & Winston, 1969) p. 76.

6. Maslow on the basis of a study of highly "self-actualized" persons describes such persons as unusually capable of reconciling such oppositions in their own personalities as selfish-unselfish, adult-child, male-female. *Motivation and Personality,* (New York: Harper & Bros., 1954). Similar findings about highly creative persons have been reported by several psychologists, such as D. W. MacKinnon, "Creativity and Images of the Self" in R. W. White, ed., *The Study of Lives* (New York: Atherton Press, 1963.)

7. Albert Hofstadter has said that philosophy's great task is "to find the key to the problems of meaning and existence faced by man just because he is human." *Agony and Epitaph* (New York: George Braziller, 1970), p. 17.

8. Henri Bergson, *Laughter, op. cit., passim.*

9. Carl R. Rogers, *On Becoming a Person* (Boston: Houghton Mifflin Company, 1961), p. 195. See Søren Kierkegaard, *Fear and Trembling.*

10. Martin Buber, *I and Thou,* Ronald Gregor Smith, trans., (New York: Charles S. Scribner's Sons., second edition, 1959) p. 3.

11. William Arrowsmith, *op. cit.* On the problem of integrating the humanities themselves and a hopeful solution, see James H. Stone, "Integration in the Humanities: Perspective and Prospects," *Main Currents in Modern Thought,* (Sept.-Oct., 1969). The standard work—and there are not many —on integration in education, though not having much to do specifically

with integration in the humanities, is Nelson, B. Henry, ed., *The Integration of Educational Experiences,* the Fifty-Seventh Yearbook of the National Society for the Study of Education, Part III (Chicago: National Society for the Study of Education, 1958).

AUTHOR'S NOTE

Carrol Grabo in an unpublished dissertation, Theoretical Models of Integrated Humanities Programs (University of California, 1972), has conducted a sustained analysis of the relations between psychological integration and integrated humanities subject matters.

Only after completing this work did I come upon Henry B. Veatch's very valuable study, *Two Logics: The Conflict Between Classical and Neo-Analytic Philosophy,* in which an exceptionally strong case is made out against the exclusive reliance upon a kind of logic that is suited only to the natural sciences, and the consequent neglect of the humanities as importantly cognitive. (Evanston: Northwestern University Press, 1969.)

Index

Abelard, Pierre, 14
Ackerman, James, 118-119, 235n
Adler, Alfred, 243n
Aeschylus, 101
Alan, S. C., 229n
Alberti, Leon, 27, 224n
Allport, Gordon, 90, 243n
Andersen, Hans Christian, 5
Anselm, 14
Aquinas, Thomas, xv, 14, 28
Archimedes, 60
Aristophanes, 8-9, 13, 71, 142,
    222n
Aristotle, 2, 9, 18, 28, 31, 43, 60,
    68, 125, 141, 168, 171, 176, 177,
    208, 209, 217, 222n, 224n, 228n
Arnold, Matthew, 41, 42, 59, 103,
    226n
Arnold, Thomas, 41
Arnstine, Donald, 237-238n
Arrowsmith, William, 163, 220,
    238n, 244n
Athenaeus, 19
Augustine, St., 102, 110

Bach, Johann Sebastian, 101, 103,
    111, 216, 237n
Bacon, Francis, 30, 31, 34

Bacon, Roger, 14
Balboa, Vasco de, 142
Bantock, G. H., 194, 241n
Bardi, Giovanni, 28
Barkan, Manuel, 240n
Barron, Frank, 244n
Barzun, Jacques, vii
Baumgarten, Alexander, 34, 37
Beardsley, Aubrey, 146
Beardsley, Monroe C., 225n, 238n
Beatles, The, 138
Beethoven, Ludwig van, 101, 110,
    120, 133, 142, 148, 176
Bell, Clive, 102, 233n, 239n
Bennett, Dorothy, 239n
Bentham, Jeremy, 33, 39
Bergmann, Ingmar, 181
Bergson, Henri, 44-45, 89, 226n,
    244n
Berkeley, Bishop, 233-234n
Bibbey, Cyril, 226n
Bible, The, 72
Billington, J. H., vi, 221n
Birckhoff, G. D., 74
Blake, William, 172, 224n
Bloom, Robert, 234n
Boccaccio, Giovanni, 18
Boehme, Jakob, 89

Boileau, Nicolas, 31
Brahms, Johannes, 101, 176
Brancusi, Constantin, 85
Brandwein, Paul, 239n
Brecht, Bertolt, 112, 116-117, 143
Brinton, Crane, 16, 21, 223n, 224n, 229n, 230n
Bronowski, Jacob, 64, 65, 69, 71, 74, 229n, 231n
Broudy, Harry S., 235-236n, 237n
Brown, Norman O., 119, 203-204, 214, 242n, 244n
Browne, Thomas, 224n
Bruner, Jerome, 90
Bruni, Lionardo, 22
Bruno, Giordano, 14
Buber, Martin, 56, 111, 161, 220, 238n, 244n
Bullough, Edward, 88
Burckhardt, Jacob, 14, 43, 223n
Burns, Robert, 150
Burstyn, Harold, 66, 229n
Butler, Joseph, 34

Caesar, Julius, 17
Campanella, 14
Camus, Albert, 85
Cary, Joyce, 177
Cassidy, Harold Gomes, 228n
Cassirer, Ernst, 53, 207, 227n, 242n
Castelvetro, Lodovico, 28
Castiglione, Baldassare, 20, 223n
Cato, 19
Celine, Louis Ferdinand, 120
Cezanne, Paul, 101, 110, 148, 176
Chapman, Laura H., 240n
Chase, Richard, 205, 206, 242n
Chaucer, Geoffrey, 18, 101, 110, 176, 223n
Chesterton, G. K., 43
Chirico, Giorgio de, 87

Chrysoloras, Manuel, 23
Cicero, 8, 11, 12, 14, 17, 19, 23, 34, 35, 96, 174
Classicism, 96
Clemens, Samuel, 61
Coleridge, Samuel Taylor, 38, 89, 202, 225n, 242n
Coles, Robert, 118, 235n
Collingwood, R. G., 84, 154, 237n
Combs, Arthur, 106
Comenius, John Amos, 20, 223n
Comte, Auguste, 43
Conant, James, 230n
Conrad, Joseph, 89
Copernicus, Nicolaus, 22, 71
Corneille, Pierre, 28
Cornford, F. M., 222n
Crane, Ronald S., 35, 58-62, 83, 224n, 225n, 228n
Crary, Ryland W., 234n
Crockcroft, John, 233n
Cromwell, Oliver, 41
Curricula, humanities, 165-185

Dante Alighieri, 60, 85, 101
Darwin, Charles 43, 60, 68
Daumier, Honoré, 110, 120
Davitz, Joel, 241n
Debussy, Claude, 85, 97, 148
Delbrück, M., 230n
Demosthenes, 17
Descartes, René, 14, 29, 31, 34, 200, 215
Dewey, John, xvi, 125, 165, 209, 231n, 232n, 238n, 243n
Dickens, Charles, 182
Dickinson, Emily, 52
Donne, John, 28, 128-129, 199
Dostoevsky, Feodor, 61, 110, 133, 183
Dryden, John, 30, 31

Ducasse, C. J., 195, 241n
Dufour, Richard, 238n
Durant, Will, 170
Dürer, Albrecht, 27
Dworkin, Martin S., 233n

Edwards, Jonathan, 101
Einstein, Albert, xv, 60, 68, 201, 218, 226n
El Greco, 101, 197
Eliade, Mircea, 98, 232n, 243n
Eliot, Charles William, 70
Eliot, T. S., 72, 113, 199-200, 241n
Elyot, Sir Thomas, 59
Emerson, Ralph Waldo, 38-39, 61, 225n
Epictetus, 85
Epistemon, 19-20
EPOCH, 173
Erasmus, Desiderius, 16, 21, 22
Erikson, Erik, 85
Euclid, 66

Feldman, Edmund, 172, 221n, 239n
Felelfo, 23
Fellini, Federico, 181
Ficino, Marsizlio, 15-16, 27, 224n
Flew, Antony, 236n
Fliegel, Norris, 226n
Ford, G. W., 230n
Forster, E. M.; 227n
France, Anatole, 76, 162
Frankl, Viktor, 90, 106
Freud, Sigmund, 43, 69, 89, 99, 193, 199, 201, 203, 214
Friedenberg, Edgar, 109, 234n
Froebel, Friedrich, 165
Fromm, Erich, 90, 106, 188, 240n

Galilei, Galileo, 22, 60
Gauguin, Paul, 144, 148

Gayley, Charles Mills, 205, 242n
Genêt, Jean, 120
Giacosa, La, 17-18
Gibbon, Edward, 34-35, 43, 60, 101, 154, 199
Gieseking, Walter, 151
Gilbert, Katharine, 224n
Glasser, William, 242n
Goodman, Paul, 109, 234n, 236n
Gorgias, viii, 6, 23
Goethe, Johann von, 37, 61, 101, 197
Gospel According to Matthew, The 3
Graeffe, A. D., 244n
Greeks, The, 1-12
Greene, Maxine, 242n
Greene, Theodore Meyer, 227n
Grimm, Brothers, 5
Grunewald, Matthias, 133
Guarino, 23
Guevara, Che, 119
Gutenberg, Johann, 16, 18, 223n

Halley, Edmund, 30
Hals, Franz, 28
Hamilton, Richard, 239n
Hampshire, Stuart, 119, 235n
Handel, George Frederick, 145
Hanslick, Eduard, 102, 233n
Harvey, William, 71, 183
Havelock, Eric, 24, 224n
Haydn, Franz Joseph, 143, 171, 197
Hegel, Georg Wilhelm, 38, 44, 73, 75, 81, 89
Heidegger, Martin, 89, 121
Heisenberg, Werner, 87
Hellas, 6
Henry VIII, 142
Henry, Nelson B., 245n
Heraclitus, 209
Herder, Johann Gottfried von, 37

Herodotus, 7, 22, 171
Hesiod, 3, 14, 171
Hesse, Hermann, 119, 146
Hilbert, David, 87
Hilton, Peter, 229n
Hippias, 6, 7
Historicism, 97-98
Hobbes, Thomas, 30, 113, 155, 237n
Hofstadter, Albert, 244n
Hogarth, William, 110
Holbein, Hans, 30, 84
Holbrook, Clyde, 238n
Hölderlin, Friedrich, 37
Holt, John, 100, 232n
Homer, 2, 4, 14, 17, 22, 60, 163, 171
Horace, 14, 17
Hubris, 1
Hufford, Frances, 238n
Hull, C. L., 90
Humane, The, 105-120 passim
Humanistic, The, 81-93, 105 passim
Humanitarian, The, 105-120 passim
Humanitas, 11, 12, 16, 223n
Humanities, definitions of, vi-ix, 47-62, 82-83, 228n
Hume, David, 33-34, 35, 36, 61, 143, 172, 174, 225n
Hutcheson, Francis, 33, 34
Huxley, T. H., 41-42, 59, 96, 226n

Ibsen, Henrik, 182, 197
Iliad, The, 3, 74, 110
Illich, Ivan, 109, 234n
Ionesco, Eugene, 71
Irving, Washington, 96
Isocrates, 7-8, 11, 23, 222n

Jackson, Andrew, 76
Jaeger, Werner, 222n
James, Henry, 118, 146, 148

James, William, viii, 60, 82, 88-89, 96, 106, 134, 183, 197, 228n, 231n, 241n
Jarrett, James L., 221n, 222n, 226n, 231n, 235n
Jaspers, Karl, 121
Jeffers, Robinson, 85
Jefferson, Thomas, vii, 87, 176
Jesus, 111, 120, 148, 219
Job, 3, 61, 219
Johnson, Samuel, 32, 171, 225n
Jones, Howard Mumford, vi, 221n
Jones, W. T., 227n
Joyce, James, 84
Jung, Carl Gustav, 89, 90-91, 106, 199, 212-213, 214, 218, 232n, 241n, 242n, 244n
Juvenal, 17

Kahn, Wolf, 234n
Kallen, Horace, 241n
Kant, Immanuel, 36-37, 53, 89, 101, 110, 143, 171, 225n
Kaplan, Abraham, 239n
Kaufmann, R. J., 240n
Keats, John, 144, 148, 177, 198, 225n, 237n
Keeney, Barnaby, 225n
Keller, Charles, vi, 221n
Keller, Hans, 231n
Kerenyi, C., 242n
Kern, Evan J., 240n
Kierkegaard, Sören, 44, 84, 102, 220, 244n
Kodol, 181
Kohl, Herbert, 109, 234n
Kozol, Jonathan, 109, 234n
Kristeller, P. O., 16, 223n, 224n
Krutch, Joseph Wood, 44
Krutchfield, Richard, 168
Kuhn, G., 224n

Langer, Suzanne, 231n, 241n
Lavoisier, Antoine Laurent, 66
Lawrence, D. H., 193, 240n
Learning, humanistic, 187-210
Leavis, F. R., 103
Leibnitz, Gottfried Wilhelm von, 29-30, 34, 200
Levi, A. W., 241n
Lewis, C. I., 188-189, 235n, 240n
Lewis, C. S., 223n
Lincoln, Abraham, 142
Livy, 17, 96
Locke, John, 30, 31, 34, 96, 224n, 232n
London, Herbert I., 233n
Longfellow, Henry Wadsworth, 96
Lossu, René Le, 32
Luca, Mark, 239n
Lucretius, 215
Lullius, Raimundus, 20
Luther, Martin, 21, 85, 154, 224n

Machel, Frank, 239n
Machiavelli, Niccolo, 18
Machotka, Pavel, 241n
Mackinnon, D. W., 244
Mahler, Gustav, 146
Malinowski, B., 205, 242n
Mandeville, Bernard, 34
Manning, Duane, 234n
Mao Tse-tung, 75, 231n
Marcuse, Herbert, 115-116, 119, 235n
Marquis of Mantua, 17
Marrow, H. I., 11, 222n
Marx, Karl, 43, 75
Maslow, Abraham, 90, 106, 129-131, 210, 236n, 244n
Max, Peter, 184
May, Rollo, 90, 106
McCarthy, Desmond, 149
McClellan, James E., 236n

McCullers, Carson, 118
McKeon, Richard, 24, 224n
McKuen, Rod, 146, 184
McLuhan, Marshall, 24, 119, 224n
Melancthon, Philipp, 22
Melly, George, 239n
Mendel, Gregor Johann, 43
Mendelssohn, Felix, 143
Merleau-Ponty, Maurice, 226n
Meyer, Leonard, 236n
Michael, Donald, 237n
Michelangelo, 101, 111, 182, 216, 219
Michelet, Jules, 21
Mill, James, 33, 39
Mill, John Stuart, 33, 39-40, 59
Milton, John, 28, 59, 101, 146, 148, 176
Molière, 219
Mommsen, Theodore, 98
Monet, Claude, 72, 144
Montague, W. P., 240n
Montaigne, Michel, 16-17, 21, 22, 34, 61, 95, 162, 174, 223n, 232n
Montesquieu, 171
Monteverdi, Claudio, 28
Moore, Marianne, 201, 241n
More, Thomas, 21, 22, 84
Mozart, Wolfgang Amadeus, 54, 87, 101, 138, 139, 143, 171, 182, 183
Muller, Herbert J., 229n
Mumford, Lewis, 230n

Nagel, Ernest, 230n
Napoleon, 142, 148, 215
National Endowment for the Arts and the Humanities, 225n, 227n
Neill, A. S., 236n
Newman, John Henry, 40-41, 59, 225n
Newton, Isaac, 29, 30, 34, 37, 60, 171, 224n

New York State Education Dept., xiv
Nietzsche, Friedrich Wilhelm, 44, 174
Novalis, 37

O'Brien, Conor Cruise, 231n
Occam, William of, 14
O'Connor, Flannery, 118
Odyssey, The, 3, 10, 74, 110, 222n
Olafson, Frederick, 228n
Ong, W. J., 24, 48-49, 112, 222n, 224n, 226n
Ortega y Gasset, Jose, 102, 233n
Otto, Rudolph, 207, 242n
Ovid, 17

Paideia, 12
Panofsky, Edwin, 226n
Papinian, 19
Parker, De Witt H., 127, 235n
Parmenides, 6
Pascal, Blaise, 61, 109
Pater, Walter, 113-114, 234n
Paul, St., 110
Pausanias, 19
Peckham, Morse, 243n
Pepper, Stephen, 235n
Pepys, Samuel, 85
Percy, Walker, 118
Perls, Frederick, 106
Perry, Ralph Barton, 49-53, 134-135, 227n, 235n, 236n
Pestalozzi, Johann Heinrich, 39, 165
Petrarch, Francesco, 18, 21
Phenix, Philip, 54-58, 227n, 237n
Piaget, Jean, 69, 168
Picasso, Pablo, 120
Pico della Mirandola, Giovanni, 15, 223n
Plato, 2-8, 10, 14, 15, 17, 19, 24, 27, 28, 32-33, 60, 61, 68, 71, 87,

89, 101, 110, 141, 148, 155, 171, 176, 183, 190, 200, 215, 216, 222n, 223n
Plotinus, 89
Plumb, J. T., 221n, 233n
Plutarch, 17, 19, 22, 61
Polanyi, Michael, 54, 56, 63-64, 65, 69, 229n
Politian, 23
Pope, Alexander, 29, 32, 54, 225n
Popular Arts, 182-185
Postman, N., 222n
Pratt, Carroll C., 208-209, 243n
Prior, Moody E., 227n, 230n
Prodicus, 6
Propertius, Sextus, 17
Protagoras, 6, 13
Psychology, humanistic, 106-107
Ptolemy, 71
Pugno, Lawrence, 230n
Purcell, Henry, 28, 142, 182
Pythagoras, 174

Quintilian, 8, 11, 14, 23, 35

Rabelais, François, 16, 18-19, 20, 95, 223n
Racine, Jean Baptiste, 162
Randall, John Herman, 33, 37, 225n
Ransom, John Crowe, 217, 231n
Ravel, Maurice, 148
Read, Herbert, 63, 64, 168, 228n, 244n
Reich, Wilhelm, 131
Reid, Louis Arnaud, 231n, 240n
Reimer, Bennett, 240n
Religious humanism, 107-108
Rembrandt, 28, 118, 182
Renaissance humanism, 13-25, 27-30, 107, 108
Reynolds, Joshua, 32, 225n
Rhetoric, 23-24

Rich, J. M., 236n
Richards, I. A., 242n
Richter, Sviatoslav, 151
Rilke, Ranier Maria, 240n
Robinson, W. R., 239n
Rodin, Auguste, 142
Roethke, Theodore, i
Rogers, Carl, 90, 106, 188, 189, 190, 220, 240n, 244n
Rohwer, William, 231n
Romans, The, 11-12
Romanticism, 36-39
Root, Robert Kilburn, 227n
Roper, Elmo, 239n
Rosenberg, Bernard, 226n
Rosenfeld, John M., 236n
Roush, John, vi-vii, 221n, 232n
Rousseau, Henri, 148
Rousseau, Jean Jacques, v, 32, 33, 36, 39, 44, 143, 172, 221n, 225n
Russell, Bertrand, 55, 66, 213

Sandys, John Edwin, 22, 224n
Santayana, George, 42, 45, 61, 208, 243n
Satin, Joseph, 171, 239n
Scaliger, Joseph Justus, 28
Schaeffer-Zimmern, Henry, 168
Schelling, Friedrich Wilhelm, 37
Schiller, Friedrich, 37-38, 225n
Schlegel Brothers, 37
Schleiermacher, Friedrich, 37
Schoenberg, Arnold, 112
Schopenhauer, Arthur, 89, 120
Schubert, Franz Peter, 143, 176
Schwab, Joseph, 229n, 230n
Schwartz, Scheila, 221n, 235n, 238n
Science, i, 39, 41-44, 55, 63-79, 95
Scotus, Duns, 14
Seneca, 17, 22
Shaftesbury, Anthony Ashley, Third, Earl of, 32-33, 34

Shakespeare, William, i, 28, 60, 72, 76, 101, 110, 128, 144, 148, 162, 163, 170, 176, 182
Shattuck, Roger, 237n
Shelley, Mary, 95
Shelley, Percy Bysshe, 130
Shumaker, Wayne, 241n
Sidney, Philip, 28, 58
Simonides, 2
Skinner, B. F., 108
Smith, Adam, 33
Smith, C. M., 238n
Snell, Bruno, 223n, 224n
Snow, C. P., 41, 43-44, 63, 70, 228n, 233n
Soame, William, 31
Socrates, 7, 13, 14, 24, 82, 171
Sontag, Susan, 232n
Sophocles, 2, 73, 110, 222n
Sousa, John Philip, 138
Spencer, Herbert, 40, 91, 225n
Spengler, Oswald, 73, 120
Spinoza, Benedict, 29, 34, 89, 100, 101, 120, 219
Steiner, George, 103, 233n
Stenhouse, Lawrence A., 239n
Stevens, Wallace, 201-202, 242n
Stone, James H., 242n, 244n
Strauss, Jack, 238n
Stravinsky, Igor, 97, 110, 147, 148
Symonds, J. A., 23, 224n

Tacitus, 101
Taylor, Harold, vii, 221n
Tchaikovsky, Petor Ilich, 73, 110
Teaching, humanistic, 141-164
Thucydides, 7, 71, 101, 155, 171, 237n
Tolstoy, Leo, 73, 120, 232n
Toynbee, Arnold, 73
Transcendentalism, 38-39

Turner, Joseph Maylord, 149
Tuveson, Ernest Lee, 224n

Unamuno, Miguel de, 174, 191, 240n

Value, 121-140
Van Gogh, Vincent, 118, 176
Villemain, Francis T., 239n
Vinci, Leonardo da, 22, 27, 32, 142, 224n
Virgil, 14, 17, 22, 96, 142, 183
Vittorino da Feltre, 17-18
Vives, Juan L., 21, 58
Voltaire, 120

Walker, Jerry L., vi, 221n
Warren, Robert Penn, 118

Warshaw, Thayer S., 238n
Watts, Harold H., 242n
Webster, John 30
Weinberg, Carl, 234n
Weingartner, C., 222n
Welty, Eudora, 118
Wheelwright, Philip, 206, 231n, 242n
White, R. W., 244n
Whitehead, Alfred North, 67, 89, 207, 209, 237n, 241n, 243n
Wittgenstein, Ludwig, 82-83, 89, 91, 199, 231n, 241n
Wright, Frank Lloyd, 142
Wright, Richard, 118
Wordsworth, William, 38, 40, 101